UNSTUCK

ASCD MEMBER BOOK

Many ASCD members received this book as a member benefit upon its initial release.

Learn more at: **www.ascd.org/memberbooks**

BRYAN **GOODWIN**
TONIA **GIBSON**
DALE **LEWIS**
KRIS **ROULEAU**

UNSTUCK

How Curiosity, Peer Coaching, and Teaming Can Change Your School

 Alexandria, Virginia USA
 McREL INTERNATIONAL Denver, Colorado USA

1703 N. Beauregard St. • Alexandria, VA 22311-1714 USA
Phone: 800-933-2723 or 703-578-9600 • Fax: 703-575-5400
Website: www.ascd.org • E-mail: member@ascd.org
Author guidelines: www.ascd.org/write

Deborah S. Delisle, *Executive Director;* Stefani Roth, *Publisher;* Genny Ostertag, *Director, Content Acquisitions;* Julie Houtz, *Director, Book Editing & Production;* Liz Wegner, *Editor;* Donald Ely, *Senior Graphic Designer;* Mike Kalyan, *Director, Production Services;* Keith Demmons, *Production Designer*

McREL International
4601 DTC Boulevard, Suite 500
Denver, CO 80237- 2596 USA
Phone: 800-858-6830 or 303-337-0990
Website: www.mcrel.org • E-mail: info@mcrel.org

PAPERBACK ISBN: 978-1-4166-2590-2 ASCD product #118036
PDF E-BOOK ISBN: 978-1-4166-2592-6; see Books in Print for other formats.

Quantity discounts are available: e-mail programteam@ascd.org or call 800-933-2723, ext. 5773, or 703-575-5773. For desk copies, go to www.ascd.org/deskcopy.

ASCD Member Book No. FY18-6B (Apr. 2018 PS). ASCD Member Books mail to Premium (P), Select (S), and Institutional Plus (I+) members on this schedule: Jan, PSI+; Feb, P; Apr, PSI+; May, P; Jul, PSI+; Aug, P; Sep, PSI+; Nov, PSI+; Dec, P. For current details on membership, see www.ascd.org/membership.

Library of Congress Cataloging-in-Publication Data
Names: Goodwin, Bryan, author.
Title: Unstuck : how curiosity, peer coaching, and teaming can change your school / Bryan Goodwin, Tonia Gibson, Dale Lewis, and Kris Rouleau.
Description: Alexandria, Va. : ASCD, 2018. | Includes bibliographical references and index.
Identifiers: LCCN 2017060451 (print) | LCCN 2018009317 (ebook) | ISBN 9781416625889 (PDF) | ISBN 9781416625902 (pbk.)
Subjects: LCSH: Educational change--United States. | Educational leadership--United States. | Teaching teams--United States. | Teachers--Professional relationships--United States.
Classification: LCC LA217.2 (ebook) | LCC LA217.2 .G668 2018 (print) | DDC 371.2/07--dc23
LC record available at https://lccn.loc.gov/2017060451

27 26 25 24 23 22 21 20 19 18   1 2 3 4 5 6 7 8 9 10 11 12

UNSTUCK

Introduction: Running in Place

Coming up with ideas is the easiest thing on earth. Putting them down is the hardest.

Rod Serling

Let's step back for moment and survey the current landscape of U.S. education, drawn from recent headlines and news stories. It all seems vaguely reminiscent of a *Twilight Zone* episode, something Rod Serling might have written and narrated himself:

> Picture, if you will, a teacher, commended by her peers and superiors for being among the very best. Her students know her to be tough, but fair. Enter now a principal who says she must alter her grades so more students pass her course. Resistance is futile, the principal says. It's a directive handed down from on high (Williams, 2015).

> Now picture a single square of light shining from a school window late at night. Inside, a school principal is checking boxes on a teacher evaluation form. For one teacher in question, he stares at a particular box: cooperative learning. Although he has seen this teacher's students learning in groups, on the day of his official classroom observation she taught a good lesson, but the students weren't in groups. He weighs his decision, then rates her "unsatisfactory." Later, he'll admit that his rating was unfair and inaccurate, but he was simply following orders handed down from on high (Anderson, 2012).

> Now picture, if you will, a courtroom. A dozen teachers stand trial, accused of doing something verboten in their own classrooms: cheating. They altered students' responses on the state test to make their own performance look better. The verdict is read: guilty, the court ignoring their pleas that they acted in response to pressure from edicts coming from on high (Fantz, 2015).

You might ask yourself, what is this place?

This is the land of unintended consequences. It is a land where people use outside forces to alter behaviors by handing down edicts, following a kind of outdated groupthink called Theory X. It is a place that lies between the summit of our highest hopes and the pit of our darkest fears. It is a place called here, a time called now. Welcome to the *Twilight Zone.*

Teacher stress.

Student disaffection.

Leader burnout.

These seem to be the plague of our modern system of education. It wasn't always this way, of course. Many educators recall how, not too long ago, the job was, if not easier, at least less stressful and more joyful. Of course, everything wasn't necessarily right with the world back then: Many students fell through the cracks; some got a decent education, and others didn't.

How Did We Get Here?

Roughly 30 years ago, with our ears ringing of warnings that we were facing a "rising tide of mediocrity" (National Commission on Excellence in Education, 1983) and seeing unacceptable gaps between disadvantaged students and others, we set off, with good intentions, down a path of reform with what seemed like a business-minded focus on the bottom line of student achievement. We created standards. We developed assessments. We set goals for the year 2000. Of course, the year 2000 came and went and our goals remained unmet, so we redoubled our efforts, setting even higher goals and tougher consequences to leave no child behind. And who could argue with that?

Yet our current path of reform has had numerous *Twilight Zone*-like unintended consequences. We have consumed educators with making sense of vague standards (Schmoker, 2014) that have been too voluminous to possibly cover in 13 years of education (Marzano & Kendall, 1998). We have created layers upon layers of assessments for students, who now take 20 or more standardized tests per year (Lazarín, 2014). Teachers and school leaders now find their performance rated on complex, yet error-ridden, formulas and on assessments that are suspect in and of themselves, especially when (as we'll see in a later chapter) we can give students a $10 bribe that suddenly makes them appear to be six months smarter.

It's perhaps no surprise, then, that educators at all levels are under more stress than ever before, resulting in churn among principals and teachers fleeing the profession (Béteille, Kalogrides, & Loeb, 2011; Butrymowicz & Garland, 2012; MetLife, 2013; Strauss, 2015). And there's plenty of evidence to suggest that such high levels of stress—we might call them *threat conditions*—actually *reduce* performance, making people more likely to make mistakes and less likely to try new things (Bronson & Merryman, 2013), including the very new approaches we most need to apply now.

Our students, meanwhile, drop out of school when they don't see how standardized learning is relevant to them (Bridgeland, DiIulio, & Morison, 2006), and we respond by creating what *New York Times* columnist David Brooks (2016) has described as the "mother of all extrinsic motivations," the grade point average (GPA), which "rewards people who can grind away at mental tasks they find boring" and "encourages students to be deferential and risk-averse" even though what we want from them in life is to be "independent thinking and risk-taking." And as we'll see later in this book, the more pressure teachers feel to cover content and prepare students for standardized achievement tests, the less apt they are to encourage student curiosity and engagement—so it's perhaps no surprise that the longer students stay in school, the less motivated, curious, and creative they become (Gottfried, Fleming, & Gottfried, 2001).

Perhaps, though, the biggest unintended consequence of our top-down approach to change has been performance plateaus. As we'll see in the next chapter, in state after state and district after district—and indeed, across the globe—early gains engendered by top-down measures begin to fade and performance levels off. Nation-wide, the United States has fallen into this pattern. For a decade or more, U.S. students have demonstrated only incremental gains while their peers in other nations, including those that have taken a radically different approach to reform, have seen their achievement continue to rise.

Is It Working?

Some might argue, of course, that our top-down "tough love" directed much needed attention to our most marginalized students—focusing our whole system of education on students who were previously falling through the cracks. That much is true. Yet we might ask this question: Has it worked? The answer (which we'll also explore in more depth in the next chapter) is, well, not exactly.

It's true that accountability pressure in the United States appears to have helped the lowest performing students in the lowest performing states improve; the pressure has also had some benefits for low-achieving students enrolled in schools under the most pressure to improve (Deming, Cohodes, Jennings, & Jencks, 2016). That's the good news.

The bad news is that nationwide, achievement gaps appeared to be closing more rapidly *before* the top-down pressure of high-stakes testing kicked in (Nichols, Glass, & Berliner, 2012). Moreover, in true *Twilight Zone* fashion, there's evidence to suggest that for many low-performing schools, the increasing weight of tough-love sanctions—including giving students the right to transfer to other schools and providing tutoring services—did little to bolster their performance. If anything, they proved to be a bit like quicksand: the more sanctions were placed on schools, the more their performances sank, finding bottom only after the final and most severe sanction—restructuring, when the school's principal was usually replaced—resulting in a modest uptick in achievement (Ahn & Vigdor, 2014).

Moreover, despite shining the bright light of accountability on the success of all students, the high school graduation rate in the United States remains below that of other developed nations, and student success is still more strongly tied to parents' income than in other countries (OECD, 2011). In fact, the United States has proportionally *fewer* high-performing students than 24 of 34 developed nations (West, 2012).

In short, it would appear that decades of test-driven reforms may have helped a few students at the very bottom perform a little bit better, but has done very little to raise average student performance or propel more U.S. students into the top echelon of performance worldwide. The bottom line is that the educators in the United States appear to be working harder (and believe it or not, spending more on education than nearly every other nation in the world [OECD, 2011]), without much to show for it.

Right Idea . . . Wrong Response?

Some might say, of course, that these unintended consequences are not so much a reflection of having the *wrong approach* to accountability (i.e., we ought to stick to our guns) but, rather, the *wrong response* to it—perhaps among a few bad apples. If only those students/parents/teachers/principals would get with the program, some might argue, we'd all be fine. Alternatively, others might think the problem is just that the message still isn't getting through to these people; we should talk slower and louder, ratcheting up the pressure even more or creating even more precise accountability systems or market mechanisms to drive performance.

As we'll show in this book—by unpacking decades of psychological research, extensive studies in business and schools, and real-life examples in actual schools and districts—these *Twilight Zone*-like unintended consequences are not simply unexpected anomalies. They are quite predictable outcomes of what's become for us an ingrained way of thinking about how to drive change in people's behavior.

Or Maybe It's Just the Wrong Idea

Granted, in today's high-pressure, high-stakes environment, educators could be forgiven for being short on patience with seemingly highfalutin theoretical discussions. "Just tell me what to do and I'll do it" has become a default response for many educators.

We understand that. Yet we also understand something else: Ideas are powerful. How we *think* about a problem guides how we respond to it, which, in turn, affects the reality we create for ourselves and our students. Some of the most powerful ideas—perhaps even the most pernicious ones—are those that have become so ingrained in our thinking that we hardly pay attention to them anymore.

Behind all our top-down approaches to reform are many unspoken ideas and tacit assumptions that have become so much a part of our mindsets that they seem axiomatic—our default operating system, if you will. And yet, to understand why all of this is happening and how we've come to find ourselves in this *Twilight Zone*, we must step back for a moment and call out the theoretical underpinnings of the reform efforts that are driving us to distraction. Only by putting these ideas on the table, as we'll do in the next two chapters, can we begin to see that it doesn't have to be like this: we don't have to feel this way with all of this pressure and fruitless exhaustion. There *is* a better way forward.

Getting Unstuck

In many ways, the U.S. education system has gotten stuck in a rut. The top-down approaches that may have worked once upon a time (however briefly or limitedly) just aren't working anymore. Yet we have remained so committed to them that we keep doubling down on them, finding new ways to ratchet up the pressure on students, teachers, and school leaders, creating ever more complex systems and schemes.

As the saying goes, when you find yourself in a hole, stop digging.

This book is about finally putting down our shovels and finding a way out of that hole. We'll point to examples from around the world of schools and school systems—including a large, successful effort in the northern suburbs of Melbourne, Australia—that not only point to a better way but also show that it *is* possible. Beyond that, we'll provide a straightforward road map for getting from where we are now to where we want to be.

Although some of the ideas in this book may seem radical, we don't call for a radical dismantling of everything we've been doing for the past 25 years. Our point is not to swing the pendulum all the way back to evidence-free approaches to schooling that ignored large swaths of students. Getting clarity about what we want students to learn and seeing how well they're doing is important. So too is using data to guide our efforts. Perhaps most important of all is focusing on the success of *all* students to create an education system that lifts people from poverty rather than reinforcing privilege. We should retain all of those important elements of what we've been doing.

With all of that in mind, our point is this: We've been going about this current approach to reform for nearly a quarter century now, and with the exception of some small pockets of higher performance here and there, student performance overall has not gotten much better than when we started out. So, we could keep doing exactly what we've been doing and expect different results (famously called the definition of insanity). Or we could look for a better way forward—one that starts not with a policy edict handed down from on high but, rather, with helping students become more motivated, curious, and engaged and helping teachers find passion and joy in the profession while continually improving their practices. We could also help and encourage school leaders to create environments that feel less like an uninspired bureaucracy and more like a Silicon Valley startup, where people are encouraged to experiment and engage in rapid-cycle improvement efforts.

A Better Way Awaits

If you're content with the way things are—your students are flourishing, your teachers are happy, and your leaders inspire continuous improvement in your schools—we're tremendously happy for you. We'll also spare you the trouble of reading this book: It's not written for you. Rather, it's for those who have found themselves feeling burned out, feeling frustrated, or hearing a nagging voice in the back of their heads that asks, *Is this really the right way to do things?*

The book is written for malcontents and people frustrated by what they see, yet not quite sure how to get from their current state of frustration to where they want to be. If you have ever felt like Lassie pawing the ground, desperately trying to get your colleagues, friends, and community members to understand that something has gone badly awry, yet unable to help them see *what* exactly ought to be different about our current system of education, this book is written for you. We hope it's something you can share with others to spark a conversation, even a movement, in your school community.

Or maybe you feel overwhelmed by the complexity of the multiple mandates being thrown at you and the enormity of the challenge of trying to change so much at once in the name of school "reform"—a word which itself suggests a kind of deficit thinking about people who have dedicated their lives to educating our youth. At times, it can feel a little like trying to turn an oil tanker around in a harbor. At other times, it can feel beyond your grasp. It's the system—something out there beyond the walls of your classroom, your school, or even your district or state—that's causing all of this.

How can one person, or an even a small group of inspired people, change all of that? This book will show how one step at a time—through courageous acts that in our current milieu of reform may seem to verge on civil disobedience—we can loosen the chains that bind us and move toward a better system for learning.

Certainly, others have written about these ideas in the past. We don't pretend to have the lock on good ideas. In fact, throughout this book we will be sharing many other people's insights and voices. Yet we believe this book still offers something new and different—namely, a more complete picture of what it could look like to pull these great ideas and thoughtful voices together into something resembling a new approach to teaching and learning.

Nonetheless, we know that good ideas, the best intentions, and a stirring vision aren't enough to effect change. That's why this book also aims to provide a very practical road map for getting from here there, one step at a time. We will offer plenty of tips, real-life examples, and next steps throughout this book for those of you who share our own practical bent.

We understand these changes won't take place overnight. The process will be a journey, but a rewarding one. Like climbers ascending a mountain, each bend in the road will provide new vistas that can inspire us to journey on.

So, let's get started.

1

When Delivering Well Stops Delivering Well

It isn't what we don't know that gives us trouble, it's what we know that ain't so.

Will Rogers

In late 2002, professor David Hopkins found himself called to 10 Downing Street to meet with Tony Blair. The prime minister was, to put it mildly, irate. Hopkins, newly minted head of the standards and effectiveness unit at the national education department—essentially the chief education advisor to Blair—found himself in the unenviable position of needing to explain why, seemingly under his watch, national reading and mathematics scores that had once been on a steady upward trajectory had hit a plateau (Hopkins & Craig, 2011).

It didn't help, of course, that Hopkins's predecessor, Michael Barber, had a made a name for himself by evangelizing a method known by the tongue-in-cheek moniker *deliverology*. Known as "Mr. Targets" in the British government (Smithers, 2005), Barber had gotten all schools in the United Kingdom to adopt standardized approaches to reading and mathematics instruction and focused everyone's attention on delivering the new approaches well (i.e., meeting his famous targets).

The gains had been impressive: Between 1997 (when the National Literacy and Numeracy Strategy was adopted) and 2000, the percentage of students testing at proficient levels in reading and mathematics rose from 63 to 75 percent and from 62 to 73 percent, respectively (Olson, 2004). "We got something quite rare," Barber would later comment, "which is, across a whole system, to get rising average standards and a narrowing of the [achievement] gap" (Olson, 2004).

So successful was his method that Barber, in fact, went on to write a field guide for the deliverology method (Barber, Moffit, & Kihn, 2011) and founded a nonprofit organization in the United States dedicated to its principles, the Education Delivery Institute. Yet shortly after Barber's departure from the Blair government, something seemed to have gone wrong: Student achievement scores leveled off. They weren't getting *worse*, but they certainly weren't getting better. Across the Atlantic, *Education Week* picked up on the story, citing it as a cautionary tale for U.S. reformers who were heading down a similar path (Olson, 2004).

Had teachers lost their focus? Had people stopped paying attention to deliverology? No, Hopkins explained carefully to Blair. Nothing had changed. In fact, *that* was the problem. The performance plateau they were experiencing was quite predictable—a natural result of the top-down approach to reform that the United Kingdom had taken, which had been necessary to begin with, but was now yielding diminishing returns.

"I would make no apology for what Michael et al. did in 1997," Hopkins told *Education Week*. To so dramatically move the needle on such a large system "has to be a stunning achievement. But," he added, "and this is a big but, that was only the first stage in a long-term, large-scale reform. And one of the reasons why we've stalled is that more of the same will not work" (Olson, 2004).

To understand why, empirically, that should be the case, let's back up a bit to understand what we know from research about the complexities of change and program implementation.

Getting from Knowing Better to *Doing* Better

The first point we must acknowledge is that doing *anything* well—sometimes referred to as *closing the knowing-doing gap*—is no small feat. Like most organizations, schools have yet to perfect the art of implementation. Case in point: A few years ago, the U.S. government supported more than two dozen scientific studies of popular interventions through its Regional Educational Laboratory (REL) program. The hope was that in doing so, the so-called regional labs could separate the wheat from the chaff and add the good programs to the newly created What Works Clearinghouse, an online repository designed to provide educators with gold-star reassurance of which programs they could go forth and use with confidence.

There was just one problem with the raft of studies: In every case but one, the popular and widespread approaches, when put under glass, were found to have *no* positive effects on student achievement (Goodwin, 2011b). If we dig more deeply into those published studies, though, it becomes apparent that in most cases, the programs studied were so poorly implemented that researchers were unable to discern whether the fault lay with program itself or poor deliverology. To wit:

• A study of 2,140 6th graders using Thinking Reader, a software program designed to improve reading comprehension by asking students computer-adaptive questions about young adult novels, found no effects on reading comprehension, yet fully 69 percent of students wound up using the Thinking Reader software less often than the program's developer has specified; in fact, software usage dropped off so much that by the end of the school year, just 8.9 percent of students actually finished the third and final novel (Drummond et al., 2011).

• A study involving 2,446 4th graders found no higher mathematics achievement for students working with the popular Odyssey Math software, which at the time was in use by 3 million students across the United States. However, during the course of the study, students used the software on average only 38 minutes a week, well below the minimum of 60 minutes the program developers required; moreover, of 60 classrooms studied, students in only *one* classroom actually used the software for the full time period required (Wijeku-mar, Hitchcock, Turner, Lei, & Peck, 2009).

- A study of nearly 10,000 4th and 5th graders found that students whose teachers were trained in another popular program, Classroom Assessment for Student Learning, demonstrated no higher levels of achievement than control group students. Yet teachers spent, on average, only about half the recommended time in training (31 versus 60 hours) and, perhaps not coincidentally, demonstrated no observable changes in their teaching practices (Randel et al., 2011).

- A group of more than 600 5th graders who were taught for one year with Collaborative Strategic Reading, a scaffolded approach to reading instruction, demonstrated no better achievement than con-trol group students; however, classroom observations revealed that only 21.6 percent of teachers used all five strategies that the approach comprises (Hitchcock, Dimino, Kurki, Wilkins, & Gersten, 2010).

Of the more than two dozen programs rigorously studied by the regional labs, only one was found to yield significant results, a pro-gram called Kindergarten PAVEd for Success. Interestingly, it also appeared to devote the most attention to implementation—using a differentiated coaching model that provided more intensive support for teachers struggling to apply the program's explicit vocabulary instruction methods (Goodson, Wolf, Bell, Turner, & Finney, 2010).

Applying the Science of Deliverology

All of the above suggests that Michael Barber was spot-on with his focus on deliverology. Inconsistency in implementation con-founds even the best laid plans. Bold proclamations and elaborate schemes don't amount to a hill of beans if no one follows through on them. Getting things done, according to Barber and his colleagues from McKinsey & Company (Barber et al., 2011), requires ensuring that all of these elements are in place:

- **Identifying a team or unit to focus on the implementation.** In keeping with the British adage that if everyone is responsible, no one is responsible, leaders must make clear who's responsible for what and what they expect of everyone.
- **Maintaining clear performance targets and expectations.** In keeping with another adage—if you don't know where you're going you'll probably wind up somewhere else—deliverology requires long-term goals and interim targets with progress indicators to track implementation (and celebrate accomplishments) along the way.
- **Creating new routines.** Any new program or approach requires creating new habits. One way to instill them is through regular progress monitoring and reporting, which sends the message to everyone that those pesky new expectations aren't going away.

The early results in the United Kingdom bear witness to the importance of following principles of deliverology, especially when what needs to be done is fairly straightforward. And to be clear, there *are* a lot of fairly straightforward things that, done well, can significantly improve student success.

The Power of Doing the Right Things Right

In our previous books, we've identified many simple (though not necessarily *easy*) things that system leaders, school leaders, and teachers can do to move the needle on student performance, starting with nine key categories of effective instruction in *Classroom Instruction That Works* (Dean, Hubbell, Pitler, & Stone, 2012) and a broader set of teaching behaviors in *The 12 Touchstones of Good Teaching* (Goodwin & Hubbell, 2013), as well as three core elements of effective school leadership in *Balanced Leadership for Powerful Learning* (Goodwin, Cameron, & Hein, 2015), five key components of effective school systems in *Simply Better* (Goodwin, 2011c), and six correlates of district leader success in *School District Leadership That Works* (Waters & Marzano, 2006).

We have seen schools and districts nationwide move the needle on student achievement when they get these things right, which led us to conclude as we did in *Simply Better,* "One of the most powerful things school systems can do to change the odds for all students is simply doing *well* what they already know they must do" (Goodwin, 2011c, p. 134). Put simply, big gains in student achievement come from doing the right things right. That's why sometimes the most effective improvement efforts aren't terribly flashy; they can be quite ordinary, even plain vanilla.

Plain Vanilla Improvement

In the summer of 1989, Sam Stringfield, a professor and researcher at Johns Hopkins University, stumbled onto a mystery. He and his colleague, Charles Teddlie, had been staring at a "mountain of data" gathered through the Louisiana School Effectiveness Study, an examination of eight pairs of matched schools of similar size and demographics in which one member of the pair had strikingly high performance and the other strikingly low performance. A team of observers had gone to all 16 elementary schools to gather qualitative data that the researchers hoped would tease out the disparities among the different sets of schools. No observers (many of whom were non-educators) were told which schools were doing well or poorly, yet they had *all* been able to separate the princes from the frogs. Stringfield spent the summer sifting through the observers' case studies, trying to figure out what had tipped them off. After all, the low-performing schools weren't *obviously* inadequate. Each had a star teacher or two, several programs in place, and other seemingly positive things going on in them. On the other hand, the top-performing schools were, to be frank, a little boring. Some were underfunded. None were implementing the latest reform du jour. As Stringfield later recalled, "Several were as plain vanilla schools as could be imagined" (Stringfield, Reynolds, & Schaffer, 2010, p. 14).

There was, however, one striking difference between the two sets of schools that the observers seemed to have picked up on. In the low-performing schools, an "anything goes" attitude appeared to prevail; they tolerated a wide range of teacher and student behaviors. In contrast, the high-performing schools had a much clearer focus on student achievement and maintained much more consistent standards of teacher and student behavior.

The high-performing schools had routines and followed them. Observers could walk into different classrooms in these schools and see the same thing occurring—good teaching. Classrooms in the low-performing schools, on the other hand, were more like Forrest Gump's box of chocolates: You never knew what you were going to get. As it turns out, the key to going from low performance to better performance often appears to be one word: *consistency*.

Better Routines, Better Results

All of that is easier said than done. Simply knowing *what* to do is not the same as doing it. The key is employing effective practices with quality, intensity, fidelity, and consistency—doing them so well in every school and classroom that they become routine (Goodwin et al., 2015). In our previous books, in fact, we've borrowed a page from surgeon Atul Gawande, whose *Checklist Manifesto* (2009) demonstrated the power of simple checklists in emergency rooms to help health professionals establish new routines and avoid critical oversights and mistakes. To help school leaders and teachers develop new routines and stay focused on doing what matters most, we've provided our own model checklists (which, we should note, we've always presented as "do-confirm" lists to help people stay focused on meaningful practices, rather than as less mindful "read-do" lists or lockstep procedures).

In struggling schools or those with low capacity, these new routines may need to come from outside the system—in the form of a new leader bringing new ways of doing things, an off-the-shelf curriculum, a new behavior management program, or a prescribed instructional framework. For example, a series of case studies of high-performing, high-poverty schools conducted by Karin Chenoweth (2007, 2009) of the Education Trust found that many had started on their pathway to improvement by adopting prepackaged curricula, such as America's Choice, Success for All, or Core Knowledge—exactly *which* program they chose seemed to matter less than picking one and doing it well to overcome what one leader described as a "Burger King" culture in which teachers "got to have it their way" (Chenoweth, 2007, p. 128). In similar fashion, many of these turnaround schools gathered model lesson plans from teachers and put them in binders to give to novice teachers so they would have concrete examples of well-designed lessons to emulate. Soon after getting everyone on the same page, achievement rose.

Hard Habits to Break

It's important to note that low-performing schools often fall into the pattern of unchallenged "habits" and dysfunctional ways of doing things that must be broken and replaced with new and better routines (Brinson & Rhim, 2009). Of course, breaking habits and establishing new routines is never quite as easy as it sounds. For starters, there's the challenge of getting the new practice to stick. Charles Payne (2008) recounts, for example, the story of an urban high school where teachers came together to establish a new routine for reducing the excessively high number of students cutting class and loitering in the halls during class: Teachers with preparation periods would spent the first few minutes of those periods combing the hallways for students skipping class and send them all to the school's auditorium where punishment (e.g., afterschool detention) would be meted out.

The new routine worked. Within a few weeks, student absences from class dropped and a growing sense of order and safety began to take root in the school. But then one day, one teacher decided not to follow the routine; other teachers soon followed, the routine faded, and the school reverted to disorder.

A second, and often more difficult challenge, is that the new routines don't always make things better—a phenomenon referred to as the "implementation dip" by Canadian researcher Michael Fullan (2001), who observed that when the fear of change collides with lack of know-how, performance slumps. To overcome implementation dips, Fullan encourages schools and their leaders to

• Maintain focus and urgency to quash any this-too-shall-pass syndrome.

• Monitor implementation to avoid backsliding into familiar (yet inferior) practices.

• Listen to naysayers and, as appropriate, incorporate their ideas into change efforts.

• Work as teams to buck each other up when the going gets tough.

By employing these strategies (as well as those Barber encourages for deliverology), school leaders can usually help their teams overcome implementation dips and experience success, which can feel like heady times. Data start trending upward, people start pulling together, and things feel different—a new culture begins to take root. People feel optimistic. They may begin to develop what's known as a sense of "collective efficacy"—a shared belief that they can pull together to have a positive effect on student success.

Then the Pixie Dust Wears Off

This upslope period may last a few years or more, but eventually the pixie dust starts to wear off. The routines employed to address obvious shortcomings begin to reveal shortcomings of their own. Maybe it becomes evident that the adopted reading program works great for 80 percent of students but not the other 20 percent. Or maybe the off-the-shelf curriculum that sparked initial gains by creating coherence and vertical articulation fails to engage students. Or the classroom walkthroughs that initially surfaced obvious opportunities for instructional improvement begin to feel rote and tedious, no longer uncovering straightforward ways to improve teaching. Or maybe the behavior management program that initially restored order and safety now begins to feel oppressive, focused more on creating compliance than building character.

When any of these things start to happen, the data begin to show it, too, as previous performance gains turn flat. It is precisely in these times that we realize we now face a new problem, one that, if we don't know how to address it, can feel even more pernicious than implementation challenges or dips: the performance plateau.

The Dreaded Performance Plateau

Almost anywhere you look, performance plateaus abound in education. Here are a few examples:

• In Virginia, many so-called turnaround schools improved for three years, then hit a performance plateau (Hochbein, 2012).

• In Texas, test-based accountability drove performance gains for a while, then levelled off (Schneider, 2011).

• In 25 states, testing pressure created initial gains before student performance plateaued and declined (Nichols et al., 2012).

• Worldwide, education systems show a "pattern of a steep rise followed by a plateau," likely because "once the 'easy wins' have been achieved in classroom instruction, further improvements take longer to embed and are harder to achieve" (Mourshed, Chijioke, & Barber, 2010, p. 50).

School systems are not alone. Plateau effects are common in other areas—from exercise to the arts to business (Sullivan &

Thompson, 2013). In exercise, the recommended treatment is to switch up one's routine. In business, the treatment is much the same. Business coach Bill Bishop (2010) says that companies typically hit a performance plateau when they stop improving their products, believing they've found that *one* right way to do things. Similarly, Jim Collins (2009) has observed that one of the first signs of trouble among declining companies is that they lose "sight of the true underlying factors that created success in the first place" (p. 21). They come to believe they were successful "because we do these specific things" instead of understanding "why we do these specific things and under what conditions they would no longer work" (p. 21). In short, there's a tendency to cling to the old routines that sparked initial success. Over time, though, those routines start to become mindless. People may still use them without fully understanding *why* they are doing them, *when* it's time to change or improve upon them, or *what* they ought to do when the old routines no longer work.

When schools and districts hit performance plateaus, there's a tendency to double-down on what they had been doing—tightening the screws, so to speak, to get everyone to follow the prescribed mathematics program to a T. Or having seen plug-and-play approaches work before, they try to patch the shortcomings of the original approach by plugging yet another new program into the gap.

The Trap of Technical Solutions

The trouble with these responses, though, is that they treat performance plateaus as what business researchers Ron Heifetz and Donald Laurie (1997) long ago referred to as *technical problems*— something for which there's an existing solution; we just need to go out and find it and implement it well. However, performance plateaus tend to be much thornier and more complex, often because the obvious things have all been done so it becomes less clear where the solution lies—or what the deeper problem might be in the first place. Tackling this second breed of problem, which Heifetz and Laurie call *adaptive challenges*, tends to require a different set of behaviors and tools, including collaboration, creativity, and experimentation—or, innovation.

We often encounter performance plateaus when we've exhausted all the obvious solutions or plug-and-play approaches: Better curriculum? Check. Ninety-minute reading blocks? Check. Professional development for teachers? Check. Behavior management program? Check. You can imagine the rest of the list. What this means is that performance plateaus themselves are often *adaptive challenges*. As a result, often the only way to push through them is to recognize that what created success in the past (e.g., plugging in externally developed solutions) won't ensure continued performance gains in the future. What's needed is a more adaptive and entrepreneurial spirit, which (as we'll discuss in more depth later in this book) requires a different style of leadership—one that's less directive and more empowering.

The Problem with Technocratic Fixes

More than a decade ago, when then U.S. Secretary of Education Rod Paige (2002) heralded the passage of the No Child Left Behind Act, he wrote, quite insightfully, that "Never in the history of human civilization has a society attempted to educate all of its children." In hindsight, his words may illuminate why the very reforms enacted by the landmark legislation missed the mark. Clearly, if no one in human history has figured out how to do what you're setting out to do, there's no blueprint or obvious solution set to get you there. It's the equivalent of a moonshot—of President Kennedy declaring that Americans would land on the moon within the decade, even though it wasn't clear at that moment exactly how we'd get there. Because the challenge was so immense, it was no coincidence that the Apollo mission begat a whole series of innovations—including computing, jet propulsion, Velcro, and dehydrated foods.

And yet, for a variety of reasons, including political expedience (Ravitch, 2010), we attempted to tackle the very complex challenge of leaving no child behind like a technical problem, assuming that we could cobble together existing tools such as standards, assessments, and accountability to get us there. This disconnect between the aspirations and provisions of the bipartisan No Child Left Behind Act seems, in retrospect, a little like trying to get to the moon with slide rules, combustion engines, and scuba gear.

Sure, setting high standards for learning (provided they are clear enough) can drive important changes to the curriculum, and accountability can focus attention on data and data-driven decision making to improve instruction. But when compared to the immense challenge of trying to help millions of students with different needs all achieve high levels of learning, standards, assessments, and accountability are limited tools.

So, it's not surprising, then, that reforms driven solely by high-stakes testing have had diminishing returns, resulting in the kinds of performance plateaus we've seen in the United States and elsewhere (Barber & Mourshed, 2007; Fullan, 2011; Hopkins & Craig, 2011). What's worse is that continued reliance solely on technocratic solutions was not only limiting but may have been *counterproductive,* as it only served to increase stress and anxiety, which in turn diminished people's capacity for collaboration, experimentation, and innovation.

Higher Pressure, Lower Performance

Data suggest that our teachers and school leaders are under a tremendous amount of stress these days. In a recent MetLife Foundation (2013) study, for example, fully three-quarters of principals reported that their jobs—much of which now entail responding to external pressures—have become too complex. Nearly half (51 percent) of teachers and principals (48 percent) report being under great stress several days per week—a significant increase since 1985, when this data point was last measured.

The problem with this level of stress, as Po Bronson and Ashley Merryman (2013) note in their book *Top Dog*—a sweeping synthesis of research on the relationship between pressure, competition, and performance—is that it's not conducive to better performance. In many ways, the kind of stress many educators face right now seems to be tantamount to *threat* conditions, which prevent the kind of creative and collaborative thinking most needed to move beyond reliance on simple solutions and toward the sort of deeper analysis and inventive thinking necessary to tackle adaptive challenges.

Learning to Unplug from Plug-and-Play

In short, the real challenge of performance plateaus is learning to let go of the approaches we took to get early gains when they no longer work. Policymakers and leaders in the United States have been slow to recognize this reality and pivot to a different set of strategies. As a result, we keep relying on what Michael Fullan calls the "wrong drivers of reform" (2011). Smitten with the initial results of plug-and-play approaches, we keep hoping to push technical solutions from the top down, issuing policy from a central authority and expecting it to reach classrooms.

Indeed, the entire federal effort to employ scientific research to create a What Works Clearinghouse, well-intentioned though it may have been, reflects this kind of thinking. It assumed we could plug-and-play our way to best-in-the-world performance when, at best, off-the-shelf programs will only get us to a minimum threshold or acceptable baseline of performance. Going beyond that will require a different set of strategies.

Let's be clear: Making this shift is never easy, especially when we've grown accustomed to using one set of leadership styles to achieve initial gains. Powering through implementation dips often requires some top-down direction—leaders must assign roles, monitor performance, and hold people accountable. Sure, they listen to concerns, but when confronting a technical problem, there's little question about what needs to be done. Research suggests, in fact, that these top-down or directive leadership styles can be effective when the solution is obvious or at hand (Goodwin, 2015b).

However, when schools face thornier challenges, a different approach is needed. It's far more effective to drive improvement not from the top down but from the "inside out." Thus, the first thing we may need to do when confronted with performance plateaus is acknowledge that the things that once worked for us—including a steely eyed focus on implementing off-the-shelf solutions—are likely to have diminishing returns.

Adopt, Then Adapt

Studies of schools that have managed to engage in continual improvement—that have been able to push through performance plateaus and sustain performance gains—show that they have learned to do exactly that: demonstrate a recurring pattern of *adopt, then adapt.* In her previously noted profiles of high-poverty, high-performing schools, Karin Chenoweth (2007, 2009) observed that many of these adopted pre-packaged curricula, such as America's Choice, Success for All, Everyday Math, Open Court, and Core Knowledge, were used to spark initial gains. Yet over and over again, they pivoted to a different approach to sustain those gains. Often within a few years of *adopting* the curriculum, most schools saw it wasn't a perfect fit for their students. Those that kept improving their performance began to *adapt* the off-the-shelf curriculum to align with their own student needs. Unlike businesses that lose their way, they weren't wed to the specific approach that led to their early success; instead, they understood the principles underlying their success (e.g., having a strong, consistent, and aligned curriculum). And because they remained focused on their "customers" (i.e., student needs), they saw that the curriculum they had adopted was only a starting point and version 2.0 was now needed.

McREL's own research on high-performing, high-poverty "beat-the-odds" schools (as reported in Goodwin, 2011c), which surveyed and compared the responses of hundreds of teachers in high- and low-performing, high-poverty schools found a similar pattern of empowerment. Teachers in beat-the-odds schools were more likely than teachers in low-performing schools to report having influence in school decisions and a shared vision for success. In short, they had learned to come together to develop new approaches and ways of working together to get things done. As schools improve, they're likely to reach a performance ceiling where the way forward becomes less clear and more ambiguous. A school that has seen gains by enacting an external curriculum or reading program and ensuring greater consistency in learning experiences may now find itself facing a thornier challenge—perhaps motivating students to engage and buy into their own learning. When they reach this point, the way forward is less clear—the solutions are likely to lie in teams of teachers coming together to identify new ways to ignite students' passion for learning, perhaps by unleashing their creativity and passions through immersive project-based learning. Basically, to tackle adaptive challenges, schools must adopt a different approach to leadership and improvement —one that drives change not from the top down, but from the inside out.

The Limited Half-Life of Top-Down Approaches

David Hopkins understood all of this as he sat in 10 Downing Street, trying to explain to the prime minister why the pixie dust of the United Kingdom's heavy emphasis on literacy and mathematics had worn off. As he would tell the prime minister (and later write), top-down approaches can provide a "short, sharp shock" that jolts systems "out of complacency" and helps them focus on a few "measurable goals" (Hopkins, 2013, p. 9). For truly low-performing schools, urgency and focus are often exactly what's needed. Thus, Barber's focus on deliverology had been right at the time; it had compelled teachers across the United Kingdom to employ, with greater consistency, better approaches to reading and mathematics instruction. And it had worked: Student achievement had improved.

Yet there was a problem baked into the overall approach. Although teachers were employing better teaching techniques, they had simply been following someone else's paint-by-numbers program and hadn't really gotten much smarter about teaching, improving their own knowledge or skills for teaching, or understanding what to do when the prescribed approaches stopped working under certain circumstances or with certain students.

That's why top-down approaches, Hopkins observes, "have a very limited half-life" (2013, p. 9). Continued outside pressure becomes "oppressive, alienating, and counter-productive." Once the pixie dust of technical solutions wears off, sustaining performance gains requires a different, "inside-out," approach.

An Opportunity to Take a Different Approach in Australia

A few years after his tense conversation with Prime Minister Blair, Hopkins returned to academia, accepting a temporary teaching position halfway around the world at the prestigious University of Melbourne. As fate would have it, nearby, a newly minted regional director, Wayne Craig, found himself grappling with the question of how to help the Northern Metropolitan Region—a large, loose-knit school system serving more than 75,000 students, many of them immigrant students living in impoverished neighborhoods—overcome a long history of languishing for years as one of the worst performing regions in the state of Victoria.

Victoria: A Glimpse into Our Own Future?

Let's pause here a moment because at this point, some readers, especially those in the United States, may wonder what they could possibly learn from Australia—a place that seems worlds apart and very different from the United States. In some regards, that's true:

Many aspects of education in Victoria, Australia, *are* different (albeit in ways that can provide eye-opening insights for U.S. educators). In many ways, though, Victoria and its capital city of Melbourne reflect many of the same realities experienced by education systems across the United States and the rest of the world. Here are a few:

It's populous—and growing. Victoria's population recently passed the 6 million mark. If it were a U.S. state, it would be in a virtual tie with Missouri for the 18th most populous in the nation. Most of its residents are concentrated in the Melbourne metropolitan area, which has a population of close to 4.5 million people, which would make it the 12th largest U.S. city—close in size to Phoenix or San Francisco. And it's been adding close to 100,000 residents each year (Martin, 2016), most of them arriving from outside Australia, bringing us to the next point.

It's diverse. One quarter of Melbourne's population was born overseas, hailing from 180 different countries and speaking more than 200 languages. Across most of the northern Melbourne metro area (where we focus our narrative), that proportion is closer to one-half.

Its educators feel underpaid. On paper, Australian teachers look slightly better paid than teachers in the United States, making $60,589 Australian dollars (or $44,000 U.S. dollars) per year, compared to $41,460 (U.S.) per year on average in the United States (Ricci, 2015). However, Melbourne is the sixth most expensive city in the world; a loaf of bread costs more than $4 and an average bottle of wine more than $23 (Calligeros, 2015). In fact, researchers speculate that a key reason that up to 50 percent of Victorian teachers leave the profession within their first five years is they simply feel underpaid and undervalued (McMillen, 2013).

Its educators belong to unions. The Victoria branch of the Australian Education Union represents 48,000 teachers, principals, and education support staff. Like unions in the United States, it provides professional learning services for educators, represents individual educators in contractual disputes, and lobbies the state government for better salaries and working conditions for educators.

Its students are tested—and results matter. Student achievement is measured on a regular test called the National Assessment Programme for Literacy and Numeracy (NAPLAN). These results are partially used to guide decisions about principals' employment. In addition, a high-school exit exam called the Victorian Certificate of Education serves as a high-stakes test for students, as scores on the test often determine their placement into university or Technical and Further Education (TAFE) school upon graduation.

Despite these many similarities with the U.S. context, there are some important differences:

Schools operate mostly autonomously. In the early 1990s, the entire state of Victoria adopted what was called "self-management," giving school leaders control over hiring, budgeting, curriculum, and professional learning. While the state is divided into what are now four regions, regional offices are skeletal in size compared with central offices of large, urban school districts in the United States. Many schools band together in networks to pool resources for services like professional learning.

Schools operate in a highly competitive environment. In effect, Victoria has long had what amounts to a voucher program: Public, private, and parochial schools are publicly funded, and parents have the right to choose among them (though the tuition at private and, to a lesser extent, parochial schools often tends to exceed the government benefit). Thus, schools operate in something akin to a free market, competing for students and their associated enrollment dollars.

Accountability is simple and direct. As noted earlier, students are regularly tested in Australia. Results from these tests feed into a two-pronged system of accountability. First, the state of Victoria requires a regular school review—the equivalent of accreditation in the United States—during which third-party teams visit schools and provide an analysis for school leaders and officials from the state. Generally, these reviews are formative in nature, yet for schools mired in low-performing status, they can contribute to a principal being recommended for "non-renewal" or termination. In short, principals in Australia face many of the same pressures as school leaders in the United States.

In many ways, then, Victoria reflects what could be the future of education in America, with every public school in effect operating as a school of choice, competing with parochial and private schools for student tuition dollars, and in some cases, their very survival. Right now, in fact, across the United States, many school districts (from Boston to Houston to Chicago to Denver) have moved to or are gravitating toward granting schools greater autonomy—not unlike what happened 20 years ago in Australia. Moreover, as of this writing, 31 states are considering creating or expanding school choice programs (Goldstein, 2017), and the U.S. Secretary of Education, Betsy DeVos, has been a vocal supporter of vouchers and school choice. Thus, regardless of one's view on the merits of such changes, peering into system-wide change in Melbourne may be instructive as it may provide a glimpse of the future of U.S. school systems.

Planning for Change in a Loosely Coupled System

In his more than 30 years as a principal and administrator, Wayne Craig had seen many reform efforts come and go. With great fanfare, someone atop the system would cook up a bright idea and attempt to foist it upon everyone else. Yet by the time the bright idea filtered down through layers of bureaucracy into school improvement plans and teacher behaviors, it often became so distorted, diluted, or lost in translation that nothing ever really changed. And that was before the move toward self-management in the 1990s had made the system even more "loosely coupled" and, thus, made the task of being an effective regional director imminently more complicated.

The last thing Craig wanted was for his tenure as regional director to be similarly futile. By chance, he bumped into Hopkins at a conference and learned that he had a taken a position at the nearby university. Craig later picked up the phone and struck up a conversation with the Englishman. Before long, Hopkins found himself, at Craig's request, touring the region's schools to offer his own honest assessment of what was at the heart of their struggles, including the root causes of their endemic low performance.

After he toured the schools, Hopkins wrote back to Craig that the situation was indeed dire—student performance was low across most of the region and there were simply too many schools with too few students. Yet in his conversations with school staff, Hopkins had also caught a glimmer of hope, namely "a willingness to change and to face the challenges of school transformation" (Hopkins & Craig, 2011).

The challenge, as Hopkins saw it, would be to both address the urgent financial need to close schools (which would cause considerable disruption) while simultaneously engaging in much needed transformative school improvement efforts. The peril, of course, was that the hue and cry over school closures would distract from the more important effort to improve teaching and learning in the remaining schools. Yet, both needed to be done: Students couldn't wait for the fuss over school closures to quiet down while they sat languishing in poorly performing schools.

After talking it over with Hopkins, Craig decided the best thing to do would be to redirect everyone's attention to the real matter at hand: providing a high-quality education for all children regardless of their background. From the outset, it was clear that simultaneously shaking up and rebuilding a large school system would be an *adaptive challenge*; there was no set script or program to follow. Even if there were, Hopkins and Craig knew from experience it wouldn't get them too far.

Sure, Craig could bring in some new reading or mathematics program and ride herd over public school principals to get them to monitor and enforce its implementation. He and his leadership team could also create a complex system of rewards and punishments to ensure teacher compliance with the program. Yet doing all of that would be akin to using a technical solution to solve an adaptive challenge, which they saw as one of the fundamental flaws with most complex reform efforts. Indeed, as they would later write together, "often we try to solve technical problems with adaptive processes, or, more commonly, force technical solutions onto adaptive problems" (Hopkins & Craig, 2011, p. 154).

No, what was needed was a different way of thinking about reform—not another prescribed approach, but one that could truly increase teachers' professional capacity, inspiring and helping them to *help one another* develop better teaching practices that would aim to increase both student learning and motivation.

It was a simple idea: What if they started with *teachers*? What if they placed teachers and their motivation to change students' lives at the center of the effort, reminding them why they became educators in the first place? Moreover, what if they started not with a glass-half-empty approach, wagging their fingers at what teachers were doing wrong, but rather with observing what the best teachers were doing right and systematically sharing those bright spots?

Better yet, what if they also started with *students*, learning what they liked and disliked about school? What if they asked students what would make them more excited about coming to school and what their teachers could do to make them more engaged and motivated as learners—in a word, *curious*?

That one idea, *curiosity*, was something that Craig couldn't get out of his head. In the years he spent as a principal of a vocational school on Melbourne's east side, transforming it from a school of last resort to a school of first choice for students from across the city (many of whom traveled three to four hours per day just to attend), he had seen the power of students becoming passionate about and self-directing their learning. *Curiosity*. The word kept buzzing like a neon sign. What if *that* could become the focus of schooling?

Balancing Outside In with Inside Out

Conceptually, the two men were in agreement: Instead of simply trying to push ideas or directives from the top down, they would try to make them happen *from the inside out*. It wouldn't be solely one approach or the other, of course. They knew, after all, that sometimes a leader must lead. Sometimes new habits need to be adopted and new routines put into place. Yet as Hopkins observed to Blair that day in 10 Downing Street and in a subsequent book, *Every School a Great School* (2007), the key to sustaining system reform over the long haul is to continually rebalance "top-down and bottom-up" change.

That would need to be the case in the Northern Metropolitan Region. Some of the worst-performing schools would likely require a healthy dose of top-down direction to establish order. Others, though, would need to push through performance plateaus by rethinking how they went about their business, starting perhaps with placing student curiosity at the center of their efforts. Ultimately, even struggling schools, once they had established some order and consistency in their practices, would need to make the transition to "inside-out" approaches as well. Helping leaders make this pivot—especially those who had found success with top-down directivity—would not be easy, of course.

 PAUSE AND REFLECT

- What habits are ingrained in your school or district? Are they productive or unproductive?
- In what areas might you be experiencing an implementation dip?

- In what areas might you be experiencing a performance plateau?
- Do you need more consistent and effective routines (technical solutions)?
- Do you need to adapt what you've adopted (adaptive challenges)?

ENVISION A BETTER WAY

Inside-out approaches are, by definition, local and individualized with no lockstep program to follow. Nonetheless, it can be helpful to imagine new paths forward. With each chapter, we'll suggest a few roads less traveled to help you and your colleagues envision inside-out change in your schools.

- Reanalyze trend data for implementation dips and performance plateaus.
- Inventory your organizational routines and categorize them as productive or unproductive.
- Create three lists: (1) keep doing, (2) do more consistently, and (3) stop doing.
- Reassess your improvement plan(s) to identify which strategies are technical solutions and which are more complex adaptive challenges.

Sailing into Uncharted Waters

From the outset of their efforts in Melbourne, Craig and Hopkins were in agreement that, conceptually, leading a reform effort that sought to engender change from the bottom up by empowering educators to build their professional capacity made a lot of sense. Yet they understood that they were sailing into relatively uncharted waters.

What they were attempting to do—place student curiosity and teachers' intrinsic desire to change students' lives at the center of an improvement effort—was a radical idea, nothing short of a complete paradigm shift when it came to education reform. Focusing on *curiosity*? *Encouraging* teachers instead of browbeating them? Reforming from the *inside out*? It seemed crazy, but also made a whole lot of sense.

But could it really work? Could they really pull it off?

2

Flipping the Paradigm

It is a miracle that curiosity survives formal education.

Albert Einstein

Australia's most iconic denizens are, in a word, strange. Consider the kangaroo—the only creature in the world to move by hopping on uniquely formed hind legs that consist of short thighs, long shins, and enormous feet. Then there's the lovable koala; it's turned something poisonous to most other animals—eucalyptus leaves—into the staple of its diet. And let's not forget the platypus. The first European scientists to see one thought it was a hoax—a beaver's tail and a duck's bill stitched onto an otter's body. The strange biology, though, serves a purpose: They use their bills to scoop grubs and shellfish from river bottoms, using their beaver-like tails to propel themselves. Although it may seem strange at first, upon closer examination, it all makes sense.

That's how we might also describe the approach Craig and Hopkins took to systems improvement in Melbourne. Yes, it may appear strange at first, running counter to how school systems have tried to engineer change in almost every other corner of the world, yet when examined more closely, it seems more like common sense. Of course, common sense isn't always that common. If you spend much time Down Under, though, it seems a little less surprising that an "uncommon sense" approach to education improvement might emerge from a land that prides itself on being a nation of inventive iconoclasts.

Made in Australia: Counterclockwise Improvement

A long list of innovations—from the boomerang to ultrasound to the black box flight recorder—have come from Australia. In their usual self-effacing way, though, they tend to credit their inventiveness not to a particular talent or aptitude but simply on, as the saying goes, necessity being the mother of invention. Living on a faraway continent and in remote places like the Outback demanded that Aussies develop a sort of adaptive ingenuity—reengineering what had arrived from foreign lands to serve a new purpose, just as Mother Nature seems to have done with the unusual flora and fauna on the continent.

Something Borrowed, Something New

Australians tend to be a nation of borrowers—in the best sense of the word. Unlike Americans, whose worldview can be a bit ethnocentric, if not egocentric (as British comedian John Cleese once observed of the World Series, "When we hold a world championship for a particular sport, we invite teams from other countries to play, as well"), Australians are far more attuned to goings-on beyond their borders. Their broader worldview is plainly evident in their newspapers, which tend to dedicate as much space to world affairs as domestic ones.

If you speak for even a few minutes with rank-and-file educators in Australia, you'll hear how much they know about education innovations occurring elsewhere in the world. Most have heard about Elizabeth City and Richard Elmore's "instructional rounds," and they're well versed on Bruce Joyce's research on professional development, Carol Ann Tomlinson's work on differentiated instruction, Michael Fullan's work on leadership, and McREL's research on leadership (which is, in part, where this story begins). To top it off, Aussies also have plenty of local experts, like New Zealander John Hattie, whose syntheses of research have landed him on a global stage.

You also see their iconoclastic inventiveness in their sports, such as Australian Rules Football (called "footy" for short). The sport resembles a rough-and-tumble playground game (usually played when the teacher's back is turned); when one kid throws a ball into the air, someone else catches it and runs for dear life as everyone else tries to gang tackle him. Throw in some goal posts on an oval field and a perplexing scoring system, and you've got footy—a perfect reflection of Australian imagination, reimagining rugby and football with a dollop of ingenuity and a dash of insanity and turning it into something unique.

Australians also have tendency for inventive integration in their music. Paul Kelly is probably the most famous singer-songwriter you've never heard of, sometimes referred to as the Bob Dylan of Australia. His music blends country, rock, R&B, new wave, reggae, Irish folk, and the occasional didgeridoo. The sound is vaguely familiar, yet unconventional—like his holiday season classic sung from the persona of a prison inmate calling home before Christmas to give his brother a recipe for "How to Make Gravy."

So perhaps it was only in Australia that David Hopkins, a well credentialed and widely published British academic, could put some of his ideas to the test in a real-world laboratory. Or maybe it was the environment of northern Melbourne itself, where nothing else seemed to be working, that buoyed Craig and Hopkins with the idea that, well, we can't do any *worse*.

Make no mistake. These *were* radical ideas—they pushed against many elements of the prevailing mindset of education reformers. To understand just how radical and against-the-grain these ideas were, let's take a step back to understand the paradigm under which we've been operating for close to two decades now.

Seeing the Water in Which We Swim

The trouble with any pervasive paradigm is that sometimes it so surrounds us that, like fish in water, we no longer pay attention to the environment in which we find ourselves. But if we take a moment to crawl out of the water and look back on the pond in which we've been swimming, we can better understand the shortcomings of the overall approach and (perhaps more importantly) see a better way forward.

A good place to reexamine some of the key ideas that undergird top-down approaches to reform are found in a book written more than two decades ago by Harvard professor Alfie Kohn (1993). Titled *Punished by Rewards: The Trouble with Gold Stars, Incentive Plans, A's, Praise, and Other Bribes*, Kohn's exhaustive, well-documented 300-page treatise surveyed the damage caused by the so-called behaviorist school of psychology's influence on almost everything we do in education.

Behaviorists Gone Wild

In the 1940s, Harvard researcher B.F. Skinner set out to create a modern, scientific form of psychology in hopes of moving the field of study from its roots in the speculative proclamations of Freud and Jung and the quackery of phrenology (the so-called "study" of people's intelligence and personality based on the bumps on their skulls). Skinner's big idea was that, to be a science, psychology should be based on observation. Thus, he began using "conditioning"—the provision of small rewards and punishments—to train pigeons and rats (Skinner, 1969). Based on his observations, he concluded that all behavior, including human behavior, was driven by the quest for pleasure and the avoidance of pain or discomfort—in short, rewards and punishments.

Skinner called these dual drivers of behavior "reinforcements" and used them to train his lab animals—offering them, for example, a pellet of food for one move in the right direction, followed by another, and then another. Before long, his pigeons were playing Ping-Pong with one another and his rats were running through mazes. It was a simple, empirical idea, and it caught on. Soon business managers began applying these ideas to drive employee behavior—offering bonuses for high performance and pink slips for low performance—all under the aegis of what were considered "scientific management" principles.

Eventually, these ideas wormed their way into education. Although educators typically shy away from words like "punishment," preferring more nuanced terms like "consequences," the same general idea underlies our pervasive use of external motivators in education: We reward students for desired behavior and dole out consequences for undesired behavior. We give tests and assign grades to get students learn what we want them to learn. We give out prizes for good behavior and take away recess for bad behavior. And in what now seems like an inevitable extension of these practices, we have begun applying these same testing and grading schemes—the stock and trade of education since early in the 20th century—to schools and teachers themselves in an effort to "reform" education by applying scientific management principles to school systems.

A Growing Global Epidemic

It's not just in the United States that behaviorism has dominated education policy. A few years ago, Pasi Sahlberg (2011), architect of Finland's much-vaunted reform efforts, observed that top-down approaches to reform—namely, using external pressure in the form of standards, high-stakes testing, test-based teacher performance evaluation, and school accountability to drive performance improvements—have spread, virus-like, throughout education systems worldwide. He cleverly dubbed the phenomenon the Global Education Reform Movement, or G.E.R.M. for short.

In simple terms, the last two decades of reforms have attempted to push new ideas and ways of working into the system, including federal mandates for testing, school improvement, and teacher credentialing. In turn, many states have resorted to dictating policies to districts, often defaulting to heavy-handed monitoring as the main tool to ensure compliance. Districts, in turn, employ their own compliance monitoring schemes to get schools to toe the line and principals find themselves becoming drill sergeants issuing marching orders to teachers, who, in turn, resort to rewards and consequences to cajole or force students into learning.

We might describe the whole approach as "outside in" and describe its symptoms accordingly:

Starting with the glass half empty. Outside-in approaches often begin with deficit thinking. We dwell on "achievement gaps," "at-risk" students, and "poor performance," which leads to a generally dim view of the system and the people in it.

Scripting one-size-fits-all solutions. If we view the system as a hopeless mess, we're naturally inclined to bring in outside solutions to fix it, often in the form of scripted solutions (e.g., "teacher-proof" curricula and programs) that we command educators to *adopt* with so-called "fidelity of implementation." However, because they're so scripted, these imposed solutions often do little to develop any real expertise in the system.

Giving orders. To get people to employ the scripted solutions, leaders resort to delivering edicts or issuing orders and principals (operating as middle managers) are tasked with enforcing the orders, with teachers expected to follow them dutifully.

Relying on summative measures. Outside-in reforms typically rely on externally administered *summative* measures (i.e., high-stakes tests) as the prime (if not *only*) data point that matters or can be trusted. These data, of course, often come too late for educators to do anything about them—the students tested have already left the school or classroom in which they were tested. Thus, educators find themselves trying to drive by looking through the rear window.

Using coaching to ensure compliance. Outside-in approaches also tend to warp one of the more effective strategies for improving performance: collaboration and coaching. As we'll see later in this book, when administrators operate with top-down behaviorist mindsets, they tend to recast coaches as confederates of the central office, tasked with ensuring compliance and reporting on those who don't toe the line.

Employing extrinsic rewards and punishments. The default motivational device for top-down reform efforts is carrots and sticks—sanctions for poor performance and rewards for good performance. Yet as we'll see, these extrinsic rewards have diminishing returns over time.

Maintaining pressure. Frustrated by diminishing returns, administrators often feel the continual need to turn up the heat to get the gains experienced from the initial dose of extrinsic motivators. Yet, as we'll see, increased pressure often impedes performance and thwarts collaborative and creative thinking.

Collectively, these outside-in approaches are not only exhausting but also counterproductive, due to some serious, fundamental flaws.

Fundamental Flaws with Outside-In Approaches

Perhaps the most fundamental flaw with top-down approaches is also the most commonsensical one: Namely, we can't *force* anyone to learn anything. With the possible exceptions of subliminal advertising and brainwashing, knowledge never enters anyone's head involuntarily; to learn something, we must *want* to learn it. Students are no different, of course. We can tinker all we want with the system of education that surrounds them, but if they aren't motivated to learn, they won't.

At this point, given how pervasive and ingrained outside-in thinking is, some readers might be asking, But don't people sometimes need good, old-fashioned top-down direction and pressure to, as the old song goes, straighten up and fly right? Didn't we need to force teachers to take their jobs seriously and care about *all* students? Prior to top-down reforms like No Child Left Behind, weren't we doing too little to keep students from falling through the cracks? Wasn't that what high-stakes testing was really all about—forcing the system to focus on all students? And at the very least, didn't it give superintendents and school leaders the license to employ some tough love to get everyone focused on the real problems at hand? What's so wrong about that?

Some of that may be true. Certainly, it's important to focus on the success of all students. And some studies have shown that the initial threat of sanctions did, in fact, cause some schools, especially those with small numbers of underperforming students, to pay more attention to them and improve their outcomes (Ahn & Vigdor, 2014). Yet given that student motivation contributes as much to students' success as the quality of their teachers (Hattie, 2009; Marzano, 1998), we might wonder if we've spent endless time and energy devising sophisticated formulas for calculating school performance, value-added gains, adequate yearly progress, and teacher performance—which collectively account for about 20 percent of the variance in student achievement (13 percent for teachers, 7 percent for schools)—while overlooking an equally large leverage point for student success, namely student motivation, which accounts for roughly 14 percent of the variance in student achievement.

Rewards *Can* Focus Our Attention, But . . .

Moreover, while tracking student achievement is important, it's possible that we've put too much faith in the accuracy of these data. Consider the following experiment: Steven Levitt, author of *Freakonomics* (and a self-avowed behaviorist), led a team of economists in a series of studies involving some 7,000 students in the Chicago area to see whether incentives—like cold, hard cash—could entice students to perform better on tests. As they sat down to take the standardized test, students were told that if they did well, they'd receive an award, ranging in size from $3 trophies to $20 cash awards (Levitt, List, Neckermann, & Sadoff, 2012). Generally speaking, the small rewards worked: Students performed at significantly higher levels, equivalent to demonstrating about five to six months of additional learning. The economists patted themselves on the back for demonstrating that financial incentives could work in the classroom. Yet this study really seems to have other, more profound implications: Recall that the students had *no prior knowledge of the reward system* before they sat down to take the test, so they weren't studying any harder or preparing any differently for it; they were just buckling down and taking the exam a bit more seriously. In other words, the small bribes made the students *care enough* about the test to miraculously appear six months smarter—all because they suddenly applied themselves on a test that heretofore had been meaningless to them. Yet these were often the same standardized achievement tests on which the students' own teachers and school leaders were being evaluated. That fact alone should give us pause.

Rewards Don't Provide Clarity

With that in mind, some might argue that perhaps we should force students to care about the tests by making them high-stakes for kids, too—for example, linking promotion, graduation, or college admissions decisions to them. For the sake of argument, let's say we did exactly that (the ethics of doing so notwithstanding given concerns about their validity and reliability). We might then ask: Would it make a difference? That's exactly what Ronald Fryer Jr., a researcher at Harvard University, sought to find out when he attempted to use external rewards to drive student behavior. He offered 18,000 students in four cities a total of $6.3 million in rewards to show up to school, behave better, and get better grades. In New York City, where he paid students for good test scores, he found no effects. "As zero as zero gets," he told *Time* magazine (Ripley, 2010, n.p.).

Fryer chalked up the disappointing results to students' genuine confusion about *how* to improve their performance; many reported, for example, that they hoped to raise their grades by "reading the test questions more carefully" or "not racing to see who could finish first" (Fryer, 2010, p. 33). "Not a single student," Fryer observed, mentioned "reading the textbook, studying harder, completing their homework, or asking teachers . . . about confusing topics" (p. 33). The point here appears to be that external rewards alone (or sanctions, for that matter) don't drive better performance if students (or teachers, for that matter) don't know *how* to achieve better results.

Rewards Can Backfire

All right, then, some might say, let's use rewards *and* better guidance to drive the better behaviors we want to see in students, such as reading more and studying harder. That should work, right? Yes, perhaps it would, at least *for a little while*. And that's the real problem with external motivators (even positive rewards); they *can* drive behavior, but ultimately erode internal, or *intrinsic*, motivation for engaging in that same behavior.

As Deci, Ryan, and Koestner (1999) reported in a sweeping synthesis of research on intrinsic motivation, when researchers rewarded young children with cookies for drawing pictures (something they had been doing for fun prior to the study), afterward those same students became less likely to entertain themselves by drawing pictures. Those rewards, it seemed, had the effect of turning the once fun activity of drawing into a chore—something done to please others, not themselves.

In other words, if we reward kids for doing what they ought to find naturally rewarding (including learning), we may inadvertently send the message that learning is a chore and not enjoyable. And if our entire system for motivating learning is based on external rewards, like grades, gold stars, report cards, and pizza parties for finishing summer reading lists, we could be sending a strong message that this whole enterprise of learning is a kind of unpleasantness to be tolerated or endured—which may explain why research has found that the longer students stay in school, the less intrinsic motivation or interest they report in core academic areas (Gottfried et al., 2001).

Rewards Work Until They Don't

So, if these behaviorist-inspired, outside-in approaches are making us so miserable, why are they so darn pernicious?

One likely reason is that behaviorism often rings true to our own experience. At some point, we have all probably used old-fashioned returns and consequences and seen them change behavior—whether it's threatening the removal of TV privileges if our kids don't clean their rooms or creating late fees to get adults to pick up their kids from afterschool care on time. We have likely seen them work in schools, too, especially chaotic ones where establishing some routines, order, and better habits are needed. In short, there's a time and place for employing top-down efforts and external rewards to establish better routines and get our house in order (sometimes literally).

The trouble is these extrinsic motivators have diminishing returns over time. Like drugs, their effects begin to fade the longer (and more) we use them. As a result, we must continually amp up the rewards or punishments to achieve even the *same* results. Instead of having kids who naturally appreciate being tidy for its own sake, we find ourselves needing to devise and monitor ever more complex weekly allowance schemes. Or instead of creating more punctual parents, we may encourage more parents to show up late, unapologetically paying what they've come to see as a surcharge granting them permission to leave their kids in afterschool care a bit longer. Or instead of having kids who want to behave, we create compliant students who revert to bad behavior as soon as the teacher's back is turned.

Shifting to a Better Kind of Motivation

In many ways, then, the notion that we can drive sustainable change with external rewards is a myth. The problem with myths, though, as David Hopkins noted in his book *Exploding the Myths of School Reform* (2013), is that deep inside most of them lies a germ of truth. We've all seen external rewards work in *some* circumstances, so we start to assume that they ought to work in *all* circumstances. And that is precisely where the trouble begins; it's also what makes outside-in approaches to change so pernicious, like a bad cold (or G.E.R.M.) that keeps hanging around.

So how might we begin to cure ourselves?

One starting point would be to recognize that behaviorism isn't the only school of thought when it comes to motivation. Indeed, for the past four decades, a growing body of research has begun to emerge to show that *internal* motivators are often more powerful than *external* ones when it comes to driving behavior. Consider, for example, those moments when you've become so enraptured by something you're doing (e.g., something you're intensely passionate about, like playing a musical instrument) that you find yourself utterly losing track of time. Or recall the times that you've felt such a deep sense of purpose or solidarity with your fellow human beings that you've voluntarily sacrificed your spare time for no tangible reward at all. Or maybe you've found yourself so wrapped up in getting better at something that you've stuck with it—whether it's repeatedly picking yourself up off the ice while learning to skate, casting a fishing lure into a river over and over until you get it just right, or blowing $10 on Skee-Ball at a carnival midway because you're oh-so-close to hitting the 100-point slot.

Motivating with Choice

Psychology researcher Edward Deci, who conducted a meta-analysis of 128 studies on motivation, has theorized that intrinsic motivation percolates out of two deep psychological needs: (1) self-determination and (2) competence (Deci et al., 1999). For starters, we're more motivated to pursue a task when we feel we have some choice in how to accomplish it. Researchers have long observed a link between intrinsic motivation and freedom of choice. A 2008 meta-analysis of 41 studies, for example, found a strong link between giving students choices and their intrinsic motivation, task performance, and willingness to take on challenging tasks (Patall, Cooper, & Robinson, 2008). Second, we enjoy activities when we choose them and when they offer a sort of "Goldilocks" level of challenge—something that's neither too easy nor too difficult to accomplish. Video games, from their earliest days, have tapped into this intrinsic motivation: Each level offers a progressively greater challenge—more Space Invaders marching down the screen or faster ghosts chasing Pac-Man around the maze.

There's a third factor, too, one that bubbles out of something motivation researcher Mihaly Csikszentmihalyi (1993) calls "flow"—that experience marked by "losing track of time and being unaware of fatigue and of everything else but the activity itself" (p. 14). In a groundbreaking study, Csikszentmihalyi, Rathunde, and Whalen (1993) attempted to find "flow" in students by tracking their engagement in learning throughout the day using what was, at the time, cutting-edge communications technology: a pager. At random intervals during the day, the pager would go off and students would write down what they were doing and their emotional state while doing it. Generally speaking, the researchers found that while in class, students were concentrating hard but disinterested in what they were learning—due in part to teachers perfunctorily plodding through the curriculum and teaching what was necessary with little attention to explaining why students ought to be interested in learning it.

A few teachers stood out as exceptions for students, though, stoking their interest in learning by modeling passion for their subject areas and explaining why they were worthy of long-term, professional pursuit—in contrast to many teachers who seemed to leech joy from learning by not explaining its purpose or applying it to the outside world. As one talented yet disengaged math student plaintively observed, "Once you have the theorem down, it would help you to know how you could use it, instead of just strictly what it is. I think it makes it more interesting and easier to learn" (Csikszentmihalyi et al., 1993, p. 183). In short, what students were saying is they felt more motivation to learn when they understood the *purpose* of learning.

Fueling Change with "Motivation 3.0"

In his book *Drive: The Surprising Truth About What Motivates Us*, Daniel Pink (2009) simplifies and synthesizes these ideas into a concept that he calls "Motivation 3.0," a wholesale upgrade over what he labels "Motivation 2.0"—in essence, a behaviorism-driven system of rewards and punishments. Motivation 3.0, writes Pink, taps into the power of (1) autonomy (providing people with some choices in their actions), (2) mastery (helping people continually advance toward higher levels of performance), and (3) purpose (providing a rationale of why something is worth doing or a deeper purpose for doing it).

All of this raises an important question: What might it look like if we were to upgrade the operating system, so to speak, of school improvement? What if we were to move beyond a heavy (if not almost exclusive) reliance on behaviorist notions of Motivation 2.0 and instead begin to employ these Motivation 3.0 drivers for improving educational outcomes? What if we were to start with *intrinsic motivation* for students and built our approach to improvement—inside out—from there? Could it be possible that if students were more motivated, everything might get a lot easier and a whole lot more joyful for them ... and their teachers?

Imagining a Better Approach

Let's imagine for a moment what such an approach might look like. If we were to build upon what we know about intrinsic motivation—for both students and professionals—we might design a whole approach to improvement (or better yet, *innovation*) around these elements in Figure 2.1:

Figure 2.1 | A Better Approach

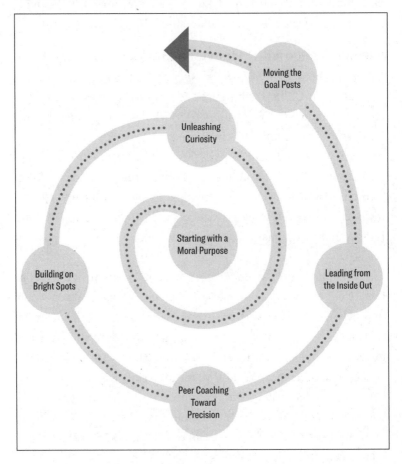

1. **Starting with a moral purpose.** Instead of using "because I said so or else" rationale or putting people on a need-to-know basis,

we'd start with grounding everyone in deep conviction or a shared moral purpose of why they were called to education in the first place.

2.   **Unleashing curiosity.** Instead of creating a system that revolves around tests, we'd start with student motivation and engagement, tapping into a familiar, yet often overlooked, motivator of learning: *curiosity*.

3.   **Building on bright spots.** We'd also recognize that answers often lie within finding "positive deviants" in people's current practices and finding ways to expand what's already working more broadly and consistently.

4.   **Peer coaching toward precision.** We'd give teachers ownership (i.e., autonomy) over their professional lives and encourage true peer coaching—teachers working together in small teams to hone their skills on best practices identified from "positive deviants" or "bright spots" in the system.

5.   **Leading from the inside out.** Real solutions come from better insights, so instead of being tasked with merely enforcing orders, school leaders would ask powerful questions that help turn *threat* conditions into *challenge* conditions, encouraging people to "fail forward" in rapid improvement cycles and develop greater precision of practice.

6. **Moving the goal posts.** Because what we measure is what gets done, we'd also reframe the goals, using more robust measures for student learning and success, including formative and performance assessments.

Can It Really Be Done?

At this point, some readers may be thinking that all of this sounds lovely, but can it really be done? That question is, in many ways, where an important chapter in our story begins—with the leader of an American education nonprofit research and consulting organization being invited to meet a local school official in Melbourne. Initially, the American imagined he would impress the official with his own organization's approaches to improving instruction, leadership, and school performance, which had been forged in the crucible of top-down reform and designed to help struggling schools boost student performance on standardized achievement measures.

Out of politeness, though, he first asked the local official, Wayne Craig, to talk about his own improvement efforts in the Northern Metropolitan Regional District. As Craig related how he and his colleagues had focused on curiosity and inside-out approaches, it soon became apparent that they had engineered a unique and refreshing approach to school improvement—one that drew from great ideas abroad while weaving in homespun insights and a dash of, well, counterintuitive craziness. The more Craig spoke about the successful effort in the northern suburbs of Melbourne, the less crazy and more compelling the whole approach began to sound, especially since it laid bare many unexamined ideas behind high-stakes testing approaches to reform—policy levers that were never really grounded in real research but, at best, extrapolated from experiments on pigeons and rats and assumed to work on humans.

Yes, It's Already Being Done

What the northern Melbourne experience revealed is that an inside-out approach to improvement was more than just a nice-sounding theory or wishful thinking; it was already being done and working. Moreover, it wasn't just a clever way to transform a single classroom or school but a way to propel an entire system forward and point toward a better way to improve learning on a large scale that contrasts sharply with the counterproductive, top-down approaches to reform. What Craig's experience in Melbourne showed—and what we describe in the rest of this book—is that it's possible to drive systems change from wholly different assumptions about motivation and system change. Ultimately, what the Melbourne experience revealed is that this seemingly crazy idea might not be so odd after all, but something, like professional football without pads or a Christmas song from a prisoner's point of view, that maybe only Australians—with their willingness to scan the world for ideas, mash them up, and season them with a dash of this-is-crazy-but-just-might-work ingenuity—could dream up. Before long, the American CEO quietly put the materials he'd intended to share back inside his bag and let Wayne Craig tell the rest of his story.

PAUSE AND REFLECT

- What motivates your students to learn?
- What motivates your teachers in their work?
- Can you clearly identify your purpose?
- What motivates you in your work?
- Do you need to "buck the trend" in an area of your practice?
- What are you doing that might be perceived as new or innovative?
- Do you see student learning through a deficit or opportunity lens?

ENVISION A BETTER WAY

- Conduct your own learning walks and observe which teacher practices are likely to encourage intrinsic motivation in students.
- Conduct a staff survey to find out what your teachers believe motivates students to learn.
- Create a list of behaviors or actions you observe that either encourage or discourage student motivation.

- Enlist the help of an objective "critical friend" to discuss current practices to help inform improvement.

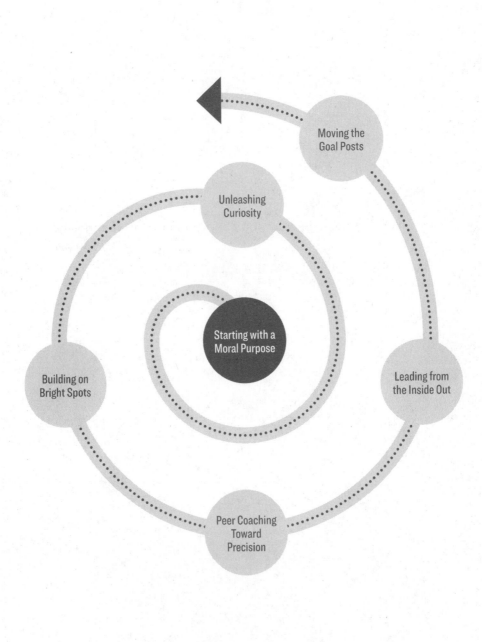

3

Starting with a Moral Purpose

I think, at a child's birth, if a mother could ask a fairy godmother to endow it with the most useful gift, that gift should be curiosity.

Eleanor Roosevelt

One of the most celebrated events in Australian history seems to be, to outsiders at least, a tragic case of senseless futility. On April 25, 1915, the untested Australian and New Zealand Army Corps (ANZAC) joined British, Indian, and Canadian troops in an assault on the Ottoman Empire in Gallipoli, Turkey. From the outset, nothing went as planned. A navigation error along with a strong current caused the first 1,000 troops to drift off course and land in the wrong spot—on more formidable terrain than expected. Unable to take the high ground, 700 of 1,000 troops died the first night of the invasion. A subsequent wave of troops advanced a bit farther, but were pinned down under heavy Turkish fire. Ian Hamilton, the British commander, safely ensconced on a nearby battleship, commanded the Aussies via radio to stand their ground. "Dig! Dig! Dig!" he ordered.

So that's exactly what they did—for months, they hunkered down in trenches and endured withering sniper fire and disease until Hamilton was finally replaced and the new commander ordered a retreat. By then, roughly 8,000 soldiers from Australia and 3,000 from New Zealand had lost their lives. Every April 25, Australians celebrate Anzac Day and the perseverance of the so-called "Diggers" who fought so bravely on that beach. For foreigners, it might seem odd to celebrate a frustrating defeat, yet for many Aussies, it was on the beaches of Gallipoli that the former penal colony finally stepped out of the shadow of the British empire and forged its own national character as one of fearless, fiercely loyal, and scrappy survivors. In the words of the Anzac veteran Charles Bean, "Anzac stood, and still stands, for reckless valor in a good cause . . . an endurance that will never own defeat" (1946, p. 181). Australians still relish their image as an indomitable people who "punch above their weight," enduring even when all hope seems lost.

The Undignified History of Systemic Reform

For much of education history, district-level reform efforts have also reflected "reckless valor in a good cause"—with similarly disappointing results that culminate in one leader's removal and the next one beating a hasty retreat from the futile effort. Sometimes, even uttering the words "systems change" may evoke eye-rolling because we've seen too few examples of school systems, especially large ones, pulling off comprehensive improvement efforts with much success. It's far easier to point to disappointments, like the Annenberg grants from years ago, Mark Zuckerberg's efforts to improve Newark Public Schools, or the turbulent era of reform in San Diego in the 1990s that Diane Ravitch chronicled in her book *The Death and Life of the Great American School System* (2010).

So-called systemic change often seems to result in people doing too much and accomplishing too little. In *So Much Reform, So Little Change*, University of Chicago professor Charles Payne suggests with tongue firmly in cheek that when people talk about systemic reform, the "wise will gesture as if to ward off evil; garlic has been known to help" (2008, p. 169). For Payne, when the word "systemic" gets thrown into conversations about school improvement, it means, "Let's pretend to do on a grand scale what we have no idea how to do on a small scale" (p. 169).

That's often true, of course. Yet we often see the opposite problem: Simply fixing a school or two is nice but does little to improve learning at any kind of scale. At best, it merely creates an island of excellence that all too quickly sinks back into the sea of mediocrity. Moreover, providing students with a better elementary school experience is important, but it is all for naught if those students subsequently land in an inadequate middle or high school. So, too, is high school reform an endless uphill climb if students continually enter 9th grade unprepared for more rigorous learning—and the same can be said of middle schools receiving students who are behind academically. In short, it takes a village—or a system—to prepare a child.

Nonetheless, the trash heap of history is littered with many failed systemic improvement efforts. So why does systems change—arguably the right approach—so often come out wrong?

Articulating the Commander's Intent

One reason for the dearth of positive results is that leaders may operate from flawed assumptions about what it takes to inspire real change in people—the equivalent of issuing commands from the safe confines of a battleship with scant understanding of what's really happening on the front lines. Back in his days as a teacher educator and school principal, Wayne Craig had watched from the trenches as plenty of Gallipoli-like disasters played out in education systems in which he found himself. He had seen many regional directors come and go, often dreaming up ideas from the central office and attempting to push them down to the troops, so to speak. But simply barking orders, Craig had observed, did little to effect change.

He wasn't alone in his dim view of trying to push orders into a system from the top down. In recent years, the U.S. military has, in fact, come to much the same conclusion. For decades, military plans were among the most meticulous imaginable—which only stands to reason, of course, as soldiers' lives depend on their commanders developing winning strategies. Yet as Chip Heath and Dan Heath note in their book *Made to Stick* (2007), military leaders have learned through trial and error that even the best-laid plans are often upturned a few minutes into a military engagement. Unexpected events always occur. Cloud cover blocks aerial surveillance. Equipment fails. Weather blows in and supply routes become impassable. Opposing armies respond unpredictably and have unanticipated cards up their sleeves. As one military commander ruefully observed, "no plan survives contact with the enemy" (Heath & Heath, 2007, p. 25).

In light of these realities, the military determined that it doesn't need more *sophisticated* planning—creating decision trees that branch off in every imaginable direction—but rather simple, guiding ideas that capture the key concept or objective and then letting people on the ground make real-time decisions about how to accomplish that objective. In military parlance, it's called the "commander's intent." Instead of crafting and sending out a lengthy plan and commanding everyone to hew closely to it, a general simply says, for example, "Break the will of the enemy in the Southeast region" (Heath & Heath, 2007, p. 26), and leaves it up to the soldiers in the field to make it happen. Thus, even if the original plan doesn't withstand contact with the enemy, the intent remains.

Tapping the Power of Intrinsic Motivation

As it turns out, a leader clearly articulating her intent also reflects one of Dan Pink's (2009) key drivers of Motivation 3.0—*purpose*. Articulating the deeper purpose behind what we're asking people is often a powerful motivator because, despite what we might like to believe about ourselves, logic and reasoning are *not* what guide most of our behaviors—rather, emotions and gut instinct do. Indeed, we tend to use reasoning and logic to justify (after the fact) what our emotions and instincts have already decided we are going to do. Chip and Dan Heath (2010) employ the metaphor of an *elephant* and *rider* to describe the power of our more primitive limbic brains (home to emotions and unconscious responses to our environment) over our more sophisticated prefrontal cortexes (home to logic and conscious thought). Our logical, conscious brain is but a rider on the elephant; it likes to think it controls the elephant (and sometimes it does), but for the most part, the elephant pretty much goes where it wants to go.

No One Cares What You Do . . . They Care *Why* You Do It

Simon Sinek (2011) has observed that the greatest leaders in history were able to inspire action by *starting with why*. Martin Luther King Jr., for example, became the leader of the U.S. civil rights movement not because he capably articulated the *what* or *how* (calling upon people to march or conduct sit-ins), but because he touched people's hearts with a deeper, spiritual *why*—namely, that decent people must act when man-made laws conflict with higher laws and degrade our fellow human beings. In Sinek's words, "people don't buy *what* you do, they buy *why* you do it." The same might be said of systemic improvement efforts. What people are likely to find more compelling is not the *what* (e.g., ensuring everyone follows the curriculum guides), but the *why* (e.g., providing every student with a pathway to a fulfilling life).

As evidence of the power of starting with *why,* Sinek points to the fanatical customers of Apple who, for example, are willing to pay a steep premium for a product that in reality is fairly comparable to less expensive products. Apple customers have shown they're willing to buy not only computers but also phones, TVs, or computers (and likely, cars) from Apple, yet when Gateway computer tried to sell TVs, they flopped badly. So, what's different about Apple? They *start with why*, Sinek asserts. Through their advertising, marketing, and product design, they make it clear that at the core of everything they do is a goal to upend the status quo. Every new product is an attempt to do something radically different than what's been done before.

Sinek depicts this *why, how,* and *what* as concentric circles with *why* in the center, *how* in the middle ring, and *what* in the outer band. For Apple, the *why* (challenging the status quo) drives the *how* (sleek design and packaging) which in turns drives the *what* (a wide variety of cutting-edge products).

Most companies and leaders, however, start from the outside in, communicating *what*, not *why*, according to Sinek. Apple's competitors, in essence, ask customers, "Hey, do you want to buy a computer from us?" (which often evokes a *meh* response), whereas Apple asks, "Hey, do you want to challenge the status quo with us?" The second message—an invitation to join a movement—tends to be far more appealing. It's a great marketing technique, notes Sinek. And the reason it's so powerful is that it's an inside-out approach—one that starts with what's deep inside the psyches (or limbic brains) of Apple's customers.

Achieving Something Bigger Than Ourselves

Being clear about *why* is vitally important because in the crush of daily events, it's easy to lose sight of our purpose for doing almost anything. Yet we know from research on school districts that maintaining clarity around shared goals is strongly linked to district success (Waters & Marzano, 2006). Researchers are also finding that believing in something important or bigger than ourselves seems to have a spillover effect into believing that *change is possible* (Duhigg, 2012). When leaders continually link improvement efforts to a bigger picture that resonates with people's ideals and beliefs, they're more likely to get people to follow them—to, in effect, join the movement with them.

A "Catch Cry" Emerges

In Melbourne, Craig spent his first few months in his new director role engaged in countless meetings with students, parents, and teachers, asking them a simple question: *Why* are we here? Sure, it might have seemed like a question with an obvious answer, but as it turns out, it was one that seemingly hadn't been asked enough. Giving people a moment to step back from the fray of school closings and other challenges and contemplate what mattered most to them and what they really wanted to accomplish helped to foster some fresh thinking and optimism.

Craig walked away from his conversations with students, parents, and teachers feeling heartened from what he heard: Everyone wanted something better. When he talked to students, he heard them say they wanted to be challenged. They wanted to feel proud of their schools. Some even begged for uniforms so they could look as respectable as students who were attending more expensive private schools.

When he talked to students' parents, he heard most of them say they wanted a better life for their children. In fact, that's why many of them had sacrificed everything they had to move to Australia in the first place: not so *they* could be more comfortable as adults but so their children could have a brighter future.

When he talked to teachers and administrators, he teased out that they, too, wanted something better: They wanted to feel successful at their jobs. They wanted to feel they were doing good work and changing children's lives.

During those conversations, he bounced a single word off them: *curiosity.* Do you feel *curious* at school? he would ask students. *Not much, but occasionally,* was the usual reply. Would you like to feel curious more often at school? *Absolutely.*

Parents quickly grasped the concept, too. Would I want my children to be passionate about their studies? *Yes, of course,* parents would reply. What would that look like? *Well, they'd immerse themselves in something they found interesting and pursue it because they were . . . curious.*

Educators also saw the value. He'd ask them, if our students were always curious, wouldn't everything else get easier? *Yes, of course.* What would it feel like if *you* were curious as a professional, trying to figure out, for example, how to help curiosity flourish in students?

It was certainly a compelling vision: schools where *everyone* was curious. Soon, a slogan (or what Australians call a "catch cry") began to emerge: creating students who were "literate, numerate, and curious."

Communicating Moral Purpose

Craig began repeating those three words, like a mantra, all over the northern suburbs of Melbourne to keep everyone focused on accomplishing something bigger than themselves. *Literate* students, he would say, can acquire and apply knowledge. *Numerate* students can think logically, think systematically, and employ quantitative reasoning to solve problems. And *curious* students have a fire burning inside them; they want to learn, ask questions, and challenge themselves to build a better world around them.

By repeating the mantra, Craig reminded people of their *moral* purpose—not just their job roles or individual responsibilities, but the bigger picture that gave their jobs meaning and a compelling reason for why they must work together to prepare students for an unpredictable future.

Staying Focused on *Why*

In short, Craig and Hopkins understood intuitively that what people find most compelling is not the outer *what* of their efforts (e.g., using better instruction techniques), but the inner *why* (e.g., providing students with gifts, like curiosity, that they could carry with them for the rest of their lives). Craig also understood that one of the most important roles for a leader is to stay on message with oneself.

Over and over, Craig beat the drum of *literacy*, *numeracy*, and *curiosity* to ensure people wouldn't lose sight of the *why* behind *what* they were doing. With every group he met, he'd speak of making kids literate, numerate, and curious. He made sure those themes were woven into every teacher training supported by the regional office. He spoke everywhere with school leaders and teachers about students being literate, numerate, and curious. And before long, he began to hear his words repeated back to him and saw them popping up in school mission statements and performance reports.

Most important, though, people began internalizing the moral purpose and making it their own driving reason for coming to school every day. He saw veteran teachers who had been burned out and ready to retire become re-inspired to stay on to see if things might actually change. At the beginning of a training session, they might start out by sitting in the back of the room, arms folded, too jaded to participate. But as the moral purpose began to sink in and they saw the practicality of what was being asked of them, they would say things like, "You know, we've been talking about this kind of stuff for a long time. I don't know why we haven't actually done it." The mantra of helping all students become literate, numerate, and curious provided a sense of moral *purpose*—the deep *why* that would unite educators around doing something bigger than themselves.

A Picture Comes into View

As the new sense of *why* became clearer, a funny thing happened. The better habits and more consistent teaching routines (i.e., the *how* that so many previous improvement efforts had sought, and failed, to instill) began to stick. And the usual threats—the brow-beating, bird-dogging, or finger-wagging—aren't what led to the change in behavior. Nor was it a hyper-complex road map or multi-page Gantt charts that did it. Rather, it was encouraging people to buy into the big, compelling idea that powered the whole effort.

Once people grabbed ahold of that big idea, it became their own and they no longer thought the same way about teaching. They started to reexamine their practices and work together to figure out how to make curiosity and student engagement happen—not unlike soldiers grasping a commander's intent and figuring out how to rise to the challenge.

A Tale of Two Schools

Among the many schools where curiosity took root and began to transform teaching practices, two were Greenhills Primary School and William Ruthven Secondary College. In a lot of ways, the two campuses could not have been more different. Greenhills was a mid-sized elementary school in a leafy suburban enclave. When its principal, Rowan Kayll, arrived there in June 2010—the middle of the school year in Australia—he found a school that was *good*, but not *great*. It had hit a performance plateau, yet few people in the school seemed to care. Most of its 425 students were at or above proficiency, but they weren't really growing.

As Kayll recalled, "Our student learning data showed inconsistencies. When looking at one form of data, achievement overall looked to be quite high, but then other data highlighted puzzling gaps." In short, its overall high student achievement masked performance disparities; a number of students were underperforming and teachers seemed to be at a loss for how to help them. Yes, the school had intervention programs for struggling students, noted the school's assistant principal, Tonia Gibson, who arrived six months after Kayll (and is a co-writer of this book), yet they were all fairly rote interventions—essentially, "let's drill, drill, drill, without getting to the root cause" of what was preventing some students from performing at grade level.

William Ruthven Secondary College, on the other hand, was a school in strife. It had come into being on January 1, 2010—the result of a merger between two previously under-enrolled and low-performing schools, Merrilands College and Lakeside Secondary College. Created to serve grades 7 to 12 in the working-class neighborhood, it was home to immigrants from at least 45 countries. Three-quarters of the school's students were from non–English-speaking families, many of whom spoke Arabic at home (Milligan, 2014).

Knowing the multitude of technical and adaptive challenges the principal of this new school would face, Wayne Craig tapped Karen Money, an experienced school leader and veteran of other merger efforts, to lead the freshly minted school. When she took the helm, the school faced a budget shortfall of $1.2 million against an overall budget of $5 million, which meant she immediately had to let go of 15 teachers, nearly one-third of the school's staff—hardly a positive way to start a new tenure as principal.

"To take on a new school like this . . . was frightening," Money later told a newspaper reporter. "I was conscious of the troublesome nature of the merger, but students are at the center of my work, and I resent that the system had let them down in terms of the classrooms they were forced to learn in and the underperforming teachers" (Maslen, 2013). Although she had a graduate degree in leadership from the respected University of Melbourne and years of experience as a school administrator, the challenge was nonetheless daunting: balance the school's budget, coach teachers to higher levels of performance, heal a fractured school culture, bring parents in as partners in learning, and help the entire community develop a deeper sense of purpose.

Money knew from the start that making the transition from a fragmented school community—one reeling from budget cuts and layoffs—to one focused on curiosity and accelerated learning would be an uphill climb. "I knew the change process would be hard, and that you have to bring people along with you," she told a reporter, noting that she hadn't won any popularity points by laying off staff. "But sometimes the principal has to make tough decisions so I had to put on the armor each morning" (Maslen, 2013).

Any one of these challenges by itself would have been daunting. But facing them all at once was a tall order fraught with much anxiety. Under such pressure, many leaders might have defaulted to top-down directivity—the equivalent of a commander yelling the order to "Dig! Dig! Dig!" Yet as we'll see in the next chapter, Money took a decidedly different approach.

At the same time, it would have been easier and safer for Kayll and Gibson to let Greenhills continue to coast. Their achievement scores were fine. Teachers were comfortable. Parents were happy, and the students loved being Greenhills kids. Change—especially a change as sweeping as putting curiosity at the center of learning—was risky. Yet they decided that good enough was *not* good enough. Their students deserved more. And so they decided to press ahead with flipping the script.

A New Spark

For educators in both schools and across the entire region, the idea of curiosity was at once familiar—as familiar as a toddler looking up and asking why the sky is blue—and yet unfamiliar, like a childhood companion we haven't seen for years whose face has faded from memory. Yet as the idea came into sharper focus for educators, a new picture of what education *could* be emerged with it. It was a picture that caused them to rethink what schooling was all about and reconnect to something that somehow, somewhere, many of them had lost—that deeper *why* that had drawn them into education in the first place. For most teachers, it had, of course, never been about boosting kids' scores on a national test, filling out gradebooks, or turning in report cards. What had hooked them on education was seeing a child's eyes light up with interest, jaws drop in wonder, or brows furrow quizzically.

It was an idea captured in a single word: *curiosity*.

PAUSE AND REFLECT

- What in your work sparks your own curiosity?
- Can you identify and articulate your own moral purpose?
- What *why* questions have you asked a teacher lately?
- What role does curiosity play in your life?
- What challenges might you face in enacting your moral purpose?

ENVISION A BETTER WAY

- Create a list of purposeful *why* questions to spark others' curiosity about student learning.
- Make a chart, poster, or diagram showing what you are curious about in your work.
- Think about how you might bring people together around a shared moral purpose.
- Make a list of pathways that may help you overcome obstacles in enacting your moral purpose.

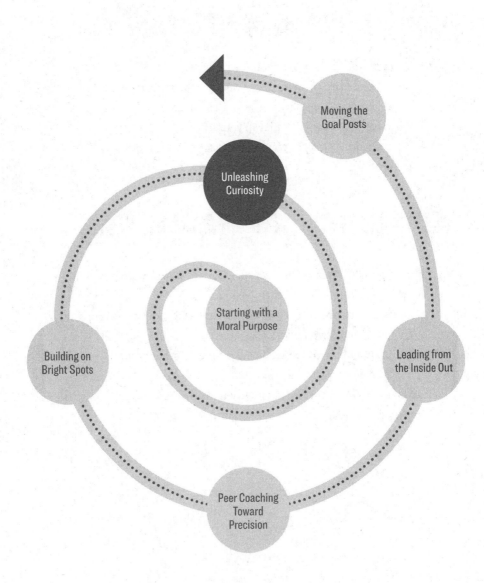

Moving the
Goal Posts

Unleashing
Curiosity

Starting with a
Moral Purpose

Building on
Bright Spots

Leading from
the Inside Out

Peer Coaching
Toward
Precision

4

Unleashing Curiosity

The mind is not a vessel to be filled, but a fire to be kindled.

Plutarch

"It's brilliant, mate, but not what I asked for," Wayne Craig told his friend and colleague John Munro. The two of them were sitting in a pub near the University of Melbourne, engaged in their Friday afternoon ritual of drinking tar-colored beer and discussing the affairs of the world. Weeks earlier, Craig had asked Munro, a respected professor of gifted and talented and special needs education, to draft a white paper on instructional strategies that support student curiosity. What Munro had come back with was, well . . . curious.

It was 20-plus pages of text that used *Alice in Wonderland* as a conceit for curious learners. Titled "Curiouser and Curiouser," the paper showed Alice's "curiosity thinking" at every step of her adventure, delighting in the remarkable things around her, exclaiming, for example, "What a funny watch! It tells the day of the month, and doesn't tell what o'clock it is!" (Munro, 2015). Curiosity accompanied Alice everywhere in Wonderland, popping up time and again, like the Cheshire Cat, accompanying her learning adventure.

Craig had originally wanted Munro to write a how-to guide for teachers, but the more he thought about what Munro had written and the metaphor he used, the more it seemed to fit. Munro had hit upon something important: Curiosity must accompany us on our learning journey. We need a sense of wonder to keep us probing deeper, anticipating what might lie around the next corner—whether it's a talking caterpillar on a toadstool or new knowledge on the next page of a book. A curious mind delights in the answers it finds. It anticipates learning something new or getting to the bottom of a nagging question. A curious mind is addicted to learning.

In many ways, curiosity itself is as strange as anything that ever came out of Lewis Carroll's pen. Often, it arrives out of thin air, materializing like the Cheshire Cat. A question pops into our minds, making us crave an answer. Yet like the Cheshire Cat, it can disappear just as quickly. And when it fades, often so too does the joy of learning.

It can also be distracting, like a topcoat-wearing rabbit running past us. We chase a question, clicking link after link on the internet until we realize we've wasted an hour or more down a proverbial rabbit hole.

As a result, we often may feel a little ambivalent about curiosity—just look at all the stories and inherited wisdom that paint curiosity as lurid fascination and temptation. In the Bible and Greek mythology, respectively, curiosity prompts Eve and Pandora to unleash evil upon the world. Folk wisdom warns us about "curiosity killing the cat." And modern-day web searchers seem to harbor the same misgivings about curiosity: Type the words "is curiosity" into Google, and it autofills with "a sin."

As parents, we may feel at times exasperated with our toddlers' incessant questions or construe teenagers' inquisitiveness as impudence. In classrooms, students' questions may feel like off-topic distractions—rabbit holes best left ignored. Or we may worry about a child becoming overly curious (i.e., "obsessed") with a single topic—be it horses, dinosaurs, or dogs.

The Power of Curiosity

And yet, there's something incredibly powerful about curiosity. It's our collective sense of wonder that prompts us to explore the deepest depths of the ocean or the moons of Jupiter. When focused, curiosity can be a powerful motivator, driving inventors to test thousands of different metals for lightbulb filaments before landing on the right one. And not all rabbit holes are bad: Einstein followed a long rabbit hole into the quantum world where he surmised that $E=mc^2$.

Better Living Through Curiosity

Moreover, contrary to time-honored stories and proverbs about the dangers of curiosity, it may not be the *death* of us, but rather the source of these positive life outcomes:

- Better job performance (Reio & Wiswell, 2000).
- Better relationships (Kashdan & Roberts, 2004)
- Greater leadership ability (Fernández-Aráoz, 2014).
- Persistence, goal-orientation, life meaning, and satisfaction (Kashdan & Steger, 2007).
- Longevity (Swan & Carmelli, 1996).

In addition, curiosity has a tremendous impact on student learning itself—it has been found to be as strongly linked to student academic performance as IQ (von Stumm, Hell, & Chamorro-Premuzic, 2011), likely for these two reasons:

Curiosity enhances memory. When we're curious about something, we're more apt to remember to learn and later recall new knowledge—even irrelevant information (Gruber, Gelman, & Ranganath, 2014).

Curiosity can fuel an addiction to learning. Satisfying curiosity fires dopamine reward centers in our brains, creating a sensation akin to receiving money, satisfying hunger, or taking drugs (Aron,

Shohamy, Clark, Myers, Gluck, & Poldrack, 2004). In short, curiosity may be habit forming. Substance abuse counselors have, in fact, long connected boredom with addiction and seek to help addicts avoid relapse by teaching them to engage in constructive novelty seeking (Heshmat, 2015).

Is It Nature or Nurture?

All of this may sound nice, you say, but can curiosity be taught, or is it simply a gift that some people have in greater abundance than others? That's an important question, of course.

Here's what we can discern from research.

One of the most powerful things about curiosity is that it *doesn't* need to be taught: Human beings are naturally predisposed to learning and exploration, following one *why* question with another in a quest to understand the world around us (Medina, 2008). Curiosity drives infants to stick foreign objects in their mouths and crawl from room to room to explore their environments. Nonetheless, early childhood researchers have found that toddlers demonstrate variable levels of *stimulation seeking,* and those who demonstrate greater curiosity as toddlers score, on average, about 12 points higher on tests of their IQ eight years later (Raine, Reynolds, Venables, & Mednick, 2002). If we stopped there, we might conclude curiosity has more to do with *nature* than nurture.

However, as dozens of studies conducted since the 1950s have discovered, *environmental conditions* profoundly influence children's openness to exploration. While studying the parenting styles of mothers in Africa and the United States, Mary Ainsworth and her colleagues (Ainsworth, Blehar, Waters, & Wall, 1978) observed that when infants enjoyed close, mutually affectionate relationships with their mothers (i.e., "secure attachment"), they were more apt to explore their surroundings than were infants with weaker maternal ties. This finding suggests that nurture—namely, how parents interact with children—influences curiosity.

Other studies have confirmed that environmental conditions—including those children encounter in school—can profoundly influence children's openness to exploration. For example, preschool children have been found to be more likely to explore their surroundings in the presence of a friendly, supportive adult than in the company of an aloof, critical one (Moore & Bulbulian, 1976). Other experiments have found that students, even those whose teachers or parents had identified them as having low levels of curiosity, were more likely to engage in exploratory behavior when adults actively encouraged their inquisitiveness with smiles, eye contact, and questions that encouraged further exploration (Henderson & Moore, 1980). Together, these studies make a strong case that the *environment* we create for children nurtures their curiosity. That's the good news.

How We Quash Curiosity in the Classroom

Here's the bad news: The longer our students stay in school—the very place we ought to help them ignite their curiosity—the less motivation and curiosity they demonstrate. Consider the following studies:

• A long-term study of student motivation, for instance, found that their interest in core academic subjects peaked at age 9 and diminished as they grew older (Gottfried et al., 2001).

• An examination of 298 students in grades 3, 5, and 7 enrolled in a predominantly white, Catholic school in a working-class neighborhood and a predominantly black public school in the Midwest found school-related curiosity decreased as children grew older (Engelhard & Monsaas, 1988).

• Classroom observations have found kindergarten students displaying, on average, 2.36 episodes of curiosity over a two-hour period, while 5th graders demonstrated only 0.48 episodes of curiosity during the same period, suggesting that many children may spend their entire day in school "without asking even one question or engaging in one sequence of behavior aimed at finding out something new" (Engel, 2011, p. 633).

• Finally, a nationwide survey of 81,000 high school students found nearly two-thirds (65 percent) reported being bored in class on a daily basis (Yazzie-Mintz, 2010).

At first blush, this last finding might not seem too surprising (after all, who *wasn't* bored in high school?), yet in a larger sense, we should find it perplexing that at the very time students have the opportunity to experience great literature, explore the mysteries of science, and use mathematics to solve complex problems, they're often bored out of their minds. In fact, given our hard-wiring for curiosity, such a dearth of student questions and engagement in classrooms seems somewhat, well, unnatural—an indication perhaps that our schools may be *driving* curiosity *out* of students.

Ambivalence About Curiosity in the Classroom

One reason for this seemingly counterintuitive outcome may relate back to adults' ambivalence about curiosity. In studies dating back to the 1960s, Paul Torrance found that while teachers said they viewed curiosity as important, few identified their *best* students as curious (1963); moreover, fully 72 percent of elementary teachers appreciated students' unusual questions, yet only 42 percent of middle school teachers shared this appreciation (1965). Engelhard (1985) found a similar pattern in a survey of classroom teachers two decades later: 65 percent of teachers in grades 2 and 3 encouraged student curiosity in their classrooms, compared with just 41 percent of teachers in grades 4 and 5. It would seem we find curiosity cute in younger children but perhaps annoying, distracting, or dangerous in older ones.

Creating Environments Where Curiosity Can Flourish

Although schools may generally discourage curiosity, that's not always the case. In a series of experiments, Susan Engel (2015) placed a "curiosity box"—a wooden box with 18 drawers containing novelty items—in the back of classrooms to see how many students would investigate it and how many drawers they would open. Some kids, she found, were more apt to investigate the box than others. That wasn't entirely surprising. What *was* surprising, though, was that student curiosity varied *by classroom*; that is, in some classrooms, kids would eagerly explore the box, while in others, few would touch it. As Engel observed classrooms more closely, she discovered something that harkened back to Mary Ainsworth's studies of mothers and children decades earlier: The critical variable in how much the children tinkered with the curiosity box was their *teacher*—namely, "how much the teacher smiled and talked in an encouraging manner" (2015, p. 635). Teachers who were warm, inviting, and nonjudgmental encouraged student curiosity. Teachers who were aloof or overly task-oriented quashed curiosity.

No Time for Curiosity

These observations all seem to suggest that while there's an element of *nature* when it comes to curiosity, there's also plenty of *nurture*—which raises the question: What's happening in school environments to cause curiosity to decline the longer students stay in school?

Engel's observations may provide some answers to that question. The longer she spent in classrooms exploring student curiosity, the more she empathized with stressed-out teachers, many of whom she observed were under enormous pressure to cover excessive amounts of material with "very specific objectives for each stretch of time," which in turn, caused them to "put a great deal of effort into keeping children on task and reaching those objectives" (2015, p. 636). As a result, they tended to treat student questions and their spontaneous sparks of curiosity as off-task distractions. Unleashing student curiosity takes time—something in short supply when teachers are under the gun to cover content and prepare students for standardized achievement tests. All of this raises an even more important question: Could our efforts to cover vast amounts of content in response to test-driven accountability be driving curiosity *out* of our classrooms?

And could it be that by the time many students reach upper elementary school, they've spent so much time hemmed in by a system of external rewards—gold stars, stickers, grades, report cards, and test scores—that they've come to see learning itself as a chore done to please teachers, parents, and others but not themselves? In short, we might ask ourselves how much of what we're doing in the interest of raising student achievement is working *against* student motivation and thus depressing achievement. Could this explain the plateaus we see in so many locations—not to mention the feeling among educators that they're working ever harder for diminishing returns?

So, what if we were to flip the script? What if we put curiosity at the center of everything we aim to accomplish in our classrooms, viewing it not as a distraction, but rather as the engine, if not the goal, of learning?

If we were to do that—to set out like the game changers across the northern region of Melbourne with curiosity as our focal point—we might want to learn a bit more about curiosity, starting with what prompts these espresso shots of motivation to pop up unexpectedly, like a Cheshire Cat.

Getting Curious About Curiosity

Curiosity is a rather strange phenomenon, coming seemingly out of nowhere, like a bolt out of the blue. Something piques our imagination. At times, it feels like an entirely irrational drive, a quest for information with little or no material benefit (Loewenstein, 1994), like becoming fascinated with supermarket tabloid headlines tattling on the lives of Hollywood stars. Just as strange, while it can often be a powerful impulse, it can also be ephemeral; once through the checkout aisle, we likely don't give another thought to those tabloid headlines.

By the same token, we have probably all experienced another kind of deeper and persistent intellectual curiosity—something that drives us to keep searching for an answer by reading lengthy article after article on the internet or filling our personal library full of books. That initial spark of interest could ignite a lifelong intellectual pursuit. It's this more profound kind of curiosity that seems to be at the heart of exploration, invention, science, and entrepreneurship—from sailors of old chasing horizons to Isaac Newton inventing calculus to Katherine Johnson, Dorothy Vaughan, and Mary Jackson calculating the complex equations ("hidden figures") required to send astronauts to the moon or Steve Jobs and Steve Wozniak building personal computers in their garage.

A Two-Sided Coin

Researchers, as it turns out, have created labels for these two types of curiosity: *diversive* and *informational* (see Figure 4.1). The first type—the spontaneous and ephemeral kind of curiosity—is sometimes also called *exploratory* curiosity (Engel, 2015; Loewenstein, 1994). Usually external stimuli trigger it—something grabs our attention, providing an initial (and often impulsive) spark to explore the environment, an idea, or a topic. Diversive curiosity often drives our initial inquiry and interest in a topic but may not serve a specific purpose—worse, it can be distracting. For example, we may wonder about a song lyric (are the Beach Boys really singing about *frying poultry in the sand?*) and go online for clarification (oh, "by a palm tree in the sand"), which leads us to look up some other misheard lyrics and before we know it, we've wasted an hour falling down one rabbit hole after another.

Figure 4.1 | **Definitions of Curiosity**

Type of Curiosity	Definition
Diversive/ Exploratory	Spontaneous and triggered by external stimuli, it drives initial interest in a topic but is often ephemeral, short-lived, and distracting
Specific/ Informational	Sustained interest in a topic that drives pursuit of knowledge and challenging or elusive goals
Trait	Curiosity internalized as a permanent disposition or aspect of one's own personality; one becomes a curious person

All of this is, of course, far different than the sustained, focused kind of curiosity that leads to the invention of lightbulbs, the discovery of a polio vaccine, or putting a person on the moon. Researchers call this latter kind of curiosity *specific* or *informational* curiosity (Engel 2015; Loewenstein, 1994). It reflects the sustained pursuit of challenging goals—an inner drive for knowledge that is maintained even when the goal may seem elusive. We tend to admire this type of curiosity while having mild disdain for the first.

This fact may explain some of our ambivalence about curiosity. In one form, curiosity can be a vice, and in another form, a virtue. This second type of curiosity, which reflects the quest "to find ever more information on a particular topic" (Engel, 2015, p. 155), is often associated with an innate drive to learn, stick-to-it-iveness, passion, and the ongoing (perhaps even relentless) pursuit of knowledge just beyond our reach.

It Takes Both Kinds

We shouldn't consider one kind of curiosity good and the other bad, though. They often work hand in hand. To pursue knowledge, we need a spark of initial interest. Yet like a temporary spark, our initial curiosity fades as we grow more familiar with something; to pursue deeper learning, we need to uncover new wrinkles or surprises in what we're learning. However, what we do in classrooms often runs counter to what nurtures curiosity: Instead of piquing students' interest in a topic and allowing them to explore it deeply, the default mode in many classrooms consists of introducing students to a topic, telling them what they need to know about it, testing them on it, and then moving onto the next thing they must learn.

Becoming Curious People

What we've described thus far about diverse and informational curiosity has been fairly task-specific, reflecting what researchers call *state* curiosity. That's still a far cry from the kind of curiosity that comes to mind when we think of Jane Goodall, Albert Einstein, Marie Curie, Benjamin Franklin, Thomas Edison, George Washington Carver, or Ellen Ochoa—people with insatiable intellectual appetites who kept asking questions even after their original question was answered. This kind of deeper, more internalized curiosity reflects what researchers call *trait* curiosity.

It's trait curiosity that's most often linked to positive outcomes in school, the workplace, and life itself. Trait curiosity gives us a fire inside to keep learning, even in the face of challenges. People with high levels of trait curiosity are curious *as people*. We might think of it as the difference between an *-ing* or *-er* suffix on a verb. It's one thing to announce that we're writing, swimming, singing, or inquiring and quite another to declare ourselves *writers, swimmers, singers*, or *inquirers*. It's this latter, inquirer type of curiosity that we hope to see in our students, helping them to grow into people who aren't curious just from time to time, but rather *all the time*.

Learning: A Long Journey That Needs a Sherpa

As it turns out, the various forms of curiosity—diverse, informational, and trait—map loosely onto phases of learning—or what we might consider the long and perilous journey that information must take before finding a home in long-term memory (Souza, 2011):

- First, to learn anything, we must notice it, putting it into our sensory register. By design, our brains ignore most stimuli that cross our sensory registry. Stimuli that make it through our filters enter immediate memory, where we hold data for about 30 seconds.
- If we consciously focus on what's in our immediate memory, we begin to move information into working memory, where we can hold information for anywhere from 5 to 20 minutes before it either decays or continues the journey to long-term memory.
- Whether information completes the final stage of the journey, finding a home in long-term memory, depends on whether our brains decide to go on more than one date, if you will, with the new information through repetition, rehearsal, or application.

These (admittedly simplified) stages of learning offer a useful starting point for considering how curiosity can serve as a Sherpa of sorts, accompanying new information on the long and winding road to memory.

Lighting the Spark of Interest

At any given moment, our brains are bombarded with multiple stimuli, like the sensation of shirt tags on our necks or the sound of air rushing through the heating and cooling vents, which we normally ignore (unless a sentence in a book brings them to our attention). To avoid being driven to distraction by these stimuli, our brains employ a sort of pecking order to help us sift through and filter out most of them. As it turns out, intellectual information usually falls pretty low on the pecking order in our brains, which makes sense; after all, for our ancestors, it was more far important to size up threats, like a lion lurking in the tall grass of the savannah, than to absorb informational stimuli, like what our hunting companion dreamt about the night before.

All of this means that for learning to occur, new information must first cut through the "static" or background noise of our environments and capture our interest, piquing our diversive curiosity.

Researchers have identified a handful of tried-and-true ways new information tends to pique diversive curiosity (Loewenstein, 1994):

Incongruity. Curiosity begins when we encounter something that doesn't fit our expectations, something that, in a word, is perplexing—like learning that winds blowing down from mountaintops are warm, not cold.

Manageable information gaps. We're also all suckers for incomplete sequences (e.g., 1, 2, 3, 5, 8 . . . what's next?), unfinished narratives (e.g., cliff-hangers), and puzzles and riddles (e.g., what belongs to you but others use more than you do?) (Lowenstein, 1994). Of course, we tend to have greater curiosity about topics we already know *something* about it (e.g., we're more likely to be more curious about the nocturnal habits of our house cat than an African serval). Also, our curiosity builds as our knowledge gaps close; we find it more difficult to put down a mystery novel five pages from the ending than five pages from the beginning. Basically, our brains hate knowledge gaps, which is why it's likely been bugging you that we didn't immediately answer the riddle about what belongs to you that others use more than you do (and why your brains will be happy that we're providing the answer now: *your name*).

Guessing and receiving feedback. Curiosity also requires knowing what we *don't* know, which is why guessing and receiving "accuracy feedback" on our guesses is a powerful way to build curiosity. Studies have found, for example, that people were interested to learn the easternmost state in the United States after they ventured incorrect guesses about the westernmost state (Lowenstein, 1994). *California? Hawaii?* Correct answer: *Alaska.* (Look on a map and you'll see why, and if you pay attention to the international date line, you'll also see why it's technically also the *easternmost* state.)

Controversy. In a famous experiment, Lowry and Johnson (1981) randomly assigned one group of 5th and 6th graders to engage in cooperative learning about a particular topic (e.g., designating wolves as endangered species) and another to focus on controversy in the topic; the students in the latter group demonstrated more interest in the topic, sought more information on it, and were more likely to give up a recess period to watch a film about it. The takeaway is that controversy begets curiosity.

Someone knows something we don't. We might consider this the "I have a secret" phenomenon. We grow curious when we hear people whispering or chuckling while reading a book. Teachers can apply the same idea by asking students to guess the content of a closed box or using Socratic questioning to draw insights from students.

Clearly, decades of research give us a good handle on some straightforward strategies teachers can use to spark curiosity in the classroom. Yet we know this impulse can fade just as quickly, likely because our immediate memory times out after about 30 seconds. So how might we turn this fleeting kind of curiosity into something that holds the attention of our working memory?

A Flame of Focused Attention

Here's where we begin to tap into the power of informational curiosity, or the need to "to find ever more information on a particular topic" (Engel, 2015, p. 155). Our working memory is thought to be comprised of a *phonological loop* for auditory signals and a *visuo-spatial sketchpad* for visual signals with a *central control mechanism* that coordinates the two systems (Souza, 2011). Research has shown that these systems appear to be most effective when they're triggered together: When we receive information orally, we only retain 10 percent of it three days later, but when a powerful image accompanies it, we recall 65 percent of it three days later (Medina, 2008). In classrooms, we know that nonlinguistic representations, like graphic organizers, are among the most effective teaching strategies available to teachers (Beesley & Apthorp, 2010).

We've also known for a long time that our working memories can hold only seven (plus or minus two) bits of information at once. If we bombard students with too much information, we stress their working memories, causing cognitive strain, mental fatigue, and frustration. That means we need to "chunk" ideas into smaller components and give students time to process them independently, eventually pulling them together (or adding them to) previously learned bigger, more cohesive ideas or themes (Bailey & Pransky, 2014).

With all of this in mind, here are few strategies we can use to help students turn their *spark* of initial interest into a *flame* of more focused attention:

• Asking **higher-order questions** that focus students' attention and encourage them to *think about* what they're learning through analysis, elaboration, synthesis, or reflection (e.g., "What patterns do you see among animals in colder and warmer climates?" "Can you think of any modern parallels to the Smoot-Hawley Tariff?" "This writer makes a lot of points, but what's the big idea, or thesis, she wants to convey?" "What would you do if you were Ralph and Piggy just died?").

• Using **lesson narrative and pace** to chunk lessons into approximately 5- to 10-minute segments that give students opportunities to process and consolidate new information (e.g., "All right, let's pause a moment. We've explored two big ideas in biology—Bergmann's and Allen's rules—that are related but different concepts. Share with the person next to you what you see as their similarities and differences and what's maybe still a little fuzzy to you").

• Helping students overcome cognitive overload by drawing discrete bits of information back together into **fertile ideas** or **driving questions** (e.g., "Okay, let's circle back to our fertile idea for this unit: that ecosystems are rarely stable but always in flux. What have you learned today that provides you with new insights into the relationship between climate change and ecosystems?").

Here, too, unleashing curiosity doesn't seem to require an elusive set of teaching practices but rather applying familiar teaching techniques more consistently and with greater precision.

Stoking an "Unforgettable" Fire

Focusing on something for 20 minutes, while important, still doesn't guarantee new knowledge will stick with us. To do that, we must reinforce newly formed neural pathways through practice and rehearsal (Souza, 2011). Not all practice is created equal, though. Studies have shown that *massed practice* (i.e., sessions bunched together, usually right after learning something new) and *rote rehearsal* (e.g., memorizing lists with mnemonics or other techniques) support automaticity and information recall, yet often fail to embed deep learning into our long-term memories.

To do that, we must go a step further, engaging in *distributed practice* (i.e., sessions spread over time) and *elaborative rehearsal* (e.g., paraphrasing or summarizing learning, engaging in reciprocal teaching, making predictions, and generating questions about our own learning) (Benjamin & Bjork, 2000; Rawson & Kintsch, 2005). Another key to embedding knowledge into long-term memory is having opportunities to *make meaning* of it, which usually requires relating it to our own experiences, beliefs, or prior learning (Souza, 2011). Collectively, more than 100 studies of this so-called "self-reference effect" found significant effects on memory when, for example, people memorize word lists by relating each word to their personal experience (Symons & Johnson, 1997). It's no surprise, then, that classroom research has found similarly powerful effects of providing students with personal learning goals and objectives (Beesley & Apthorp, 2010). Learning goals can help us focus on knowledge while it's in our working memory, which is important. Yet it appears that the real power of learning goals may lie in *personalizing* them, which supports a self-reference effect that supports long-term memory.

Lastly, we know that developing deep knowledge requires students to be more than just passive recipients of information; they must also be active learners, asking themselves questions about what they're learning, what they have yet to learn, and what they'd like to learn. Basically, we want them to demonstrate trait curiosity.

Pulling together these ideas points to some straightforward ways we can help students fuel a fire inside their minds:

Personal goal setting. Engaging students in personal goal setting to help them personalize learning and connect learning to themselves, creating a self-reference effect (e.g., "Now that you've identified a favorite animal from this list, we're going to see how climate plays a big role in where they live." "Let's complete a K-W-L chart to identify what you *know* about cylinders and what you *want* to learn. Then, at the end of this lesson, you'll identify what you *learned*." "Parabolas are all around us—from planetary orbits to roller coasters to basketball three-pointers to architecture; write a goal that defines what you want to learn about capturing these phenomena in mathematical formulas and how you'll know you've mastered this concept").

Elaborative practice. Helping students engage in elaborative practice to consolidate information into big ideas and driving questions, recalling, reflecting on and sharing with others what they've mastered, what they have yet to learn, and what questions they have now (e.g., "Winston Churchill famously said, 'Democracy is the worst form of government, except for all of the others.' Do you agree? Write an essay in which you defend your answer, first by defining each type of government in your own words and then by describing what our classroom might look like if it reflected each type of government— including what might go right and what might go wrong. You should end your essay with a thought-provoking question").

Curiosity thinking. Encourage curiosity thinking by sharing the benefits of curiosity with students and modeling positive self-talk about learning, including taking intellectual risks, making mistakes, and changing their thinking as they encounter new learning (e.g., "What changed about your thinking over the course of this history unit?" "Let's travel back in time to three weeks ago: What do you know now about writing strong, persuasive paragraphs that you didn't know then? What are you able to do now that you weren't able to do then?" "What misconceptions did you have about the quadratic formula when you first started working with it? What mistakes were you making? How did you fix those mistakes?").

Driving questions. Encouraging students to *ask their own* driving questions or what McTighe and Wiggins (2013) call *essential questions*, to experience the joy of chasing their own intellectual horizons (e.g., "Now that you've learned some things about the Renaissance, what else are you curious about? Maybe you're wondering *why* after centuries of the Dark Ages people started to ask new questions and think in new ways or whether something like the Renaissance could occur today." "What problems in the world would you like science to solve?").

Ultimately, though, a "fire inside" isn't something we can light for students; they must do it for themselves. Thus, these teaching practices reflect a process of "letting go" and increasingly turning the learning process over to students—transitioning away from classrooms we might describe as teacher-directed and student-experienced to ones that are student-owned and teacher-guided. Figure 4.2 pulls these ideas together, mapping the spark, fire, and flame of curiosity onto phases of learning and related instructional strategies.

The Missing Ingredient?

Curiosity, in all its forms, is essential to learning. On one hand, if new knowledge doesn't pique our curiosity, we tend to ignore it altogether or let it quickly fade from our immediate memories. And if we don't continue to be curious about new information long enough to focus on it while it's in our working memories, we're unlikely to learn it. Further, if we don't engage in active reflection on our learning, connecting it with prior knowledge and asking new questions, it's unlikely to

Figure 4.2 | **Teaching Strategies Linked Learning Phases and Curiosity**

Learning Phase	Curiosity as a Companion	Related Teaching and Learning Strategies
Phase I: Attention Information in sensory register (phonological loop and visuospatial sketchpad) moves into immediate memory, where it's held for roughly 30 seconds.	"Initial spark" Diversive/ informational curiosity All right, you've got my attention.	Cue and engage learning with … • Exposure to gaps in prior knowledge • Incongruity, mystery, and controversy Set challenging learning tasks with … • Personalized goals and objectives • Meaning and purpose
Phase II: Focus With focus, information moves from immediate memory to working memory (phonological loop and visuospatial sketchpad), where it's held for 5 to 20 minutes before decaying or moving to long-term memory.	"Ongoing flame" Specific/exploratory curiosity I'm still interested; tell me more.	Present information verbally and visually Advance understanding with … • Similarities and differences • Higher-order questions • Generating and testing hypotheses Support deeper processing with … • Checks for understanding • Effective pace and segmented learning • Cooperative learning • Summarizing and note-taking
Phase III: Consolidation Through encoding, repetition, and rehearsal, new knowledge is consolidated into long-term memory.	"Fire inside" Trait curiosity I want to grasp and connect this with other knowledge.	Support mastery with … • Guided practice • Independent practice • Recall and retrieval • Elaborative rehearsal Encourage reflective learning with … • Rubrics for (self-)assessing learning • Assessment for learning • Growth-minded feedback and recognition of effort Provide a bigger picture with … • Driving questions and fertile ideas

find a home in our long-term memories. And that is, of course, what happens to most new learning—it fades quickly.

On the other hand, when curiosity *is* present, our brains become primed for learning; we're more apt to pay attention to new informa-tion, focus on it long enough to hold it in our working memories, and ultimately rehearse and reflect upon what we've learned sufficiently for it to find a home in our long-term memories.

Perhaps the biggest point to draw from this discussion is this: Over the past quarter-century, we've spent a lot of time and energy to improve schools and student outcomes; we've developed higher stan-dards, more rigorous tests, and tougher accountability measures. Yet these efforts have all neglected something vitally important: namely, our students and whether they care about any of this at all. So perhaps the real question we ought to be asking ourselves is, what if we were to create schools where learning was challenging yet engaging? Where students were persistent yet passionate? And where teachers could be focused yet creative?

Surveys of teachers have found that most teachers would agree that curiosity is important, but only when prompted (Engel, 2015). That is, when asked to list important outcomes of learning off the top of their heads, teachers seldom volunteer the concept of *curiosity*. Yet when they see it on a list, they are apt to rate it highly as something that's important to cultivate in children (Engel, 2015). What that may suggest is that deep down, we all know that curiosity is important, even though it has not been a priority in our schools and classrooms. Teachers are not to blame for that.

Sure, there are some who might contend that not everything in life is interesting, so why should school be any different? We need to toughen kids up to deal with boring things in their lives. Such a response, though, as Alfie Kohn observes, suggests that "the central purpose of schools is not to get children excited about learning but to get them acclimated to doing mind-numbing chores" (1993, p. 218).

Getting kids acclimated to boredom is hardly the kind of message any school would want to hang over its front door.

Fortunately, Engel's survey findings suggest that most teachers aren't *opposed* to curiosity; it's just been the furthest thing from their minds. After all, in our current reality of high-stakes testing, value-added measures, school accountability, and focus on mathematics and reading scores, who has time to foster curiosity, let alone think about it? The current milieu of top-down reform efforts and mandates has been in subtle yet powerful ways further pushing curiosity out of our classrooms.

The good news is that we *can* bring curiosity back into our classrooms, largely by restoring what most teachers would recognize as research-based best teaching practices in their classrooms.

Tried and True with a Twist

As we've seen, curiosity comes naturally to us all. It needn't be taught, simply nurtured. Moreover, classroom practices that encourage curiosity are hardly mysterious or elusive; great teachers have long used strategies like asking thought-provoking questions, maintaining a lively pace, and engaging students in reflective practice. Indeed, in many ways, the key to unleashing curiosity in the classroom is simply good teaching—or perhaps more to the point, *teaching with precision* or developing and applying deep professional insights (i.e., an understanding of "if I do x, then y will occur"), including encouraging greater curiosity and deeper learning.

In a word, we might call that expertise.

Expertise doesn't come from an off-the-shelf program or pre-packaged curriculum. Yes, there are some tried-and-true strategies teachers can use (such as those highlighted in Figure 4.2) to nurture curiosity, but there's not really a step-by-step script to follow. Ultimately, teachers must encourage curiosity through thoughtful every-day interactions with students that help them find their own passions, see themselves as learners, and challenge themselves to keep on chasing intellectual horizons.

Creating these sorts of classroom environments is not easy. If it were, we'd already be doing it. Getting just one of these components right—whether it's framing learning around essential questions, creating learning choices, or helping students become more self-reflective as learners—takes time and energy. It's much easier, of course, to be boring—to hand out worksheets, grade multiple-choice tests, and teach like Ben Stein's character in *Ferris Bueller's Day Off*. Nonetheless, creating classrooms where curiosity comes alive *can* be done, especially when teachers have opportunities to support one another in developing greater precision with their teaching practice.

Emerging from the Rabbit Hole

Wayne Craig and David Hopkins had understood all of this from the beginning. Yet it became even more apparent for Craig after he read Munro's *Alice in Wonderland* paper. Creating classrooms where curiosity could flourish was going to be, well, an adventure. There was no how-to guide or out-of-the-box program to apply. Teachers would have to figure it out together and help one another get a little bit better every day at supporting student curiosity and learning.

Yet it was also apparent that there were plenty of teachers across the northern region of Melbourne who were already doing many things to spark student curiosity, fan the flame of student interest, and stoke the fires inside students' minds. Likely, the teaching techniques needed to help students become "literate, numerate, and curious" were already present in classrooms, just waiting to be found and shared. Identifying those practices already in use would be the first step. The second step would be helping teachers become more adept at applying those techniques. If they could do that—develop practices that foster curiosity and make powerful learning more commonplace —they could create something marvelous for students.

PAUSE AND REFLECT

- What are you curious about? Write down and reflect on the questions that pop into your head over the course of a day.
- Can you recall a time your own curiosity led to a personal breakthrough or success?
- Do your colleagues value the curiosity of others?
- How do your teachers talk about student curiosity? Is it valued or seen as an interruption?
- Actively engage with colleagues who have inquiring minds. What do they do or say differently than others?
- What questions did you get asked today? How much curiosity do you hear in your school?

ENVISION A BETTER WAY

- Ask teachers to identify practices they employ to promote student curiosity.
- Conduct your own learning walks to identify "bright spots" where teachers encourage student curiosity.
- Inventory students (or teachers) on what they're curious about.
- Model curiosity by asking colleagues for feedback on your practices, helping you to find "glow" and "grows."
- Conduct learning walks and take note of the higher-order questions being asked.

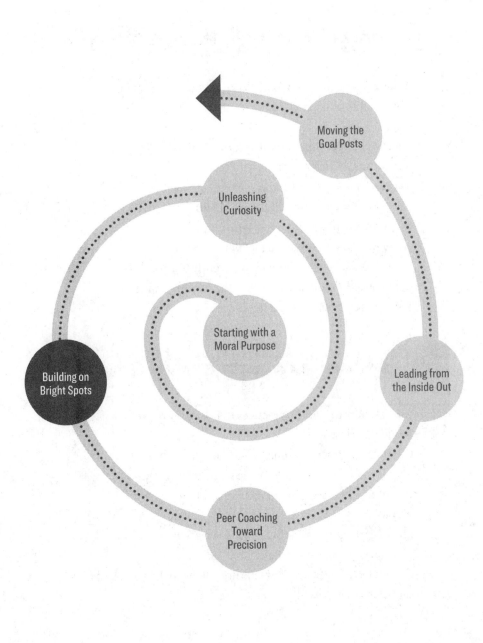

Moving the
Goal Posts

Unleashing
Curiosity

Starting with a
Moral Purpose

Building on
Bright Spots

Leading from
the Inside Out

Peer Coaching
Toward
Precision

5

Building on Bright Spots

Hope itself, of course, is not a plan. Simply wanting kids to be curious won't make them curious. You can start with *why*, but eventually, you must articulate *what* to do. In education, the breakdown often falls somewhere between good intentions and good execution. One reason for that, as David Hopkins had found in his work with teachers, is that "teaching is a profession without a practice" (2013, p. 120)— that is, unlike medicine, engineering, or law, there are few established practices or common vocabulary for teaching. In medicine, for example, a scalpel is a scalpel, and every doctor understands the difference between diagnosis and prognosis. And every lawyer understands the difference between *de jure* and *de facto*.

Yet in teaching, something as simple as the beginning of a lesson can have many different terms (e.g., hook, launch, anticipatory set, engagement) and likely means something a bit different conceptually and in practice to every teacher. Similarly, there are few agreed upon protocols for what happens in a lesson; instead, teachers are confronted with heaps of teaching frameworks and models. As a result, teaching in schools remains idiosyncratic at best. Teachers tend to teach how they were taught, their practice more influenced by their own conception of teaching or "folk wisdom" of colleagues rather than by a robust evidence base of research or observational data about what works best in their own classrooms. Moreover, teaching often becomes entwined with a teacher's identity—teachers feel that how they teach defines who they are as people (City, Elmore, Fiarman, & Teitel, 2009), which makes it difficult to step back from their practice and consider better ways of teaching.

Yet, as we've seen, one key to better school performance is creating *consistency of practice*—ensuring that all teachers in every classroom are consistently employing effective teaching techniques. Often, to solve this problem, leaders turn to top-down strategies. They identify a reading or math program that specifies what teachers ought to do in the classroom and impose it on everyone in the school or district. Sometimes that works—as it did initially when Michael Barber focused on the deliverology of the new reading and math program in the United Kingdom. Craig and Hopkins, however, wanted their teachers and leaders to go *beyond* that point. They wanted educators in northern Melbourne to get on the same page, not in a prescribed, mindless, or forced way but in a very mindful and professional way— like doctors and nurses working together in an operating room, using the same vocabulary and drawing upon the same protocols. In short, they didn't want to create a new program for every teacher to follow (especially as none existed for creating curious learners). Rather, they hoped to create what Hopkins referred to as "precision without prescription."

Precision Without Prescription

Precision, as it turns out, is another key to changing people's behaviors. In their book *Switch: How to Change Things When Change Is Hard,* brothers Chip and Dan Heath call out the importance of "script[ing] the critical moves" (2010, p. 49). They observe that "What looks like resistance is often a lack of clarity" (p. 53). For example, when two professors reframed an abstract "eat healthy" campaign in West Virginia as a simple step—buying 1 percent fat instead of whole milk—what had seemed like resistance melted away and spawned dramatic changes in behavior in two communities.

Some leaders may worry that the more they prescribe behaviors, they more resistance they'll encounter, so they speak in generalities about a change, assuming people will prefer to fill in the gaps and make meaning for themselves. Ambiguity, however, can be exhausting. It creates what psychologists call "cognitive load" and the related phenomenon of decision paralysis—as researchers found when they invited supermarket shoppers to select from a display of six different types of jam versus 30; overwhelmingly, shoppers were more apt to purchase jam from the display with just six choices (Iyengar & Lepper, 2000).

It was at this very point that Craig and Hopkins knew they faced a paradox: They wanted to provide teachers with *precision* but not necessarily *prescription*, which would inevitably not only stir up resistance but also lead back to the same troubles Hopkins had seen in the United Kingdom, when teachers become proficient with a paint-by-numbers approach (e.g., a prescribed reading program) but did not become better "artists" who could adapt and apply the new approach to novel challenges.

Looking for Bright Spots Within

Craig and Hopkins also understood that even if they could go out and find some new program to foster curiosity (or develop one themselves), it simply wouldn't work to tell teachers, many of whom were jaded veterans of prior unsuccessful reform efforts that had left them with a this-too-shall-pass skepticism, "Here's someone else's approach handed down from on high for you to apply in your classroom. Go use it in your classroom." Moreover, they understood that cataloging everything that's *wrong* with what people are doing tends to demoralize them, fails to generate buy-in, and perhaps most important, can miss bright spots already in the community that ought to be celebrated and exploited.

Another anecdote in *Switch* (Heath & Heath, 2010) illustrates this point. Jerry Sternin, an aid worker for Save the Children, was dispatched to Vietnam to help local villagers combat child malnutrition. The problem initially seemed intractable—the inevitable result of grinding poverty and lack of education. When faced with big challenges like that, people tend to dive deeply into the problem in hopes of figuring out how to fix it. Sternin, however, took a different approach. He traveled to local villages, brought people together, and asked them to weigh their children in hopes of finding children of impoverished families who *weren't* malnourished. He observed those families closely to see what they were doing differently. The solution, which Sternin had not foreseen, was a relatively simple one: Rather than feeding their infants twice a day as was common, mothers of healthy children fed them the same amount of food, but as smaller meals, conscientiously hand feeding them four times a day and mixing in discarded pieces of tiny shrimp and crawfish found in the rice paddies. As it turns out, the children were better able to digest the smaller meals, and the additional protein helped them grow.

In northern Melbourne, Hopkins, Craig, and Munro decided to go on a similar scavenger hunt for bright spots. They used instructional rounds (see Figure 5.1), a non-evaluative practice developed by Elizabeth City, Richard Elmore, and their colleagues at Harvard (City et al., 2009) that was already prevalent in Victoria, to arrange teams of teachers to visit one another's classrooms—not in a finger-wagging way to see what they were doing *wrong* but to see what they were doing *right*—that is, to identify the practices of effective teachers that already existed in the Northern Metropolitan Region that they could link to supporting student literacy, numeracy, and curiosity.

Figure 5.1 | **Instructional Rounds Process**

1. Rounds visit to focus on teaching and learning in the school.
2. Small groups visit a rotation of classes and descriptive evidence is gathered.
3. Groups analyze evidence, taking into account school context to develop theories of action.
4. Visitors provide structured feedback to school and teachers.
5. Host school uses the theories of action as a basis for planning ongoing professional development.

Source: City, E. A., Elmore, R. F., Fiarman, S. E., & Teitel, L. (2009). *Instructional rounds in education: A network approach to improving teaching and learning.* Cambridge, MA: Harvard Education Press.

Developing Teacher "Theories of Action"

Initially, through the instructional rounds process, they cataloged more than 100 effective teaching practices. Working in collaboration with teachers and school leaders, they synthesized and winnowed the list down to just over 20 effective practices. However, to provide *precision without prescription,* they knew they couldn't simply tell teachers to use the 20-some practices without first helping teachers understand *why* the practices were important and in which circumstances they ought to use them—something that's often missing from many teachers' understanding of pedagogy.

Thus, they concluded that what was needed were "when-then" statements that would describe *WHEN teachers do this, THEN this happens for students.* These when-then statements, which they called "theories of action," would provide teachers with a deeper understanding of how to respond to specific classroom circumstances or student learning needs. Framed correctly, these theories of action would also capture a sense of moral purpose—shared beliefs about what constitutes effective teaching.

The theories of action would need to be based on research, of course—to show skeptical teachers that what was being suggested to them were tried-and-true practices that met the bar for evidence set by New Zealand researcher John Hattie (2009), who coined the term *hinge point* for interventions that demonstrate effect sizes of greater than d =.40. (An effect size is the measure of the strength or overall impact of a program or intervention being studied.) Hattie writes that an effect size of .40 is strong enough for educators to see "real-world change" in student achievement (2009, p. 17). It's also the threshold point at which an innovation exceeds the average effect teachers have on student achievement, which is generally between d =.20 and d =.40. As Hattie points out, many programs and approaches that are purported to "work" are, in truth, no more effective than average classroom teachers left to their own devices. By using this cutoff point, Craig and Hopkins and their teacher collaborators further distilled their list of 20 strategies down to the following six key theories of action for teachers and individual classrooms that have been shown to have a significant impact on student learning (with, in fact, effect sizes greater than d = 0.7). The appendix provides a complete list of these theories of action, along with rubrics used to describe increasing precision with these practices.

Harness learning intentions, narrative, and pace. One of the first things that surfaced during the instructional rounds was that great teachers were consistently clear about their learning goals for each lesson; their lessons remained lively and fast-paced with a clear sense of forward momentum and progress. Research has, in fact, found strong links between student success and clear learning objectives (Marzano, 1998) and keeping lessons fast-paced, sequenced, and focused (Adams & Carnine, 2003). Based on these observations, they developed the following theory of action and accompanying belief statement:

> WHEN we harness learning intentions, narrative, and pace so students are more secure about their learning, and more willing to take risks, THEN achievement and understanding will increase and curiosity will be enhanced.

We believe that by making learning intentions and learning outcomes explicit, each student has more control over their own learning, and can contribute more effectively to learning outcomes for the whole class.

Set challenging learning tasks. In a now famous experiment, researchers (Rosenthal & Jacobson, 1992) told a group of teachers that a special Harvard assessment had found some of the students in their classrooms to be on the brink of rapid intellectual development. Unbeknownst to the teachers, though, the test didn't exist; the so-called "rapid risers" had just been randomly labelled as special. Yet a year later, those same students demonstrated higher IQs than their peers. The general principle that emerged from the study, dubbed the "Pygmalion effect," has since been confirmed in other studies (Hattie, 2009): When teachers expect more, students rise to the higher bar. The Pygmalion effect, however, is not Dumbo's magic feather. Simply believing in higher student performance doesn't make it so; teachers must make their expectations for learning explicit and translate their expectations into challenging learning opportunities for students— helping them to find their "Goldilocks" level of challenge, where learning is neither too difficult nor too easy but just right. Finding the proper level of challenge for students (sometimes referred to as the *zone of proximal development*) has the added effect of helping students see their knowledge gaps, which, as we've seen, are the essence of curiosity. With all this in mind, the team in Melbourne developed a second theory of action and belief statement for teachers:

> WHEN learning tasks are purposeful, clearly defined, differentiated, and challenging, THEN all students will experience powerful, progressive, and precise learning.

> We believe curiosity is enhanced when students work at a level appropriate to their understanding.

Frame higher-order questions. Asking questions of students has, of course, long been a mainstay of teaching. Yet not all questions are created equal. Higher-order questions—those that ask students to do more than simply regurgitate information but instead apply, analyze, evaluate, or synthesize information—not only support deeper learning and higher student achievement (Hattie, 2009) but also foster curiosity (Munro, 2015). Higher-order questioning naturally tends to be "bundled" with other techniques, including "wait time"—the practice of waiting a few seconds after each question and student response before calling on a student (Rowe, 1986)—as deeper questions require more time for students to consider and develop an answer (Larson & Lovelace, 2013). Conversely, if students can immediately answer a question a teacher asks, it probably wasn't a question worth asking. The team captured these ideas into the following theory of action and belief statement:

> WHEN we systematically employ higher-order questioning, THEN levels of student understanding will deepen and levels of achievement will increase.

> We believe that students are more likely to be curious when they are regularly asked to analyze, synthesize, and evaluate.

Connect feedback to data. As leadership guru Ken Blanchard famously opined, "feedback is the breakfast of champions." Education research affirms this assertion. In a meta-analysis of research on instructional strategies, McREL researchers (Beesley & Apthorp, 2010) found that providing effective feedback translates into students scoring 28 percentile points higher on standardized achievement tests—roughly the equivalent of a full year of learning (Bloom, Hill, Black, & Lipsey, 2008). In his broad synthesis of 800 meta-analyses of education research studies, Hattie (2009) found a similar effect size, which dwarfed that of many other common practices, including encouraging teacher cooperation or reducing class sizes. In fact, of the several hundred education practices Hattie studied, the effects of providing students with timely, relevant, and specific feedback ranked among the highest, prompting him to observe that one key to raising achievement is to provide students with "dollops of feedback" (2009,

p. 238). To capture these ideas, the team in Melbourne developed the following theory of action and accompanying belief statement:

> WHEN we connect feedback to data about student actions and performances, THEN behavior will be more positive, progress will accelerate, and curiosity will be enhanced.

> We believe that feedback based in evidence supports our students to develop independence as learners. It directs and focuses their learning. Feedback magnifies the application of our teaching expertise.

Commit to assessment for learning. It's difficult, if not impossible, to guide student learning or foster curiosity if we're not keenly aware of students' knowledge gaps, including the concepts they're struggling to comprehend and skills they still need to master. The challenge is that what students are learning and what knowledge gaps remain are usually nested inside the invisible world of students' minds. That means teachers must use frequent checks for understanding—checks that must occur not months or weeks after learning but within mere minutes, hours, or days. An analysis of more than 4,000 studies over the past four decades concluded that when done correctly—when formative assessment and checks for understanding guide instruction—formative assessment can effectively *double* the rate of student learning (Wiliam, 2007). The most adept teachers in northern Melbourne exemplified this use of powerful, motivating feedback. To capture this practice, the team developed this theory of action and related belief statement:

> WHEN we commit to peer assessment, and assessment for learning, THEN student engagement, learning, and achievement will accelerate.

> We believe curiosity is enhanced as the depth of student understanding increases.

Implement cooperative groups. Cooperative learning is in many ways the educational equivalent of work meetings; done poorly or mindlessly, they can be tortuous affairs and enormous wastes of time, yet when done well, they can be an incredibly productive means for learning together (Beesley & Apthorp, 2010). Moreover, as Kathleen Cushman (2010) discovered when she interviewed students who had developed a passion for learning, well-designed cooperative learning opportunities were where many students learned to take chances and stoke what she described (and titled her book) as fires in the mind. To capture the power of cooperative learning, the team developed the following theory of action and accompanying belief statement:

> WHEN we implement cooperative group structures, and techniques to mediate between whole-class instruction and students carrying out tasks, THEN the academic performance of the whole class will increase.

> We believe curiosity increases when students learn from each other in a structured manner. We believe that when cooperative learning is present in class, a spirit of collaboration and mutual responsibility will be apparent.

Developing Whole-School Theories of Action

These were the six practices that surfaced in instructional rounds as defining great teaching. Yet the observers also noticed other, broader phenomena at play when students were highly engaged in learning: Something "felt" different about schools where curiosity was flourishing. At first, it wasn't readily apparent what it was. But after reflecting on their numerous instructional rounds, the observers began to detect patterns that harkened back to the "plain vanilla" successes of the high-performing schools in Louisiana that Sam Stringfield and his team of observers had studied; there was a *consistency* in the schools where curiosity flourished, regular habits and routines in every classroom. These patterns of behavior weren't mindless; rather, they grew out of a handful of guiding principles—or four *whole-school* theories of action—that the best schools wove into the fabric of their school culture.

Prioritize high expectations and authentic relationships. Decades ago, Harvard-trained researcher Judith Kleinfeld, newly arrived in Alaska, conducted a series of case studies in schools in an effort to determine what made some teachers more effective than others, especially with native Alaskan students (1972). Only a few years earlier, Rosenthal and Lenore had published their now famous study of teacher expectations and coined the term "Pygmalion effect." Yet in the Alaskan classrooms Kleinfeld observed, high expectations were only part of the puzzle. Many teachers, in fact, set a high bar for students, yet often appeared to do little to connect with them or help them see they could *meet* the high bar set for them. Kleinfeld labeled this group of demanding yet unsupportive teachers "traditionalists." A few students were successful in their classrooms, but most were not. Another group, which she labeled as "sentimentalists," were caring, but set low expectations for students, perhaps out of a misguided sense of sympathy. Students didn't fare well in these classrooms, either. A third group, dubbed "sophisticates," neither held high expectations nor connected with students; not surprisingly, their nonchalance ranked them among the least effective teachers. In the end, only one group of teachers—those who both held high expectations for students and encouraged their learning, which Kleinfeld dubbed "warm demanders"—were effective with *all* students.

Engel's more recent studies (2015) further demonstrate the importance of teacher interactions and the tone they set in classrooms. It's not hard to imagine, then, the power of filling an *entire school* with warm demanders. Accordingly, the first whole-school theory of action was described as follows:

WHEN schools and teachers prioritize high expectations and authentic relationships, THEN curiosity will flourish.

We believe high expectations and authentic relationships increase our students' confidence and curiosity, energizing their commitment to learning. When we prioritize high expectations and authentic relationships, we believe the whole school's ethos and culture prosper.

Emphasize inquiry-focused teaching. Research has long pointed to generating and testing a hypothesis to be among the most effective classroom teaching and learning techniques (Beesley & Apthorp, 2010). At its heart, teaching through inquiry requires teachers to "let go" of trying to completely control the learning process by spoon-feeding, as it were, knowledge to students. This doesn't mean they surrender learning to students' whims and vagaries, but, rather, they learn how to transition learning in their classrooms from being wholly teacher-owned and student-experienced—with teachers guiding all learning and students operating as passive recipients—to classrooms where learning is student-owned and teacher-guided, with teachers guiding learning toward big picture goals or "fertile questions" (Harpaz & Lefstein, 2000) whereby students own their learning by setting their own learning objectives and engaging in self-assessment to track their own progress toward those goals.

Certainly it's possible for a few enlightened teachers to create such classrooms, but until it's part of an entire school's approach to learning, those enlightened teachers will be swimming upstream with little support from colleagues or leaders. Moreover, students are likely to experience a bit of intellectual whiplash as they move back and forth from dry, teacher-directed learning experiences in one classroom to engaging, empowering learning experiences in another. Finally, empowering student learning is no small task; teachers must work together to plan and create environments where this kind of learning can occur. With all of this in mind, the team pulled these ideas and observations together into the following whole-school theories of action:

WHEN inquiry is a defining characteristic of a school's culture, THEN the level of student achievement and curiosity will increase.

We believe inquiry-focused instruction is the foundation for high-quality teaching. An emphasis on inquiry leads to improved achievement and enhanced curiosity.

Adopt consistent teaching protocols. As we've noted, perhaps the most important key to school success lies in ensuring high-quality teaching in every classroom and avoiding the plague of low-performing schools: the Forrest Gump "box of chocolates" effect in which "you never know what you're going to get" when you enter a classroom. Pianta, Belsky, Houts, and Morrison (2007), for example, found upon closely examining the educational experiences of 994 students from across the United States in grades 1, 3, and 5 that just 7 percent of students spent all three years in classrooms where they received high-quality instruction and emotional support; fully 9 percent of students received poor-quality instruction in *all three grades*. Ensuring consistently high-quality instruction calls on teachers to operate like surgeons or airline pilots, following an agreed upon set of clearly defined patterns or protocols for teaching—such as the six teacher theories of action defined earlier. Students benefit from the consistency of these patterns as well, by, for example, knowing that every class will start with independent "bell ringer" exercises, that their daily learning goals will be visible in each classroom, or that rubrics to guide self-assessment will be provided for all important assignments.

Direct Instruction (with capital letters, as in the program developed by Engelmann, Becker, and colleagues) is one such collection of teaching protocols that more than 300 studies have shown to be highly effective (Hattie, 2009). Direct Instruction is *not* simply didactic instruction, though. Rather, it is an intensely *intentional* process that requires teachers to clarify learning objectives for students, provide information through direct instruction and modeling, engage in frequent checks for student understanding through individual interactions with them, give students opportunities for independent practice, and wrap up the entire lesson with a thoughtful "closure" that helps students make sense of what they've learned.

For some die-hard constructivists, Direct Instruction may come across as overly structured or rigid. The reality, though, is that many studies (e.g., Baker, Gersten, & Lee, 2002) have found that teacher-led instruction is best for low-achieving students, and conversely, structuring entire lessons around real-world application for students who are still learning to master basic building blocks of knowledge may only serve to confuse them. This doesn't mean, however, that sage-on-the-stage instruction is the "right way" to teach and that struggling students must be spoon-fed their learning with no larger sense of its purpose or application. The reality is more complex: Teacher-led instruction often works best for introducing new knowledge, yet to get knowledge to stick, students need opportunities to apply their knowledge in novel ways. That's where real-world application, practice, and higher-order thinking come in—to help students deepen their knowledge, attach it to prior learning, and apply it to novel situations that are meaningful to them. Direct Instruction advocates, in fact, note that giving short shrift to independent practice is usually to blame when students cannot recall information later or apply it to new situations (Hollingsworth & Ybarra, 2009).

What all this suggests is that teachers must have deep understanding of the learning process as described in the preceding chapter, have at their disposal a robust repertoire of teaching protocols or strategies to apply during each learning phase, and understand when to use different protocols accordingly. Just as doctors employ different treatments for the early stages of an illness (e.g., prescribing bed rest, fluids, and moist heat for a respiratory flu) than later stages (e.g., prescribing oxygen therapy and hospitalization for viral pneumonia), teachers, too, need to understand which teaching strategies or protocols they should apply during which learning phase. Moreover, they must understand they cannot simply throw students into the "deep end" of learning and expect them to swim. Placing a bunch of learning materials in front of novice learners and instructing them to teach themselves rarely, if ever, works. Rather, teachers must bring students to a point where they're able to construct their own knowledge, which usually entails showing students how to become *learners*— a point we'll take up in the next section.

The main point of this discussion—and what observers in Melbourne found in their instructional rounds—is that in effective schools, teachers uniformly appeared to understand these complexities. They weren't employing strategies at random or in rigidly scripted ways, but rather were operating from deep knowledge of learning and were able to use the right teaching strategies or patterns at the right time. The ideas were all wrapped up in the following whole-school theory of action and associated belief statement:

> WHEN we adopt consistent teaching protocols, THEN student behavior, engagement, learning, and curiosity will be enhanced.
>
> We believe the most powerful curricular and teaching patterns induce our students to construct knowledge—to inquire into subject areas intensively. We believe that when we use these patterns consistently, we increase our students' capacity to learn and work smarter.

Adopt consistent learning protocols. When observing classrooms, it's easy to focus solely on the teacher as the center of action. Yet the real action, of course, lies in what's going on in students' brains. During their instructional rounds, observers often tuned in to students and their activities in the classroom. Here, they noticed something else about "bright spot" classrooms. Not only were teachers clear and intentional about their teaching strategies but also *students* were clear about what learning strategies to use and when. They weren't being thrown in the deep end and expected to swim; rather, they appeared to know their goals for learning, the steps they could take to achieve those goals, and where they were in their progress toward achieving them. Researchers call this "metacognition" or *thinking about thinking*. It's having a voice in our heads that assesses where we are with our learning, saying things like, *Wait, I don't get* *this* to signal ourselves to reread a puzzling passage and *Oh, this is kind of like something else* to connect new learning with prior knowledge and relate it back to ourselves.

Although strong learners do these things naturally, they are actually teachable strategies, as Alison King (1991) demonstrated years ago when she trained a class of 9th graders to ask themselves higher-order comparison-contrast questions (e.g., "How are Shintoism and Buddhism alike?"), causal-relationship questions ("How did the rise of power of the Shogun affect the development of Japanese culture?"), and analysis questions ("Which king was best for England?") while listening to history lectures (p. 338). She also gave them "question starters" to model the sort of questions they could ask themselves during lectures and taught them about metacognition, including how to ask themselves questions like "What do I still not understand about this?" (p. 337). The results were striking: Students who had been taught to use self-questioning techniques scored about 15 percentage points (or a full letter grade and a half) higher on a quiz of the lecture content than students in a control group.

Self-questioning is but one example of learning strategies and habits of mind we can teach students; others include encouraging intellectual risk taking and a growth mindset (seeing challenges as opportunities to stretch their brains), using mnemonics to memorize lists of information (e.g., ROYGBIV for the colors of the visible spectrum), showing students how to break larger projects into smaller tasks and short-term objectives, and deliberately practicing skills they have not yet mastered (e.g., continually winnowing a deck of mathematics flash cards or foreign language vocabulary terms down to those that still cause them to stumble). It's these skills that ultimately allow students to own and guide their own learning, stoking the fire of curiosity in their own minds. This whole-school theory of action and associated statement of beliefs was captured as follows:

WHEN we adopt consistent learning protocols in all classes, THEN all students will experience an enhanced capacity to learn and to develop skills, confidence, and curiosity.

We believe that when learning strategies, and their purposes, are clear and accessible to all our students, they are better positioned to become powerful learners.

The Power of Practical

In the end, the instructional rounds and dialogue that followed identified a total of 10—four whole-school and six teacher—theories of action that provided the core of what it would take to help students become literate, numerate, and curious. The power of these theories of action lay in the fact that they had truly come from the "inside out," gathered from what the best teachers in the region were already doing. Sure, they were validated with sound research, but what was more important was that teachers could look at them and see that they made intuitive sense. That led to the obvious question: If we have colleagues who are already doing these things, why can't we do them as well?

Ultimately, these 10 theories of action came together as an *overall* theory of action for the entire effort, which was captured as follows:

WHEN teachers, strongly supported by their schools, explicitly and consistently incorporate the theories of action in their teaching, THEN our students' curiosity enriches their learning skills and their spirit of inquiry.

A Familiar Challenge Remains: Closing the Knowing-Doing Gap

As teachers and leaders in northern Melbourne came together around a shared moral purpose—or *why*—of the inside-out effort (ensuring all students were literate, numerate, and curious), the 10 theories of action helped to bring into focus *what* they must do. Using instructional rounds to call out bright spots was an important first step to generate greater buy-in among educators.

For starters, theories of action needed clarification. It wouldn't do to simply tell teachers that, for example, they *ought* to employ good learning intentions, narrative, and pace. That would be the equivalent of telling people to eat healthier. The reality was that any of the theories of action could be done poorly or well; to do them well, teachers would need to see, in concrete terms, what that looked like. Doing so would be an important element of precision.

Yet even if they could get that right, a second question remained: *How* would they help thousands of teachers in the region develop the professional expertise they needed to employ more precise teaching protocols in a consistent manner? *How* could they make inquiry the focus of the hundred-plus schools in the region? *How* could they help the more than 75,000 students in the region develop consistent learning protocols?

It's precisely at this point—closing the knowing-doing gap—that so many efforts in the past had failed—in northern Melbourne and frankly everywhere. Many leaders had come before with good intentions, hoping to rally the troops to improve student outcomes, but in the end, their efforts were akin to repeatedly storming the beach at Gallipoli—valiant but tragically futile.

Craig and Hopkins knew they would need a different strategy.

To be successful, the effort would be need to take on a life of its own. Like teachers who must learn to "let go" of teaching and let students take ownership of their learning, Craig and Hopkins would need to figure out how to let go of the effort, turning it over to others. They could not dictate every move from the top; ultimately, curiosity would have to emerge organically, school by school, teacher by teacher, and student by student. It's also at this point that we shift our own narrative—away from the commander's battleship, so to speak, to the beach itself, where the real "digging"—teachers working together to unleash student curiosity in the classroom—was occurring.

PAUSE AND REFLECT

- Do teachers at your school share a common language for instruction?
- What does "precision without prescription" mean to you?
- What "when-then" statements shape your beliefs about student learning?
- Can you see any of the theories of action already in play at your school?
- Which whole-school theory of action do you find most compelling?
- Do teachers understand the difference between teaching protocols and learning protocols?
- Do teachers have time to reflect upon their own practices as individuals? In teams? With a colleague?

ENVISION A BETTER WAY

- Conduct learning walks to identify commonalities in practice and language—or specific practices related to the theories of action.
- Collaborate with colleagues to generate a list of practices or protocols you see that could become part of a powerful, consistent teaching model.
- Ask teachers what "precision without prescription" would mean to them.
- Collaborate with colleagues to create a list of teaching and learning protocols that could be adopted by *every* teacher in the school.
- Develop an implementation plan to introduce protocols or a single theory of action schoolwide.

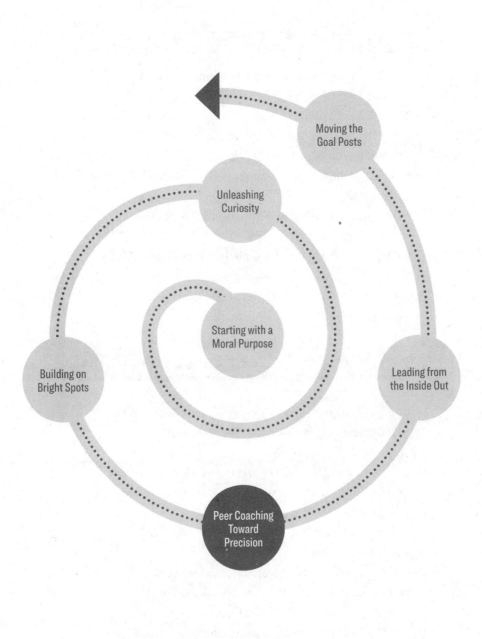

6

Peer Coaching Toward Precision

Once we believe in ourselves, we can risk curiosity, wonder, spontaneous delight, or any experience that reveals the human spirit.

E.E. Cummings

Not long ago, the U.S.-based TNTP (formerly known as The New Teacher Project) raised some eyebrows when it published a report concluding that most professional development (PD) does little, if anything, to improve teaching quality. The report, provocatively titled *The Mirage: Confronting the Hard Truth About Our Quest for Professional Development*, examined the professional growth of some 10,000 teachers in three large urban districts and a charter school management organization, hoping to uncover what distinguished the experiences and dispositions of "improvers"—the roughly 30 percent of teachers who managed to demonstrate year-over-year growth on performance evaluations—from the vast majority of teachers who appeared to be stuck in neutral as "non-improvers." As it turns out, TNTP could find few differences between the two groups, prompting them to conclude that "despite enormous . . . investments of time and money, we are much further from [creating great teaching] than has been acknowledged, and the evidence base for what actually helps teachers improve is very thin" (TNTP, 2015, p. ii).

Is PD Really a Mirage?

Some critics, like Andy Smarick (2015) of the Thomas B. Ford-ham Foundation, a conservative think tank, questioned the report's methodology—specifically, its assumption that improvements in teacher evaluation ratings reflected true teacher performance gains. Smarick also dourly noted that accepting the report's main conclusion—that we've spent billions on improving teacher knowledge and skills with little knowledge of how to actually help teachers improve—requires swallowing a bitter pill: namely, that we've adopted a new generation of "get tough" performance evaluation systems (that incidentally, groups like TNTP advocated), but now we're saying, "Oops, we actually don't know how to help you get better."

Heather Hill of Harvard found the report's "hyperbolic" language (e.g., saying teachers were "marching in place") uncalled for and noted general weaknesses in its methodology, including simply bean-counting how many hours teachers had spent in professional development without sizing up the *quality* of those hours or whether they had any relation to teachers' performance measures (2015, p. 6). Teacher, author, and blogger Peter Greene (2015) also skewered the report for jumping to the conclusion that school systems are afflicted with "a pervasive culture of low expectations for teacher development and performance" based on the single data point that two-thirds of teachers don't find their professional development to be terribly useful (TNTP, 2015, p. 2). Moreover, Greene questioned the report's entire underlying premise that if we can just get better at measuring teacher performance, highlighting teachers' shortcomings, and filling the gaps with neatly packaged training, everything will be better. The problem with this line of thinking, he argued, is its overreliance on "rewards and punishments—I mean, 'consequences.' Which takes us back to the old idea that doing a good job in a classroom somehow has no intrinsic reward or feedback, which is just a meagre view of human beings" (Greene, 2015).

Looking for the Oasis

Yet even the harshest critics of the *Mirage* report acknowledged that its general conclusion rang true and probably reflected a bitter reality: that much of what passes for professional development is fairly ineffective. Greene puts it more succinctly: "It sucks. Most professional development is like a restaurant where you don't get to see a menu, you don't get to pick your order, and the waitpersons don't even ask if you have food allergies" (Greene, 2015).

Notwithstanding the boldness of the *Mirage* report making broad-brushstroke statements about all professional development after examining just four school systems, it is true that searching for research to support the effectiveness of PD can feel like crossing a vast, empty desert where even seemingly effective teacher development practices fade as we get closer to them. We've known for quite some time, in fact, that short-term PD without follow-up doesn't work.

Years ago, Bruce Joyce and Beverly Showers (2002) demonstrated that simply introducing new ideas has little impact on professional practice, nor does modeling and practice; only when *peer coaching* gets added to theory, modeling, and practice do teachers appear to translate knowledge into action (incidentally, *informal collaboration* topped the list of professional learning activities teachers in the *Mirage* report said "has helped me learn how to improve the most" [TNTP, 2015, p. 21]).

So, does that mean peer coaching and teacher collaboration might be the "oasis" we're searching for in the otherwise bleak desert of professional development? Well, not exactly.

The Case *Against* Peer Coaching and Collaboration

As it turns out, many studies over the years have called into question the effectiveness of both coaching and teacher collaboration. Here are a few examples:

- A U.S. Department of Education–funded study (Garet et al., 2011) measured the comparative effects of adding teacher coaching to an eight-day reading institute and found no difference in teacher practices or student achievement.
- Guskey and Yoon's (2009) examination of nine rigorous studies of professional development found no instance of effective professional development programs employing peer coaching or other forms of school-based professional learning.
- The TNTP *Mirage* report (2015) itself also found little difference in quantity of coaching and collaboration for improvers versus non-improvers—improvers had 69 hours of formal collaboration and 13 hours of coaching over two years; non-improvers had 65 and 13 hours, respectively.

Sigh. So, does that mean that neither teacher collaboration nor peer coaching are as effective as Joyce and Showers found them to be? Again, not exactly. As with most things, *quality* matters more than *quantity*: It's not the *number* of hours you spend coaching that matters but what you *do* with those hours—which is exactly what Bruce Joyce had discovered years ago in a rather unusual and expected setting, with a tennis racket in hand.

Lessons from Tennis

In the 1980s, Joyce traveled to the Vic Braden Tennis College in Coto de Caza, Trabuco Canyon, California (Joyce, Hopkins, & Calhoun, 2014). The late Vic Braden was a legend in the sport, having coached countless amateurs as well as pros like Tracy Austin (you can find hundreds of Braden's videos today on YouTube), but he took a somewhat unconventional approach to coaching. Whereas many coaches immediately put students on the court and have them start hitting balls, Braden began in a darkened classroom, showing films and providing rationale for what he was teaching, going into exacting detail about how to perform it. "Essentially," Joyce later recalled, "you studied your body mechanics, ergonomics, and how to impart serious topspin to the ball . . . The introduction to a stroke was very conceptual, and the concepts were continually emphasized throughout the instruction" (p. 8).

After that, camp participants sat through dozens of demonstrations, some taped, some live, that were all tied back to the concepts they were learning. Only after several hours of demonstration were they allowed to practice.

"Each of us got a ball machine that delivered about 300 balls an hour," Joyce recounted (p. 8). "As we practiced, coaches danced around us and continued to demonstrate elements of the stroke, and repeated the rationale, politely but directly. And then back to the classroom, and then again to the courts—practice, think, practice (p. 8)."

Participants were videotaped while attempting the new strokes. Later, in playback, they would see themselves superimposed onto the image of an expert performing the same stroke—all the while being reminded of the concepts and rationale for the stroke. "By the end of Braden's sequence—rationale, demonstration, practice, video, more rationale, demonstration, and practice—could we execute our new topspin backhand stroke? You bet we could, *while practicing*" (p. 8).

Braden preached again and again to participants that when they got home, they were not to play matches. "'As soon as you do, you will revert to your old strokes because they will feel more comfortable than the new ones. The reason we want you to come here as pairs is so you can practice together for a few weeks until your new strokes are grooved,' he said. And, sure enough, if we played someone else, we reverted," Joyce recalled. "If we practiced together, the new strokes became embedded" (p. 8).

It so happens that at the same time Joyce was practicing his tennis strokes, he was designing workshops for teachers. There, he began to observe that in "both the tennis and professional development (PD) experiences, rationale mixed with demonstrations mixed with practice makes the difference in building knowledge and skill" (p. 8). He also noticed that over time, teachers would gradually lose their new practices "unless they worked together with a partner, planning lessons, trying them out, and studying student responses"—the very essence of peer practice or peer coaching (p. 8).

Rethinking Coaching

Learning. Modeling. Practicing. Coaching. Those four elements, Joyce observed—and validated through later research—were the key to helping people develop new habits, whether in playing tennis or teaching classrooms. To be effective, though, all four elements must be present. Like tennis players, teachers need to learn ideas and see them modeled, often over and over again. They also need support and lots of feedback as they transfer new ideas into practice.

Certainly, coaching can be top-down (coach-to-mentor), but it's often more powerful when it's reciprocal (teacher-to-teacher). As Bruce Joyce, David Hopkins, and Emily Calhoun observed in an article written for McREL (2014), for professional development to produce long-lasting and significant change, peer coaching duos or triads must take what they learn in training sessions, apply it in classrooms, study student responses to the new strategy, and help one another perfect the practices. "Everybody from the leaders to paraprofessionals," they noted, "needs to engage in continuous action research that links PD content to the study of implementation, engagement in problem-solving, and the study of student response (learning) in the short and long term" (p. 10).

Tapping the Power of Groups

The key here is that the work isn't done in isolation but in groups, which are often key to changing behavior. If you're a fitness buff, you've probably noticed the power of groups. When exercising alone, it's easy to slack off. But in a class, we tend to push ourselves more, maybe from peer pressure or a trainer's encouragement.

In *The Power of Habit*, Charles Duhigg (2012) recounts a 1994 Harvard study that found that when people change, it's usually because they belong to a group that helps them change, such as a sports team that pushes all of its players to work harder, a group of outgoing friends that brings an introvert out of his shell, or an Alcoholics Anonymous group helping members stay sober. Duhigg points to research conducted by Doug McAdam that found that the most important determinant of whether college students in the 1960s decided to participate in the Freedom Summer campaign to expand voting rights of African Americans in the South wasn't whether they were altruistic or unencumbered by relationships or employment obligations, but whether they were "enmeshed in the types of communities where both their close friends *and* their casual acquaintances expected them to get on the bus" (Duhigg, 2012, p. 228). Students who got on the bus, McAdam found, had both religious beliefs *and* belonged to religious organizations. In short, they had a sense of moral purpose *and* belonged to a group that reinforced their moral purpose.

As it turns out, one of the key events of the Civil Rights movement, the bus boycott in Montgomery, Alabama, also spun out of social ties. For starters, Rosa Parks had many friends and belonged to many formal and informal social groups across the city. So, when she was thrown in jail for refusing to give up her seat on the bus, her many friends quickly rallied to her cause. One such friend was E.D. Nixon, who placed a call to a 26-year-old preacher, Martin Luther King Jr., asking him to use his church as a meeting place to talk about a potential boycott of the bus system. King, still relatively new to the community, hesitated. Nixon reached out to another friend, Ralph D. Abernathy, who persuaded King to let the meeting take place in his church.

A few days later, when the local newspaper got wind of the meeting, it ran a story that said every member of the black community would be participating in the boycott. At the time of its printing, the article was factually incorrect—only a small group had committed to the boycott—yet it was prophetic. When members of the Black community in Montgomery read the story, it pinged their sense of community obligation. Thus, on the day of the boycott, the buses were *completely empty* (Duhigg, 2012).

This power of groups is one underpinning of professional learning communities (PLCs)—using collaboration and shared accountability to encourage better performance. With the right conditions in place, PLCs can, indeed, raise student achievement (Vescio, Ross, & Adams, 2008). However, not all PLCs succeed; they can fall flat if they fail to coalesce as a group that holds itself accountable for changing practices or, conversely, become too tight-knit to look beyond themselves for answers. Both shortcomings—tolerating free-riding and becoming too myopic—reflect well-documented problems with groups.

The Promise and Peril of Small Groups

We've long known that when individuals find themselves in group settings, they often don't pull their own weight—sometimes literally. In the 1880s, Max Ringelmann (1913) conducted an unusual experiment. He attached weights to a rope and tallied how much people could pull as individuals and then as a group. The more people added to the group, he found, the less weight they pulled relative to what they had pulled as individuals. Researchers have since labeled this phenomenon "the Ringelmann effect" or alternatively, *social loafing*. J. Richard Hackman (2011), a Harvard psychologist who devoted his career to studying groups, observed that "The larger the group, the higher the likelihood of social loafing (sometimes called free riding) and the more effort it takes to keep members' activities coordinated. Small teams are more efficient—and far less frustrating." As it turns out, in Melbourne, through trial and error, a group size of three emerged as a sort of magic number for peer-coaching groups in many schools—just large enough to encourage challenging conversations, yet as an external evaluator observed, still small enough to be "safe and manageable" (Zbar, 2013, p. 8).

Small groups, however, pose a different challenge, according to business researcher Morten Hansen (2009), because they can become subject to what sociologists call the *law of homophily*, the natural tendency to cleave to the familiar, be it long-held practices or people with whom they share an identity. A study of how elementary school teachers used social networks during reform efforts, for example, found that they interacted primarily with fellow teachers in the same school and grade level, with few interactions beyond those groups, not even with their own principals and instructional coaches (Daly, Moolenaar, Bolivar, & Burke, 2010).

What this suggests is that on the one hand, we're more apt to change when other members of our group change. Yet on the other hand, these same social groups can be the source of our inertia—unless they change, we don't change. So how can we introduce new knowledge to tight-knit groups?

Connecting Groups to Support Change

One answer may be found in an intriguing study. A team of industrial researchers interested in figuring out how good ideas spread from say, one factory floor to another, invited a group of 144 students into a large room and divided them into triads with the ostensible purpose of seeing which teams could fold the most origami sailboats during a short time (Kane, Argote, & Levin, 2005). Initially, groups were shown a process requiring 12 folds. Midway through the task, a new person approached each threesome and introduced a more efficient process that required only seven folds. Despite the superiority of the new method, *only 25 percent* of groups adopted it. Consider that for a moment: three in four groups *saw* the better approach modeled for them—one that could make the task easier and help them win the "game"—but they essentially shrugged their shoulders and said, "Nah. That's not for us."

So, researchers tried a different approach. In a second condition, they ensured that the person who introduced the new method wore the same color name tag and shared the same team name as the receiving group. This simple change essentially flipped the results: fully *75 percent* of groups adopted the better technique. Under these conditions, *homophily* seemed to support, rather than hinder, the uptake of new practices. In short, people appear to be more willing to try something if the idea comes from someone within the "group"— even a group that had been created rather artificially only a few minutes earlier.

In Melbourne, a similar strategy emerged. Because the region was a loose-knit confederation of schools—the central office itself had only a skeletal staff—they couldn't turn to hordes of central office personnel to roll out the program. So instead, 140 teachers from 55 low-income schools came together to deeply immerse themselves in the theories of action. These teachers were then tasked with returning to their schools to work with triads of teachers as *peers* (not as finger-wagging administrators) to adopt the strategies (Hopkins & Craig, 2011).

Creating Critical Friends

As these 140 teachers went to their schools, they faced another challenge. Often peer coaching breaks down for one simple reason: Teachers tend to be too nice to one another. A small study of a mathematics intervention in Kentucky (Murray, Ma, & Mazur, 2009), for example, found that although peer coaching conversations were positive and supportive, they lacked depth; 100 percent of comments offered were positive, with no critique. "Overall," the researchers observed, "peer partners did not challenge or question one another's classroom practices" (p. 209). So how can we prevent peer coaching from turning into vapid I'm-okay-you're-okay conversations?

A recent small-scale qualitative study in Canada (Jao, 2013) points toward a potential answer. It found that when teachers were given *guiding questions* for their collaborative conversations and *protocols* for observing classrooms, peer coaching became far more incisive and productive. In other words, to help teachers really push one another to improve their practices—to become critical friends to one another—it's necessary to clearly delineate for everyone what better teaching looks like. We can do that by using a tool that's commonplace yet widely misunderstood in education: rubrics.

Providing Precision with Rubrics

At first blush, we might think that the purpose of a rubric is to help teachers be more fair and consistent graders—allowing us to see how student work stacks up against the objective criteria of the rubric. However, a review of 75 studies on the benefits of using of rubrics found that rubrics don't really make teachers better or more consistent graders; like any tool, they can be used (or interpreted) well or poorly (Jonsson & Svingby, 2007). Nonetheless, the rubrics were found to be a powerful tool to raise student performance. How?

As it turns out, the real value of rubrics lies in placing them in the hands of students, enabling them to size up their own performance, become more receptive to feedback, and feel more motivated to improve their performance because they own the process. As the researchers concluded, what rubrics really do is put learning in the hands of students so they can "know why they are doing what they are doing" (Jonsson & Svingby, 2007, p. 139). A small study of college students illustrates this point. Students given a rubric for a writing assignment scored an average of a *full letter grade* higher (84 percent vs. 72 percent) on the assignment than a similar class without the rubric (Howell, 2011).

Creating Rubrics for Teacher Learning

In Melbourne, some schools that embraced the Curiosity and Powerful Learning approach took the six teacher theories of action and turned them into in-depth non-evaluative rubrics to serve as the basis for teachers working together. Each rubric described, in concrete terms, what increasing *precision* of practice looked like as teachers moved from the categories of *commencing* practice to *intermediate* practice to *accomplished* practice to *expert* practice. For example, for the theory of action about asking higher-order questions, teachers were given a rubric that described this progression:

• At the commencing practice level, "Teacher often asks questions that require students to repeat information."

• At the intermediate practice level, "Teacher often asks questions that allow students to demonstrate their thinking."

• At the accomplished practice level, "Teacher usually asks questions that assist teacher and students to revise tasks and review explanations in ways that improve learning."

• And finally, at the expert practice level, "Teacher uses questions skillfully to check understanding and uses student responses to intervene in ways that have a noticeable impact on learning."

At each step along the way, the rubrics offered clear examples of what these levels looked like in the classroom so teachers could see what they needed to do to move from, say, commencing to intermediate practice by, for example, going from a classroom where "Response to student answers is often 'yes,' 'no,' or praise for correct answers rather than praise for effort and thinking strategy" to a classroom where "The ratio of low-order and high-order questions is about

50/50. [And] most teacher questions are referenced to the fertile question, the learning intention, and task objectives."

Embedded in these progressions were positive messages about teachers' ability to grow. Terms like *commencing practice* (instead of labels such as "unsatisfactory" or "basic") were intended to show that teaching quality was not a fixed trait; every teacher can get better every day. The rubrics were never about sizing up teacher effectiveness; principals did not use them to evaluate teachers (made easier by the fact that the state of Victoria did not have a heavy-handed teacher evaluation system in place). In a very real way, the rubrics were intended to help teachers develop a mastery orientation (or growth mindset) about their own teaching abilities.

The Power of Autonomy, Mastery, and Purpose

With rubrics in hand, each triad of teachers selected practices to work on with colleagues during six-week cycles. It wasn't a mix-and-match approach, though—ultimately teachers understood they needed to develop professional skills in *all* of the theories of action, but they had some latitude in selecting *which* practices to work on first, based upon what they saw as their greatest opportunity for improving their own professional practice. The whole process of creating peer-coaching triads, placing non-evaluative rubrics in their hands, and allowing them to focus on their next opportunities for improvement tapped into all three elements of what Pink (2009) dubs Motivation 3.0: Teachers had *autonomy* to choose where to focus their improvement efforts so that professional development wasn't "done" to them, and they could guide and engage in professional learning for themselves. Moreover, they developed a sense of *mastery* as they saw themselves improving and students responding in kind, which led them to say, "Well, all right. That worked. What should we try next?" And finally, because the rubrics were laid out in front of them and tied to the mantra of creating schools where students were "literate, numerate, and curious," they could connect everything back to a deeper, moral *purpose.*

Letting Go in Greenhills

Early on in their time together at Greenhills, Kayll and Gibson conducted their own instructional rounds, observing classrooms and looking for bright spots to spread to other classrooms. Doing so helped them get on the same page with one another about what good instruction looks like in the classroom; after each instructional round, they would discuss privately what they had seen and share their respective ideas about good instruction. Eventually, they sat down with teachers in small groups and informal one-on-one conversations and talked— as professionals—about the practices and structures they had seen in classrooms.

The conversations remained nonjudgmental; Kayll and Gibson simply asked teachers to reflect on the core purpose of their classroom activities. "We quickly figured out that our teachers had become really disempowered over the years with so many external mandates, so it was really important to us to keep the conversations professional and not about exposing faults," said Gibson. "We wanted teachers to arrive at their own conclusions and develop their own solutions. We communicated that we didn't have all the answers and made it clear that we'd work with teachers and listen to their ideas and opinions moving forward."

Coming Together to Fix a Habit: The Learning "Wasteland"

During these conversations, it became evident that while teachers were planning activities that directly linked to curriculum standards and outcomes, most learning tasks were just that—tasks for students to complete but without a guiding purpose or *why.* As teachers began to *ask themselves why* they were asking students to do this task, they began to scrap "busy work" in favor of more purposeful work for students.

For example, the last hour of the day had become something of a learning wasteland; students often engaged in "fun" but mostly meaningless activities with little connection to the curriculum. Some teachers had fallen into the habit of showing movies with combined classes or letting kids engage in "free play" with no real purpose other than to stay out of the teachers' way while they corrected student work or planned for the next day. Over the course of about six months, as teachers became more purposeful, they began to ask one another questions about why they were forfeiting an hour of learning time each day. Soon, they began to work together to rethink the use of that final hour of the day as an opportunity for students to apply their learning in engaging ways, rotating to different teachers' classrooms to engage in hands-on projects, like creating maps of their own "fantasy islands" that integrated math, geography, literacy, environmental sciences, and social studies lessons or translating topographic maps into 3-D landscapes using papier-maĉhé.

One Thing Leads to Another

These efforts created a sense of forward momentum that made it easier for Kayll and Gibson to insert additional concepts into their dialogue with teachers—like how they were going about creating learning intentions and success criteria for students: What do we want students to know and do, and how will we (and they) know when they've got it?

As teachers began to discuss together how to structure learning around learning intentions and success criteria, the concept of pace naturally entered into their conversations: How much time should we spend on this topic? What checks for understanding should we use? How should we design learning as a series of digestible segments that create a larger whole? "Learning intentions and success criteria were inextricably linked," Gibson observed. "The more teachers saw how they helped students reflect upon their own learning and progress, the more they used them in the classroom."

Altogether, teachers spent about 20 weeks using discussions and peer and leader observations to learn, share, and give one another feedback on how to shape and use learning intentions, success criteria, and pace to engage and focus students on their own learning. Ultimately, every teacher began using these theories of action every day in every lesson. And so it went with many of the theories of action. Like popcorn in a hot skillet, as one idea popped, another would follow. Yet teachers never felt the ideas were being imposed on them; rather, they were emerging naturally from their conversations together.

Asking a Better Question: What Do Kids Think?

The concept of "challenging learning tasks" was a case in point. At first, it was a bone of contention for some teachers: Many teachers believed they were *already* setting challenging tasks. After all, most of the kids were performing at or above grade level. Yet they didn't see what Kayll and Gibson saw: five-plus years flat-line student achievement. They could have insisted that teachers were wrong—that students *weren't* being challenged—but instead they created a *challenge condition* for teachers that started with a simple question: What would our students say about their learning tasks? Do they find them challenging or engaging?

Together with teachers, they created a short survey for students in grades 3 to 6 to get a sneak peek into what students thought about their learning tasks; although no teachers were obligated to share their student feedback, student opinion was so divided that conversations naturally occurred. "Almost half of my class tell me they are bored, but they can't even do the work I planned for them. How can they be bored?" some teachers asked, revealing a common misconception: that *difficult* meant *challenging*. Only when students find a *difficult* problem compelling does it become *challenging*; otherwise, it's just drudgery.

As teachers talked more about what they learned from students, their conversations soon turned to curriculum and lesson planning. Teachers began to open up to one another, revealing their teaching habits: Some loved using worksheets for every lesson, expecting students to sit quietly and "do" their work. Others put students in groups, directing them to work on the same task (yet not collaboratively) for the vaguely defined purpose of providing a quasi-peer support system for students to ask one another for help if they got stuck.

Where's the Fire?

As teachers talked together about their practices and their purpose (or lack thereof), they soon came to a shared realization that although their activities were designed with standards in mind and most students could reach those standards, they weren't engaging students in their own learning or challenging them to apply what they had learned to a "real world" task. In other words, even if they had managed to spark student interest and fan a flame of focused learning, the fire was going out before students could engage in deep learning.

Teachers were already planning lessons collaboratively, so they began to focus their attention on "auditing" the curriculum at each level to find ways to make it more engaging and challenging by linking assignments to a larger inquiry topic. For example, kindergarten units on measurement and shape were linked to a science unit on "minibeasts," and teachers wove together a grade 3–4 Australian history unit with lessons on understanding and creating timelines, maps, reading comprehension, and narrative writing.

Over the course of a school year, teachers collectively re-planned half their units, revamping most and replacing many they deemed too dry to engage students. Over time, they also put to rest their weekly pacing guides in favor of a more seamless, personalized model of teaching and learning in classrooms. Initially, those pacing guides had been helpful routines, getting everyone on the same page about how much instructional time ought to be devoted to particular topics.

However, as teachers began to use data regularly to guide teaching, they saw that not all students were making progress at the same pace, and thus they needed to give some students extra time to master certain topics while allowing other students to move ahead with their learning. A teacher with a combined grade 5–6 class might have a small group working on a certain math task aiming for success using outcomes at a grade 4 level because that was the students' *point of need*. Other students might be working on a similar task, but using outcomes from the grade 9 curriculum. In short, teachers began differentiating their teaching and learning to provide tasks in each student's "Goldilocks zone"—neither too difficult nor too easy.

Better Together

These changes were not always easy; teachers had grown comfortable with using the pacing guides and still had memories of being directed to use them in a very compliance-oriented way. Left to their own devices, few teachers would have made the transition. Like any ingrained habit, it required social support and relationships—along with some reframing—to break the old habits. An a-ha moment for many teachers came when they realized that it wasn't *instruction* that needed to be differentiated but rather *learning*. That is, teachers didn't need to deliver the direct instruction portion of their lessons in multiple ways; rather, they needed to provide students with multiple learning paths during the guided and independent practice portion of their learning cycle.

"In hindsight, it was a messy process," Gibson recalled. "Teachers really needed to be there for one another, experimenting together to figure out how to make it work. Rowan and I had to stand back a bit and allow teachers to use a bit of trial and error; we'd gotten to the place where there was no script to follow and even if there had been, teachers would still have needed some space to make sense of it all for themselves and their own students."

After a few months, they re-surveyed students about their perceived level of challenge and engagement in the classroom. The data showed that on the whole, teachers were getting it right; across the school students reported they were feeling more confident about their learning than they had been 12 months earlier. "I think that was a bit of a breakthrough moment for us," said Gibson. "It gave teachers the confidence that when working together, they could really do something positive for students and provide them with both an engaging and challenging curriculum."

Getting It Wrong

The overall approach in Melbourne—introducing new knowledge as concrete learning progressions, giving people latitude to work on their own most salient opportunities for improvement, and letting them practice with others in short improvement cycles—is hardly new. Indeed, the research supporting these approaches goes back years, if not decades. So why then, we might ask ourselves, does it remain so difficult to put (and keep) in place this constellation of improvement practices? Why are these stars so difficult to align?

The Hidden Factor: Mental Frames

The answer to this question may have a great deal to do with how, for decades, we have tended to *think* about professional development itself. Years ago, James Spillane (2000), a researcher at Northwestern University, examined reform efforts in nine districts in Michigan and found that, on the surface, many PD approaches look the same. The school year kicks off with everyone coming to a large session in the school's auditorium or cafeteria to learn about some new set of better practices. Afterward, teachers are told to go back and apply the practices in their classrooms. And teams of instructional coaches are dispatched to help them do it.

Yet, as Spillane observed, those surface similarities "camouflaged substantial differences in the underlying theories of teacher learning and change" (p. 23)—differences that reflected what Spillane argued were *behaviorist, situated,* and *cognitive* views of change. Spillane surveyed 40 leaders in those nine districts and found that the vast majority of them, 34 (or 85 percent), held views that reflected a behaviorist perspective; that is, they sought to motivate behavior primarily through external rewards à la B. F. Skinner teaching pigeons to play Ping-Pong. For them, staff development consisted of transmitting information (usually from outside experts) to teachers, who had to be properly incentivized and monitored to ensure adoption of new programs. For leaders who operated from this perspective, teacher coaches were basically confederates of the central office sent out to relay information to teachers (and back to leaders) to ensure everyone complied with (or implemented) the chosen program.

A small handful (5, or 12.5 percent) of leaders held views that reflected a situated perspective. These leaders sought to motivate teacher learning via peer pressure, creating a school culture where norms worked against teacher autonomy and promoted collegiality. Leaders who operated from a situated perspective often tapped early adopters of new strategies and encouraged them to proselytize others in hopes of creating a tipping point at which all teachers felt socially persuaded to adopt a new strategy. We've seen, of course, how such an approach can be effective, especially in places like Montgomery, Alabama, where social networks bolstered people's courage and created community norms that led to a universal boycott of the buses.

Only one leader in Spillane's study held views aligned with a *cognitive* perspective—one more in line with Dan Pink's Motivation 3.0, in which people are seen as natural-born inquirers motivated by a need for self-actualization. This particular leader focused on teachers as individual learners, observing them to understand their prior knowledge and beliefs so that she might tailor their professional learning to support their individual professional growth.

Behaviorism Rears Its Head Again

Once again, we see that behaviorism has a funny way of twisting what we do in education. In reality, of course, the lines between these perspectives are not as neat and simple as they might appear in theory. Consider your own reasons for reading this book: You may be naturally intrigued by human behavior (cognitive), wanting to stay abreast of your profession (situated), and looking for ways to do a better job so you can advance your career (behaviorist). Teachers are no different, which means that effecting change in teaching practices often requires incorporating and balancing all three motivators—using, for example, external experts or confronting people with some brutal facts of performance to spark change (a behaviorist impulse), encouraging schoolwide professionalism (a situated response), and giving teachers some freedom to adapt practices to their own students (a cognitive motivator), while relying on rubrics for peer coaching (more akin to a situated approach).

The real challenge, however, appears to be that, as Spillane observed, the pressure of top-down accountability prompts leaders, often unwittingly, to align staff development with a mostly behaviorist approach. TNTP's *Mirage* report itself appears to reflect a behaviorist bent in viewing professional development as a mechanism for getting teachers to adopt, not adapt, new practices. For example, it asked teachers if they received follow-up support to "ensure I am *implementing* [emphasis added] new instructional practices effectively" (2015, p. 53)—the implication, of course, being not that teachers are developing more precision or professional insights, but rather that they are applying an externally imposed approach in their classrooms.

For some, dwelling on something as intangible as people's mental frames may seem pointlessly abstract and unrelated to the day-to-day challenges of running schools and working with students. Yet how we *think* about the world influences how we act in it, which in turn can yield very different outcomes for ourselves and our students. Let's consider for a moment how behaviorism has influenced our approach to what is arguably one of the most sweeping changes in education in recent years: the adoption of new educator performance appraisal systems.

Can We Evaluate Our Way to Better Performance?

Arguably, the underlying premise behind the nationwide push for stronger educator evaluation systems has tended to be this: If we can just figure out the right elements of teacher effectiveness, turn those into the right performance criteria, train administrators to use those performance criteria to make the right judgments about educators, and then attach the right incentives and training to improve performance on those measures, all will be right with the world of education.

Consider, for example, the recent $45 million effort by the Bill & Melinda Gates Foundation to determine whether it's possible to quantify something as complex as teaching. After reviewing 20,000 classroom videos, crunching data from thousands of student surveys, and parsing value-added achievement results for 3,000 teachers in seven districts, they concluded it was, in fact, possible to accurately size up effective teaching—largely by triangulating data from student learning gains, student surveys, and to a lesser extent, sizing up teachers' "on-stage" behaviors through classroom evaluations (which they found to be fraught with inaccuracies and inconsistencies) (Bill & Melinda Gates Foundation, 2013).

Many other researchers have also busied themselves over the last several years with trying to figure out whether teachers who get better scores on performance evaluations are really more effective in the classroom. Generally speaking, the answer to this question has ranged from not really (Lazarev, Newman, & Sharp, 2014) to yes, but only moderately (Kane, Taylor, Tyler, & Wooten, 2011; Lash, Makkonen, Tran, & Huang, 2016) and with no more precision than asking principals to respond to a short list of questions about their gut-level impressions of teachers' effectiveness (Jacob & Lefgren, 2008).

Of course, all of these attempts to measure teacher quality often neglect a more important question: Do complex evaluation systems actually do anything to *improve* teacher performance? One of the few studies to examine this question looked at performance trajectories of midcareer teachers in Cincinnati who participated in an evaluation system that employed multiple structured observations conducted by experienced peers from other schools (Taylor & Tyler, 2012). At the time of the study, these teachers were evaluated only once every four years, which gave researchers a before-and-after picture they could use to see whether the evaluation process itself did anything to help teachers up their game. As it turns out, they *could* detect a small spike in teacher performance—equivalent to about a 4.5 percentile point gain in students' mathematics achievement—during the year of their evaluation (and afterward, as teachers appeared to sustain their gains). The researchers attributed most of these improvements to teachers receiving, on four separate occasions, detailed forma-tive feedback about their performance—using an explicit rubric for teaching effectiveness—and having opportunities to reflect on, and converse with peers about, their practice.

It's worth noting that the evaluation system in question was fairly lenient and low stakes, as it was only loosely tied to promotion and retention decisions. Nonetheless, on individual rubric items, rat-ers were fairly strict, leading the researchers to speculate that in the end, it may have been the "micro-level feedback" that drove improve-ments (e.g., pointers provided from one teacher to another about how to improve classroom questioning techniques) (Taylor & Tyler, 2012). Without overstating findings from one study, it appears that when it comes to driving improvement, one of the most important things a performance evaluation can provide is high-quality feed-back. In other words, just as great teachers understand about grading student work in their own classrooms, evaluation without feedback is often meaningless as it does little to help anyone improve.

Perhaps the real irony in all of the energy and resources that U.S. school systems have been compelled to spend over the past several years to adopt a seemingly more business-minded "get-tough" approach to employment decisions is that during roughly the same period, the business world moved in the *opposite* direction, abandoning annual performance reviews in favor of employees working with their supervisors to set ambitious goals and receive regular feedback about their progress toward those goals.

Why Businesses Are Backing Away from Heavy-Handed Employee Evaluations

Not long after the release of the Gates Foundation report on effective measures of teachers, Bill Gates's own company, Microsoft, announced it was moving away from rating and ranking employees and would instead give employees real-time feedback and coaching aimed at fostering professional growth (Warren, 2013). Since then, other companies, including GE and Google, have abandoned get-tough performance management approaches in favor of allowing employees to set stretch goals and receive frequent feedback and coaching from supervisors and peers (Duggan, 2015). Where did these companies get such radical, crazy ideas? Largely, as it turns out, from education research, including these findings:

• Carol Dweck's (2006) studies of middle schoolers, for example, showed the power of developing a "growth" mindset (seeing intelligence as malleable) versus a "fixed" mindset (seeing intelligence as static). Done poorly, performance ratings can reinforce a fixed mindset if those being evaluated internalize low marks as evidence of their permanent inability.

• Dylan Wiliam (2011) found that timely, targeted feedback is key to improving performance, yet often falls on deaf ears when coupled with numerical ratings. His study of 6th graders, for example, found that adding a numeric score to written comments wiped out the benefits of the comments, presumably because "students who got the high scores didn't need to read the comments and students who got low scores didn't want to" (p. 109).

 • Extrinsic rewards (the *modus operandi* of performance management) can *discourage* the very behaviors they intend to encourage. As noted in an earlier chapter, researchers have observed that when children were rewarded for drawing pictures, they later spent less free time drawing (Deci et al., 1999), which suggests that rewarding inherently enjoyable activities (be it drawing pictures or teaching well) can turn them into chores and leave us feeling cheated if promised rewards don't materialize.

 • The real power of rubrics—like those at the heart of many teacher performance evaluation systems—lies not so much in their ability to improve the consistency or fairness of evaluation but in helping people chart a course for their own performance improvement (Jonsson & Svingby, 2007).

Let's pause a moment to reflect on all of this and what it means for education systems.

Getting It Right

For starters, we've seen that most professional development efforts have not been terribly effective in helping teachers grow as professionals. At the same time, given what we know about the effect ratings and rewards can have on people's productive mindsets, receptivity to feedback, and intrinsic motivation to improve, we might wonder whether even the *most precise* teacher evaluation systems would improve performance or have *negative* effects by pushing passion for teaching, joy of learning, and student curiosity out the classroom.

Doing unto Others as We Would Have Them Do unto Others

The reality is that it's difficult, if not impossible, to create learning environments where students are curious if *teachers* aren't also allowed to be curious themselves, asking bigger questions about what new approaches they could take to allow students to flourish as learners. If teachers are simply told, "Here's the new approach, now go do it," they're unlikely to experience much professional curiosity. Moreover, under our current system of top-down pressure, it's quite likely that teachers may be doing unto their students what's being done to them—turning learning into a joyless system of external rewards where the ultimate goal is to make the grade and stay out of trouble.

In the end, how we think about change is more than just an abstract academic matter because it influences how we approach the entire enterprise of talent development. Do we create Orwellian environments in which professional development becomes a means to impose new practices on teachers and performance evaluation becomes a cudgel to pressure teachers into improving? Or do we seek to inspire teachers to set individual stretch goals, work together to meet their goals, and give them feedback that helps them to get a little better, every day, at what they do?

In fairness to school leaders, we should acknowledge that they themselves are often victims of top-down pressure. As the pressure mounts on them to deliver measurable results for students (on measures that are arguably flawed or at least limited in their ability to capture deep learning), many principals now find themselves operating as middle managers—with much responsibility but little authority—tasked with getting recalcitrant teachers to toe the line in order to implement district initiatives with fidelity.

Creating Curious Professionals

As we've seen, putting curiosity at the heart of improvement could be like casting a pebble into a still pond with ripple effects across the education system. Learning begins to look different—more engaging and empowering for students. Teaching looks different, too—focused on nurturing student interest and passion for learning. Professional learning also looks different—encouraging teachers themselves to become curious, engaged in constant inquiry and self-reflection about their own professional practices. Ultimately, the same idea applies to principals and other school leaders: They, too, must be curious.

In Greenhills, Kayll and Gibson cast that pebble into the pond in a rather inside-out way. They never proclaimed that teachers ought to focus on curiosity or plastered curiosity-themed posters all over the school. Rather, they started with helping *teachers* to become curious themselves; by asking teachers question after question, they modeled an inquiry-based approach to learning and encouraged *teachers* to begin asking their own burning questions and pursue their own curiosity. Early on, they had learned from talking to teachers that the heavy weight of top-down directives had stamped out teachers' own curiosity—sending the implicit message, "Don't ask questions; just do what you're told." As a result, teachers were downtrodden and anxious. "We pretty quickly figured out that we needed to have open discussions and encourage our teachers to deconstruct the top-down leadership style that had developed over time in the school," Gibson noted. "The new leadership team agreed we needed to give our teachers permission to ask questions and take back some of the power and decision making they'd been denied in the past."

A similar evolution took place in William Ruthven over the course of two years, noted principal Karen Money. Immediately following the merger, staff morale was discouragingly low. In many ways, the 50-plus teachers and staff members in the building still felt like two schools operating under one roof, fragmented and still clinging to old allegiances that harbored an "us versus them" mentality. Thus, from the outset, Money put building a better culture inside the building—one with a moral purpose and shared values—at the top of her list. Culture, of course, is a funny thing: You can't simply talk your way into it; you must develop one trusting relationship and shared success at a time. Money helped everyone focus on something bigger than themselves—student literacy, numeracy, and curiosity—and something they could achieve only by working together.

As the Curiosity and Powerful Learning approach began to spread across the northern region of Melbourne, it soon became apparent that the success of the entire effort would lie in the hands of school leaders. Certainly, principals would need to buy in and be vocal champions of the 10 theories of action in their schools. In many ways, though, that was the easy part. The more difficult part lay in yet another important ripple effect that placing curiosity at the center would have for leaders—one that for some leaders might feel more like a tsunami, calling upon them to develop a *whole new* style of leadership, turning their own paradigm of what it means to be a good leader *inside out*.

 PAUSE AND REFLECT

- How would you distinguish professional *development* from professional *learning*?
- Consider a professional practice you've improved; what elements helped you to develop better practices?
- How active are professional learning experiences in your school?
- Are your current professional development plans focused on programs or *practice*?
- What mental frames appear to have guided most of the PD you've experienced? How might the experiences have been different if a different mental frame guided them?

- What would an inside-out peer coaching model look like at your school?
- What might leaders in your school need to "let go of" to make that happen?

ENVISION A BETTER WAY

- List professional learning options for teachers that maximize active learning.
- With colleagues, identify what an ideal professional learning cycle (over one year) would look like.
- Survey or interview teachers on what support they need to improve professional practice.
- Develop a plan for working with influencers to develop a strong, collaborative culture in your school.
- Develop protocols to support effective peer feedback for teachers.

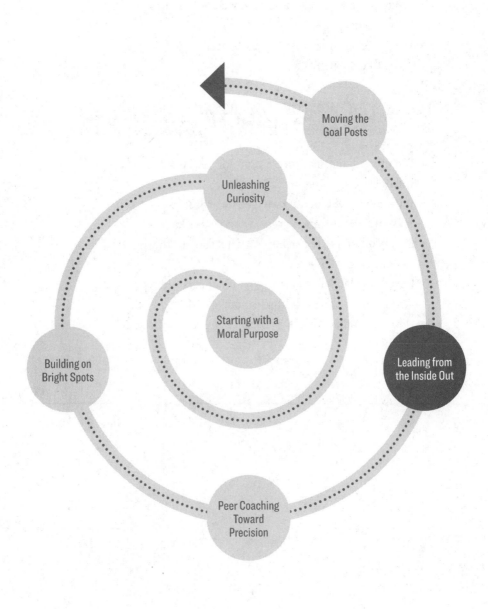

Moving the
Goal Posts

Unleashing
Curiosity

Starting with a
Moral Purpose

Leading from
the Inside Out

Building on
Bright Spots

Peer Coaching
Toward
Precision

7

Leading from the Inside Out

The important thing is not to stop questioning. Curiosity has its own reason for existing.

Albert Einstein

Imagine you're going about your regular life—perhaps standing on the sidelines of a child's soccer game—when suddenly, you feel tightness in your chest. You labor to catch your breath and begin to feel nauseated. As you look for a place to sit, you explain your symptoms to people nearby. You hear the whispered words "heart attack." Someone dials 911. By the time the paramedics arrive, there's no mistaking it: you're in full cardiac arrest. *This is it*, you think. *This is how I'm going to die.* Your last thought, while staring at the ceiling of the ambulance, is there's still so much you want to do—see Switzerland, dance with your kids at their wedding, hold a grandchild in your arms. Everything goes black.

Later, you return to consciousness and find yourself in a hospital recovery room. Eventually, a doctor pays a visit and tells you, matter-of-factly, that you're lucky to be alive; next time, you may not be so fortunate. Heart problems, she says, are caused by five major behaviors—too much stress, too much drinking, smoking, poor diet, and lack of exercise. Unless you want to find yourself back in the ER—or worse, six feet under—you must change your lifestyle. It's as simple as that.

Her bedside manner could be better, but you appreciate her frankness. You nod your assent to the doctor and assure your concerned family that you're going to change. Your new life of nicotine patches, salads, unsweetened seltzer water, and trips to the gym starts *now*. You'll even box up the liquor cabinet and donate it to the neighbors.

However, you soon fall back into your old habits. You hit the gym for a few weeks but find it difficult to squeeze workouts into your day, not to mention that it's painful and boring. You eat healthy for a month or so, then start sneaking French fries back into your diet. The same goes for the patch. You tried it for a few weeks, but the cravings didn't go away. You also tried switching to unsweetened drinks, but a voice in your head tells you you *deserve* soft drinks now and then as a reward. The same thing goes for alcohol. You'll never be able to afford a vacation to Switzerland anyway, so why not enjoy a few more trips to Margaritaville?

When you see your doctor again, you fess up that you haven't really changed your lifestyle. She warns you again that your life is at risk if you don't clean up your act. You nod knowingly but realize that you probably won't be able to change; it feels as if deep inside, a part of you has decided that living healthy is no way to live.

On your first day back at school, you find yourself in a faculty meeting where the new principal is angrily waving a report showing student achievement results from last year. Already, your school is on the "naughty list" (as everyone calls it); if student achievement doesn't improve, the school is in danger of being reconstituted, she tells you, not sugarcoating anything. That gets your attention. You're too old to be looking for a new job.

She says the best way to improve student achievement is for everyone to beef up their formative assessment practices. She and the assistant principal have done the research and found a good program. It's not cheap, she laments, so everyone needs to take it seriously. She'll be doing walkthroughs to make sure that happens. As you look around the room, you see that some other teachers plainly don't much care for her. You like her no-nonsense style, though. She reminds you a bit of your doctor; she is unflinching about what has to be done. Frankly, she had you at "reconstituted"; whatever this new formative assessment program is, you're sold; *I'm going to be a formative assessing fool.*

Failing with Three Fs

In his book *Change or Die*, Alan Deutschman (2006) notes that like doctors who try to frighten patients into changing their life habits, leaders also often resort to the "three Fs" of fear, facts, and force to drive changes in behavior. There's just one problem. These drivers (which are, incidentally, the core elements of top-down change) typically do little to change anyone's behavior, especially when the changes are complex or significant ones (2006). There's no more tragic example of this fact than this: When cardiac bypass patients are told their lives are at risk unless they give up smoking, cut back on alcohol, eat better, and exercise more, only *1 out of 10* people presented with those cold, hard facts are able to change their habits (Deutschman, 2006).

Consider that for a moment: If *fear of death* is insufficient to motivate people to change, why do we think that browbeating, shaming, or threatening loss of employment will get educators to change their habits? Once again, behaviorism fails us by assuming that human beings respond rationally to external conditioning. If that were true, then the mother of all external motivators—fear of death— ought to get people to straighten up and fly right. And yet it doesn't.

Why not?

Moving Beyond the Three Fs

One answer to this question might be found in the *outliers*—the one in 10 people who *are able* to *alter* and *sustain* healthier behaviors. When we dig more deeply into why these people change their behaviors when others cannot, we see that it has little to do with *external* motivators and everything to do with *internal* and *interpersonal* motivators—reflecting what Deutschman calls the three Rs of "relate, repeat, and reframe." People are more likely to change when they *relate* to the person asking them to change (or others changing along with them), have opportunities to *repeat* the change until the new behavior sticks, and are able to *reframe* the change in a way that helps them to dwell not on what they're *giving up* (e.g., smoking, drinking, relaxing) but on what they're *gaining* (e.g., more energy, better physique, greater self-esteem, and a longer life).

Another answer to this question is that often the behaviors we most need to change are deeply ingrained habits and difficult to break. Moreover, we seldom *break* habits altogether, but rather learn to *replace* them with new, more productive ones (see Figure 7.1 for a few examples). Seldom is that a snap decision we make—and stick to—on the basis of external rewards or punishments. We don't wake up one morning and say, "Oh, well, all right, in light of the potential consequences of my sugary, carb-heavy diet on my long-term health, I'll change my deeply ingrained behaviors, starting now."

Figure 7.1 | *Bend*, Don't *Break* Habits: Examples of Replacement Habits

Biting fingernails → Chewing gum
After-work drink to relax → After-work yoga to relax
Cookie break at work → Almond break at work
After-dinner smoke → After-dinner cappuccino
Crispy chips with that? → Yes, cucumber chips!

As we'll see, changing habits is complex, difficult, personal, and ongoing—a process that requires not a drill sergeant barking orders at us or threatening us with "or else" consequences but rather people who help us muster the will within ourselves to change and create a new set of conditions in which we can successfully stick to our better behaviors.

Replacing Old Habits with Better Ones

Habits are difficult to change even when our lives are on the line. That's largely because as researchers at MIT have discovered (and as Charles Duhigg [2012] describes in *The Power of Habit*), at the core of our habits are neurological "loops"—a *cue* (someone asks us "Do you want fries with that?") triggers a *routine* (eating fries) that creates a *reward* (a flavor bomb of salt, carbs, and fat). If we connect those cues, routines, and rewards enough, a habit loop begins to form, with those cues automatically triggering routines. The trouble is that our environments are often full of those cues or triggers. The very sight of golden arches triggers our brains to anticipate a caloric bonanza that would have been unimaginable to our great-great-grandparents.

The problem with behaviorism, especially employing fear, facts, and force, is that it addresses only one part of the loop—the reward. Yet at that moment of temptation, or the triggering *cue* (e.g., "Do you want fries with that?"), the threat of far-off consequences sits so far outside our cue-routine-reward habit loop that it really doesn't make a dent in our behavior. It would be different, of course, if every time we turned around, we saw our fellow human beings keeling over while clutching a bag of fries. That might give us pause. We don't see that, of course. Moreover, we get an *immediate* reward from the fries, the margarita, sitting on the sofa, taking a cigarette break, or whatever our vice may be. So, at best, fear, facts, and force may cause those French fries to come with a dollop of self-loathing. Yet such feelings are 90-pound weaklings compared with the sumo wrestler-sized rewards of ingrained habits. Moreover, as Duhigg notes, stress often makes us backslide into old habits, which could explain why putting people in highly stressful conditions—including giving them heavy doses of fear, facts, and force—could actually work *against* their ability to sustain new habits.

The key to changing habits, according to Duhigg, lies in manipulating the *entire* cue-routine-reward habit loop and not just the reward. We might, for example, insert a new routine—say, eating almonds in lieu of a bag of cookies to satisfy our craving for an afternoon snack. Or we might avoid the temptation of the cue altogether by ordering a salad or packing a healthy lunch. Even better, we might step back and ask why we keep hitting the drive-thru on our way home from work in the first place. Is it because we're hungry and the fast food joint is conveniently located between work and our home? Or is it because we've come to view the whole experience as a way to reward ourselves and decompress after a long day of hard work? If the latter, could we find a better, healthier way to give ourselves that same reward, such as taking our dog on a walk in the park?

So what, you might ask, do French fries have to do with school improvement?

Organizational Change: Breaking Old Habits Together

Perhaps quite a lot. That's because organizational change—at least any change worth doing—often requires *every person* in the organization to break an old habit and adopt a new one. All organizations (including schools) develop shared habits. These are often the unwritten rules about "how things are done around here." Maybe it's coasting to the end of the school year instead of sprinting. Maybe it's a mindless approach to data analysis that fixates on nudging a few "bubble kids" above the next cut score instead of reflecting on how to support the learning and motivation of *all* students. Or maybe it's wasting a school's most precious resource—instructional time— with constant interruptions by way of announcements, needless pep assemblies, or poorly paced instruction.

Whatever the habit might be, organizational change of any significance requires people to adopt *new* routines and overcome ingrained patterns of behavior. How do they do that? Leadership, of course, plays a big part. Yet as we'll see, encouraging new habits and getting them to stick requires a different style of leadership than simply barking orders and threatening consequences.

A Different Style of Leadership

Leaders themselves, of course, often fall into their own unproductive habits. For some, it could be a do-this-or-else approach to supervision. Such an approach can be habit-forming because it works, especially when we want people to follow straightforward routines, such as showing up to work on time or turning in attendance reports. A study of health care teams in Israel, for example, found that teams led by *empowering* or *participatory* leaders demonstrated greater reflection and innovation but also lower overall performance on a few key measurable yet simple outcomes—presumably because "team reflection may be important for more complex tasks, such as innovative acts, but redundant for routine tasks" (Somech, 2006, p. 151).

The same might be said for schools: To get immediate gains in achievement, reflection and innovation may be less important than simply executing more consistently on a handful of routines related to curriculum and instruction. In these circumstances, many principals have likely seen a no-nonsense approach to leadership work, resulting in a cue-routine-reward loop that creates, for many leaders, a *habit* of top-down leadership.

However, when asking people to change in more complex ways—for example, putting curiosity and student engagement at the center of learning—simply issuing orders, drill sergeant-style ("Dig! Dig! Dig!") is unlikely to foster the kind of innovative, collaborative spirit needed to move everyone forward in dynamic ways. Moreover, as we'll see in a moment, like many things related to behaviorism, such a leadership style also tends to have diminishing returns.

Empowering Change, Not Directing It

Let's consider for a moment a study involving 60 teams of college seniors engaged in a multi-person, military-style computer simulation. Prior to the experiment, the researchers identified student leaders with a penchant for two very different styles: those with a *directive* style (who defaulted to assigning individuals to roles, giving clear directions, and setting expectations for compliance) versus those with a more *empowering* style (who shared power, encouraged dissenting opinions, and promoted shared decision making). The researchers found that initially, teams with directive leaders outperformed those with empowering ones. (At this point in the study, we might imagine the directive leaders having their own habits reinforced with the rewards of higher performance.)

Midway through the study, though, things got a little more interesting. As the teams engaged in repeated trials of the simulation, the performance of teams with directive leaders began to plateau. Meanwhile, teams led by empowering leaders continued to improve and eventually eclipsed those with directive leaders. The researchers concluded that having empowering leaders made teams less productive initially as they sorted out their roles and how to work together, but ultimately their ability to engage in collaborative learning led to continued performance gains (Lorinkova, Pearsall, & Sims, 2013).

This finding shouldn't surprise us when we consider that team performance reflects the sum of people's habits and whether those habits are productive or counterproductive. We might imagine teams with directive leaders locking onto adequate routines more quickly, yet being stymied in their ability to enhance those routines or develop them into even better ones—in short, changing their habits. As we've seen, switching one routine for another is rarely easy. And the more complex the routine—or deeply ingrained the habit—the more difficult it is to change. When we do manage to change our habits, there's a kind of paradox at work: The power to change often emerges from within ourselves but is also coaxed out and supported by those around us.

As it turns out, a McREL meta-analysis (Marzano, Waters, & McNulty, 2005) found that many of the behaviors exhibited by effective leaders—especially when leading complex changes—map closely onto an empowering leadership style, including these:

Encouraging dissent and inviting questions about the purpose or logic of a change effort (demonstrating "flexibility"). Leaders do this by refraining from stating their own opinions until after everyone on the leadership has spoken their mind or assigning a devil's advocate to offer a dissenting view to the group's consensus or leader's opinion.

Inspiring people to innovate and take on challenges that may seem initially beyond their reach (helping to "optimize" performance). Leaders can, for example, encourage everyone to develop stretch goals (i.e., ambitious aims that may initially seem beyond their reach) but pair them with practical steps for achieving those goals, combining, as it were, stretch goals with SMART goals (Duhigg, 2016).

Supporting shared learning about current best practices and research (providing "intellectual stimulation"). This can take the form of a regular book or article study with thoughtful discussion about the implications of the reading for taking different approaches—or affirming the team's commitment to its current approach.

Challenging the status quo by reframing change not as a loss but as a gain and painting the picture of a better future (operating as a "change agent"). For example, school leaders might use unsatisfactory student performance data or changing conditions (e.g., student demographics or curricular expectations) to create discontent with the current reality (e.g., translating *fear of change* into fear of *what happens if* we *don't change*) while helping people to envision a brighter future.

Creating Challenge (Not Threat) Conditions

This last finding is particularly important. You may recall that one of Deustchman's 3 Rs of change is helping people *reframe* the change in a more positive light. One of the more effective ways leaders can do this is by reframing what can often seem like a threat (e.g., change or die) as a challenge (e.g., let's find new ways to get better). Consider, for example, what happened in 1994 to Italian soccer great Robert Baggio as he stood before a packed Rose Bowl stadium, a mere 12 yards from the goal with a simple task: kick the ball into the net past the Brazilian goalkeeper. Under normal circumstances, doing so would've been easy; Baggio had a nearly perfect record of penalty kicks in his illustrious career. But these weren't normal circumstances. His teammates had missed their shots in the tiebreaker shootout, so Baggio's kick was now a sudden-death affair. If he missed, his team would lose its four-year quest for the World Cup. Knowing his opponent's propensity to dive left, Baggio aimed for dead center, just above the goalkeeper's head. As predicted, when Baggio booted the ball, the goalkeeper dove left. The ball flew straight, but sailed, agonizingly, just over the crossbar (Baggio, 2002). With one errant kick, the Italian superstar lost the World Cup.

A growing body of research has found that threat conditions can *diminish* performance. Baggio's miss, as it turns out, reflects a predictable pattern. When kicking to win—that is, giving their team a lead in a shootout—professional soccer players make 92 percent of their goals, but when kicking *not to lose*, as Baggio was, they succeed only 62 percent of the time (Jordet & Hartman, 2008).

In their book *Top Dog*, Bronson and Merryman (2013) synthesize numerous studies that show our brains and bodies react quite differently when we experience threat conditions. If we fear we're being judged or watched, our brains slow down our decision making and ability to take action. On high alert to avoid mistakes, we actually make *more* of them; what normally comes naturally suddenly becomes difficult (which may explain our sudden inability to type or spell correctly when someone is watching us type). In contrast, when we have a "challenge orientation," our brains relax, allowing us to focus less on what might go wrong and more on the task at hand. In sports, athletes play looser and better when playing to win instead of playing not to lose. In academics, anxious C-students become confident A-students. And in organizations, viewing problems as challenges can turn risk aversion and anxiety into openness to new ideas, experimentation, and ingenuity.

In Greenhills, Kayll and Gibson resisted the urge to present the school's flatlined student growth data as a threat, attack past practices, or demand compliance to some new program or directive. Instead, they presented school data as a challenge. "We knew that if we simply said, 'This isn't good enough,' we'd run the risk of teachers taking it personally and becoming defensive," Gibson recalled. "So instead, we showed them the data, so they could see the flatline for themselves, and then we worked together to come up with some possible reasons for the plateau. With teachers involved in the root-cause analysis, discussions were focused on the challenge of getting to the bottom of the problem and, in turn, on coming up with practical solutions."

The Greenhills approach reflects the findings of a study (also highlighted in Bronson and Merryman's book) of the management styles of 142 CEOs of small businesses (Wallace, Little, Hill, & Ridge, 2010). Researchers found higher performance in companies led by CEOs with a so-called *promotion* focus—who encourage innovation and new ideas to achieve ambitious goals—versus companies led by CEOs with a *prevention* focus—who cautiously fixate on preventing errors. A prevention focus, the researchers observed, may be suitable in stable environments where doing business as usual is warranted, but it is ill-suited to dynamic environments where new ideas and rapid change are key. Given that most companies face ever-changing environments, the bottom line (literally) is that they perform better when leaders frame problems as challenges, not threats.

As noted earlier in this book, many educators today appear to be operating under *threat* conditions—as evidenced by the MetLife Foundation's recent (2013) survey of educators finding that nearly half (48 percent) of principals reported being under great stress several days per week and similar percentages of teachers (51 percent) feeling great stress several days per week or more—a 15-point increase since 1985, when this item was last measured. When we have a *threat orientation*, people in schools are likely to respond in counterproductive ways—being reluctant to make decisions, try new approaches, or take bold action. Thus, by reframing threats as challenges—for example, translating the fear of school failure into the challenge of helping students succeed—leaders can unleash greater creativity and collective problem solving. Such an approach might be akin to one pro soccer coach's insightful method to alleviate his players' anxieties of missing a penalty goal: He simply challenged them to kick the ball as hard as they could, figuring if they didn't know where it was going, neither would the goalkeeper (Baxter, 2010).

Creating a "Kaizen" Culture

What often seems to happen during threat conditions is that we become reluctant to admit to our mistakes or point out when things are going wrong; in short, people fail to engage in the very kind of self-reflection that's most needed to improve performance. An in-depth examination of two urban middle schools engaged in a mathematics reform (Horn, Kane, & Wilson, 2015), found that their data conversations were fairly superficial—focusing on, for example, how to present data differently or asking teachers to predict the percentage of kids who might fall into various performance categories on the upcoming statewide test—with no reflection on how to improve instruction in order to improve achievement. Another study of data teams found many similarly going through the motions, quickly working through a data discussion protocol without introspection or identifying changes in instruction before exclaiming with relief, "Yay, we're done!" (Datnow, Park, & Kennedy-Lewis, 2013, p. 355).

It doesn't have to be that way, of course. Case studies have also observed teacher teams digging deeply into data, respectfully questioning one another, and examining their own practices—typically thanks to a strong principal who clearly defines the purpose of using data (i.e., to guide instructional changes) and creates a "we" feeling in the school (e.g., making math achievement everyone's responsibility, not just the math teachers') (Datnow, et al., 2013, p. 353). These strong leaders modeled norms for data conversations, specifying what materials—and attitudes—teachers should bring to meetings, including how they would hold one another accountable, argue productively in a safe environment (adopting slogans like, "Whatever happens in your meeting, stays in your meeting"), and ensure conversations about students never turned to "nit-picking or trash talking" (p. 354). In short, these leaders were able to create what Japanese manufacturers call *kaizen*—a belief that "every defect is a treasure" pointing toward a better way of doing things.

Using Data as Mirrors, Not Windows

High-pressure environments often make it hard for people to own up to their mistakes and work together. A study of high-stakes accountability in an urban district found, for example, that the longer low-performing schools faced the threat of sanctions, the less apt they were to examine underlying assumptions and current practices and pull together to improve them (Finnigan, Daly, & Che, 2012). High-pressure environments, in fact, seem to foster decidedly behaviorist approaches to data. In one urban middle school, for example, the principal directed teachers to show kids their test scores to motivate (i.e., scare) them into doing better; he also quipped that the afterschool math program ought to be reserved as a reward for well-behaved students—with no apparent understanding that poor behavior might reflect, or be the result of, student disengagement or academic difficulties (Horn et al., 2015). The school's mindset appeared to be, *We're okay; it's our students who are the problem.*

In light of high-pressure environment in which this school found itself, its principal and teachers might be forgiven for their attitudes and behaviors. Educators who fear being adversely judged by their shortcomings are less likely to engage in self-reflection and volunteer where they can improve. Unless leaders conscientiously create a safe environment and spirit of *kaizen*, teachers can have all the data in the world but do little with them to guide real improvement.

Supporting Change with Collaboration

Empowering leaders understand that people are more likely to change as a *group* than as individuals. Consider, for example, what Mary Budd Rowe (1986) discovered about getting teachers to adopt the simple practice of wait time. Somewhat by accident, she had discovered that when teachers' questions were followed by long pauses before students responded, that students seemed to be slow and deliberate with their answers, taking time to gather their thoughts. Upon further observation, she found that when the pauses (which she labeled "wait time") extended for three seconds or more—both after teachers' questions and following student replies, student responses to teachers' questions were fully *three to seven times* longer—they were also more thoughtful and supported with evidence. Having stumbled onto a simple but powerful teaching technique—wait time—that has the added benefit of requiring teachers to ask higher-order questions and encourage better participation of all students, she set about trying to encourage teachers to use wait time. As it turns out, teachers could readily understand and see wait time working when they tried it with students. However, Rowe found that getting teachers to break their old habits of asking simple, rapid-fire questions was another matter. At first, the long pauses after questions and ensuing "crickets" seemed unbearable. With practice, though, they could implement the routine regularly in their classrooms. Yet after three or four weeks, many teachers reverted to their old habits of rapid-fire question and response.

When we consider that wait time is really a new routine inserted into the regular habit loop of classroom dialogue, we see why it can be so difficult to sustain, especially in light of what we know about stress causing people to backslide to old habits. It's not hard to imagine, for example, teachers feeling pressure to get through the curriculum and viewing reflective pauses after each question as a luxury they could ill afford. Wait time also requires that teachers ask (and thoughtfully plan) better questions, which is itself difficult and time-consuming. Moreover, the rewards can be delayed and subtle—coming in the form of longer-term improvements in student learning—versus the more immediate reward of being able to wrap up daily lesson planning and relax after a long day's work.

So, what was the solution to the backsliding? Rowe found the best way to help teachers get the practice of wait time to stick was ongoing support from peers and coaches. This same principle of using a supportive network of peers to sustain new habits has been found to work in other spheres as well—whether it's substance abuse counseling, helping parolees reenter society without recidivism, or encouraging heart attack patients to sustain lifestyle changes (Deutschman, 2006). In a dramatic experiment in Omaha, for example, 194 patients slated for heart surgery or related procedures elected to forgo the operating room and opt instead for an austere vegetarian diet and daily classes in aerobics, mediation, relaxation, and yoga. Also, for a full year, they met twice a week for supportive group conversations. Bear in mind this is the same group of people who, on average, only have a one-in-10 success rate in changing their lifestyles. Yet in the Omaha experiment, three years later (and after two years of being on their own), an astonishing 77 percent of patients had maintained their healthier lifestyles.

When we consider that organizational change is, in effect, habit change on a massive scale, it becomes more apparent that empowering leadership creates conditions, not unlike the experiment in Omaha, where people prop one another up, helping them stick with a better practice until it becomes habit. Yes, it takes time. Ultimately, though, it's far more effective than the fruitless cycle of repeatedly adopting new practices before sliding back into old habits, only to reboot the whole futile cycle with a new, doomed effort.

Asking Better Questions

Finally, it's worth noting that how schools determine a focus for their efforts (i.e., which habits they must change) is equally critical. Are they handed down from on high or developed collaboratively? Even if the school has a sense of shared moral purpose, the question remains: How do we get from here to there—that is, how do we turn a gauzy ambition to do better into concrete next steps?

Like many challenges, creating classrooms where curiosity can flourish defies easy, one-size-fits-all solutions. Rather, it reflects what Ron Heifetz and Donald Laurie (1997) called *adaptive problems,* or ambiguous challenges for which the solution and way forward is not immediately clear. Leadership in these circumstances, according to Heifetz and Laurie, requires encouraging others to engage in creativity, problem solving, and taking bold action—behaviors that are often in short supply when people operate under threat conditions.

Leading with Questions in Greenhills

When Rowan Kayll first took the helm of Greenhills Primary School, he began not with a barrage of directives but with questions. He and assistant principal Tonia Gibson spent their first few months on the job simply building relationships, talking to staff, students, and parents to find out who they were and where they'd come from. Their questions were often simple but powerful, like "Why do you come to school every day?" and "What sort of relationship should students and teachers have?"

None of their questions were intended to be judgmental or loaded; rather, they were intended to open up dialogue about important matters, like people's teaching philosophies. "We wanted teachers to understand that we respected them as professionals," Kayll noted. "We also really wanted teachers to understand that it was okay to ask questions and that it was okay not to know the answers. We'd work together to find them."

This period of reflection, observation, and structured discussions served two purposes. First, it helped the new leadership team to better understand the school's culture; like anthropologists, they could observe and bring to light, in a nonjudgmental way, the school's existing habits, routines, and beliefs. Second, their incessant questions also helped teachers see, often for the first time, the school's culture—what values and practices had emerged over time, often quite by accident and without examination (see Figure 7.2). One of the biggest things that came to light from these conversations was that the school "had a great staff, but they weren't feeling empowered in relation to teaching and learning," Gibson recalled. "So many of the decisions had been taken away from them."

Ultimately, Kayll's and Gibson's observations and questions helped teachers come to their own conclusions about the current state of teaching learning at Greenhills and helped them to identify and put to rest practices that did little to improve student learning. For example, teachers reexamined, and ultimately jettisoned, math tests that had been designed in the early '90s and no longer seemed to align with their expectations for students. Others reflected on their own classroom "presence" and practice and realized that they'd been playing too much the role of "the sage on the stage" and needed to more frequently serve as "guides by the side." Teachers throughout the school also became more comfortable with asking their own powerful questions of one another. Only then could, in Gibson's words, "the 'real work' begin."

Making Them "Thirsty"

There's an old joke about a young salesman returning to the office after losing a big sale and lamenting, "I don't know what's wrong with those people. I guess it's like they say: You can lead a horse to water but can't make it drink." A veteran salesman looks up from his desk

Figure 7.2 | **Tools You Can Use: Better Questions for Better Leadership**

Good leaders ask better questions. Here are a few basic frames for asking better questions in your school.

Bright Spot Questions (Replicating Successes)
What do we do well in this school?
Our 7th graders improved in language arts last year. How did that happen? What process did we follow?
Can we do that in other areas?

5 Why Questions: (Root Cause Analysis)
Why do we have a 4th grade reading slump?
Kids lack background knowledge. Why is that?
They don't read enough nonfiction in early grades. Why is that?

Glass Half-Full Questions (Viewing Deficit as Benefits)
Our teachers are young and inexperienced. How might we see that as a strength?
Our teachers relate well to kids and are eager to learn.

Kaizen Questions (Viewing Defects as Treasures)
What was the biggest mistake we made this month? Here's mine.

Data as a Mirror Questions (Owning Problem and Solution)
What do these data say about us, the adults, in this school?
What's one thing WE can do to improve these data?

Starting with Why Questions (Reconnecting with Moral Purpose)
What are our children calling on us to do here?
What would we want for our OWN children?

---

and says, "You got it all wrong, son. Your job isn't to make them *drink*; it's to make them *thirsty*." Empowering leadership, in many ways, reflects the wisdom of the elder salesperson by encouraging behavior through intrinsic motivation—not forcing teachers to drink, as it were, but rather, asking the right questions to make them thirsty.

In many ways, empowering leadership reflects great teaching. Just as teachers must grasp where individual students are with their learning and which teaching techniques are best suited to those needs, so too must leaders differentiate their leadership behaviors for those they're leading. That starts with understanding that different people are motivated by different things—different impulses that make us thirsty, if you will.

Years ago, McREL synthesized a large body of knowledge on change (see, e.g., Goodwin et al., 2015; Marzano et al., 2005) and concluded that when people resist change, it's often due to these four reasons:

- They view the change as an unnecessary **break from the past**—they don't comprehend the **logic** for it or remain unconvinced of its necessity.
- They **lack the skills or knowledge** they need to engage in the change—they don't know what to do or require more clarity or **details** to proceed.
- They feel the change conflicts with their **ideals and beliefs**—they don't understand or share the vision or **big picture** purpose for the change.
- They sense the change conflicts with **group norms**—they feel social harmony or their own social status is being compromised.

In a follow-up study with school leaders, the McREL researchers found that when leaders encounter resistance to change, people in their schools often feel their leaders are falling short in these four areas:

- **Input.** People feel excluded from important decisions about the change effort.
- **Order.** People feel the school lacks routines.
- **Communication.** People crave dialogue with leaders to see where things are going.
- **Culture.** People feel a diminished sense of personal well-being and group cohesion.

We might connect these dots from these two lists like this:

- If people feel change is an *illogical break from the past*, they want opportunities for **input** so they can participate in, and better understand, the logic of decision making.
- If people feel they *lack the skills or knowledge* to do what's being asked of them, they want to reestablish routines and **order** so they know what's expected of them.
- If people perceive that change *conflicts with their ideals*, they are likely to crave two-way **communication** with leaders to better grasp (and ensure they share) the same vision.
- If people feel change *conflicts with group norms*, they sense something is amiss with **culture** and feel a need to restore well-being and group cohesion.

Leadership with the Four Ps

By putting themselves in others' shoes, empowering leaders come to see that any change worth making is likely to ask many people to alter their ingrained habits, which can make them feel like they're losing control, something which William Bridges (2009) noted leaders can restore by addressing the "4 Ps" during change:

- Giving people *input* to logically understand the **purpose** of the effort.
- Restoring a sense of *order* by describing clear next steps, or a **plan,** for getting there.
- Creating opportunities for *communication* and dialogue to see **the big picture**.
- Attending to a disrupted *culture* and restoring well-being by showing everyone their **part**.

Leading with this sort of compassion and insight is at the heart of an *empowering* leadership style—and a stark contrast from a strictly behaviorist approach that assumes getting people to change is simply a matter of creating the right set of external rewards and consequences.

Leading from the Inside Out

When Karen Money arrived at William Ruthven, she understood that knitting together a fractured community and helping them to look past the trauma of consolidation and layoffs and work together toward a brighter future would be an *adaptive challenge*. There would be no paint-by-numbers program to follow; teachers would need to help one another develop more *precise* teaching practices. And to develop these new habits, they'd need to learn together and view their failures in the spirit of *kaizen*. Because of the built-up anger, resentment, and hopelessness, leading from the top down would be unlikely to work. Rather, she would need to lead from the inside out, inverting the normal hierarchy of schools. Instead of seeing herself perched atop her school, pushing directives down to teachers, she and her leadership team would need to see themselves as the *bottom* of the pyramid, supporting others in changing their habits and achieving the goals and purpose of the school—fulfilling, as it were, the "commander's intent."

Flipping the Leadership Paradigm

Flipping the leadership paradigm upside down and employing a softer approach to changing people's behaviors isn't an altogether new concept. More than a half century ago, MIT researcher Douglas McGregor (1960) observed that most companies and organizations were predicated on something he called Theory X—the presumption that work is drudgery and people shirk responsibility at every turn; thus, management needs to bird-dog them and coerce them to do the right thing with rewards and punishments. In a Theory X organization, leaders at the top of an organization give orders (like Sir Hamilton in his battleship directing Australian troops via radio to "Dig! Dig! Dig!" in the face of withering gunfire on the beaches of Gallipoli), managers hound everyone to ensure compliance, and front-line workers are supposed to follow orders unquestioningly.

McGregor, however, believed these companies had it all wrong: People weren't inherently lazy. Rather, they had a deep desire for self-actualization; they *wanted* to do work that could make them feel satisfied and fulfilled. A better management approach, one he dubbed Theory Y, was built on the assumption that people would perform at higher levels—and indeed, do almost anything asked of them—if they understood an organization's overall goals and had authority and responsibility for achieving them. In many ways, Theory Y is the antithesis of a behaviorist approach to leadership. Instead of relying on fear, facts, and force to drive change, it relies on Motivation 3.0 drivers (autonomy, mastery, and purpose), as shown in Figure 7.3.

Figure 7.3 | Theory X and Theory Y

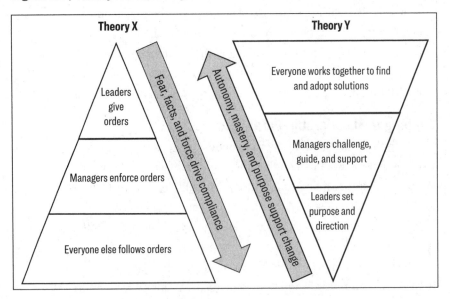

As it turns out, Theory Y isn't just a compelling idea but a more effective approach. Shortly after McGregor published his original article, an executive at Procter & Gamble who had just returned from the Korean War feeling jaded about the top-down, command-and-control approach of the military contacted McGregor to help him set up a laundry detergent plant in Georgia based on McGregor's Theory Y ideas about management, starting with organizing the factory around self-motivated teams. Ultimately, the factory outperformed others by 30 percent and became a model for Procter & Gamble, so much so that they kept the approach a secret for nearly 40 years so it would remain a competitive advantage (Hindle, 2008).

Precision Without Prescription at William Ruthven

While Karen Money was new to the staff at William Ruthven, she wasn't new to the challenge of merging schools. She had overseen the combining of four schools into one in the Heidelberg region of northeast Melbourne. It was there that she had seen how important it is to provide a vision and develop a shared culture among teachers and students when they are forced to shape a new identity as a single community. Visible, tangible improvements were one key to creating a sense of community and forward momentum. Thus, she oversaw the construction of a new language center as well as a refurbishment of the gymnasium, music, and art rooms—visible indications that new, and good, things were happening at the school. She also purchased new uniforms for the students—something students themselves requested so they might feel on par with private school students.

Beyond these important, but largely superficial, markers of community and progress, Money knew the school needed a unifying sense of purpose. For that, she turned to Curiosity and Powerful Learning. She focused much of her early efforts on developing teachers' precision of practice by sharing with them the Curiosity and Powerful Learning teaching framework—not through browbeating and prescription, but through peer coaching and being a consistent presence in classrooms herself. She also kept everyone focused on the moral purpose of the school, which, as she stated in a school newsletter, was to "build curiosity in learning and accelerate learning outcomes for all students."

"Inside Out" Takes Hold at Greenhills

Meanwhile, across town at Greenhills Primary, Kayll and Gibson also took an approach to leadership that closely resembled Theory Y.

Building on bright spots. For starters, they didn't issue any edicts, commanding people to follow the whole-school or teacher theories of action. Rather, they started with instructional rounds to find bright spots and what teachers in the school were already doing well. One bright spot immediately shone through: Teachers had strong, trusting relationships with most students. In many ways, the school had a family or "small town" feel; teachers knew many students well—they'd had their siblings in class before and were on a first-name basis with parents. However, with that silver lining came a cloud that the positive relationships weren't universal.

Indeed, the meaningful relationships with most students masked a deeper malaise in the school: negative teacher talk about certain kids. Sometimes it would surface in the teachers' lounge or in faculty meetings in how teachers would describe "the other" students with whom they hadn't formed strong bonds. Sometimes it would masquerade as sympathy: "Well, you know, [blank] really struggles in math" or "He's on the [autism] spectrum, so . . ." But nonetheless, it was often there, fueled by deficit thinking and fixed mindsets about certain kids.

Building on a glass half-full with meaningful student–teacher relationships. Kayll and Gibson wanted to stamp out such negative talk about kids quickly. Yet rather than going after it head-on by, for example, playing the shame-and-blame game, they instead chose to focus on accentuating the positive—calling out what teachers were doing well with other students. "We'd ask teachers, 'What happens when you know kids well? How do you teach them differently?'" said Gibson. Then they'd ask, "What happens when you don't know them?"

In Gibson's words, "It was really a move toward asset-based thinking, especially for those kids who were below benchmarks." They asked teachers to consider *every* student's "bright spots": What were they doing *well*? What was different about the times when they were successful? Most important, what was different about what *teachers were doing* when kids were successful?

Connecting with moral purpose and curiosity. The questions and conversations about student–teacher relationships connected everyone in the school back to their shared moral purpose (and not coincidentally, reflected one of the whole-school theories of action Hopkins and Craig had identified). Opening up this dialogue also laid the groundwork for more difficult conversations and questions to come.

During their instructional rounds, Kayll and Gibson had observed that classroom instruction was far from perfect in the school. Rote quizzes and tests were standard fare. "We still had some staff wanting to do these things," Gibson observed, adding, "Parents sort of expected them, too; they wanted to see that 10 out of 10 coming home so they could display it on the refrigerator." Moreover, some of the basics of good instruction, like learning objectives, were often missing, too.

As a teacher, it's never easy to hear that you need to improve. Teaching, by its very nature, is personal. It's a cognitive *and* caring profession; our teaching styles wrap around our intellect and personalities, so hearing that something may be missing from how we're teaching can feel like a criticism of who we are as individuals or human beings, that we're not smart enough, or don't care enough about our students.

Breaking the frame, breakthrough moments, and breaking old habits. Instead of calling everyone together and berating them for everything that was wrong with their teaching (which would only have created defensiveness and resistance), Kayll and Gibson sought to reshape people's mental models for how they approached instruction—breaking old frames, as it were, about teaching.

Building on the idea of curiosity being inextricably linked with asking questions, they started talking to teachers—and encouraging them to talk with one another—about the virtues of inquiry-based teaching and what it looked like in their classrooms. "When we changed the model to being inquiry focused, that was the real turning point," Gibson observed. "It took teachers out of their comfort zones. Students weren't just *doing* activities anymore; they were moving toward developing *understanding*." Working together, teachers began to connect instruction in both literacy and numeracy with inquiry.

"Some teachers took to it straight away," Gibson noted. But others struggled. Yet once they understood and internalized what it meant, the clouds parted, and they were never the same again. One veteran teacher, for example, took a whole year to get her head around inquiry-based learning. Just a few months from retirement, she admitted to Gibson, "I'm teaching better now than I ever have in my whole career."

Many other teachers had similar breakthrough moments—often after they were able to step back and see their teaching practices not as a reflection of their intellect or personalities but rather as a series of habits and routines they could break, if necessary. Often, this began to happen after they spent some time in other teachers' classrooms, observing their peers. "At first, some teachers didn't really want to do classroom observations because they didn't think they'd get anything out of them," Gibson acknowledged. So, they started simply— for example, having classroom teachers observe physical education teachers, which was different enough from their own regular classes that they could observe what was going on with some objective detachment, yet readily see many commonalities between teaching how to, say, dribble a basketball and how to learn the steps for solving long division equations.

Initially, the observations were simple, guided by what amounted to yes/no questions: Were lessons guided by learning intentions? Were the learning intentions evident? Did students understand them? Over time, though, the observations become deeper, guided by rubrics developed specifically for what their teachers were working on and observing in others. From the start, Kayll and Gibson made it clear that the rubrics were non-evaluative. "For Rowan and me," said Gibson, "it was really all about giving teachers those theories of action and letting them explore and learn from each other."

Collective agreements support peer coaching. During the first year, the school's leadership team—which included a broad swath of people from across the school—reflected on their observations of where staff were as a whole and collectively landed on the need to help everyone focus on and become better at using learning intentions and success criteria to guide learning. They also decided to continue their focus on meaningful student–teacher relationships. Ultimately, rather than compiling a *War and Peace*-length improvement plan with multiple strategies, action steps, and indicators, the focus became quite simply *one* teacher-level theory of action (learning intentions and success criteria) and *one* schoolwide theory of action (meaningful student–teacher relationships) at a time.

That was it.

For teachers, the focus was clear—as clear and straightforward as buying 1 percent milk from the store—and it made sense because they could see it was an area where improvements would really help students and move everyone toward more inquiry-based approaches to learning that would allow curiosity to flourish.

With a clear, single-minded focus, it didn't take long before Kayll and Gibson began to observe positive changes across the school. One of the first changes they noticed was that negative talk among teachers began to fade, replaced by more productive conversations. "On Monday, you'd hear teachers sitting in the staff room not just talking about what they did on the weekend, but about what they were doing with kids in class," Gibson recalled.

Creating challenge conditions. Ultimately, as the broader leadership team at Greenhills created *challenge conditions*—encouraging (not threatening) people to think about how things might look different for students if curiosity were allowed to flourish, teachers began to *challenge themselves*. Indeed, as the notion of student curiosity took root, teachers started to ask themselves better questions about their instructional strategies. For example, instead of simply dictating students' learning goals, they asked one another, "How about we ask the kids what *they* want to know about magnets?"

Ultimately, as we'll see later, creating challenge instead of threat conditions resulted in higher levels of implementation of the theories of action—not through browbeating, bribing, or berating people but through encouraging, empowering, and energizing them. The overall results for students were also, in a word, powerful. Yet before the entire system could move forward, there was one last element that had to be put in place—one that reflects the old adage that what you measure is what you get.

 PAUSE AND REFLECT

- What implementation efforts have you seen fail? Why did they fail?
- What motivates you to change?
- What habits have you been able to break? What helped you break them?
- What are your school's shared habits?
- How are people empowered to do their work?
- How have you seen collaboration support change efforts?
- What structures or protocols do you have in place to support people through change?

ENVISION A BETTER WAY

- With your colleagues, identify an organizational habit you've fallen into and develop a plan for mending it together.
- Identify a threat you're facing and develop a plan for turning it into a challenge.
- Categorize current improvement efforts underway as technical or adaptive challenges and consider whether they require directive or empowering leadership.
- Convert the bullet list you usually plan for group or individual meetings into thought-provoking questions.

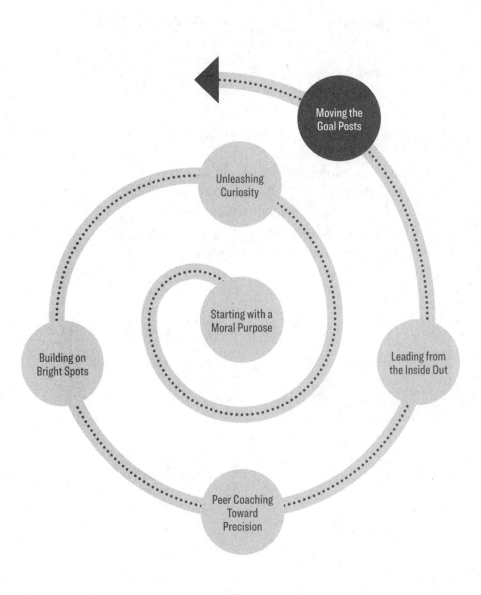

8

Moving the Goal Posts

Curiosity is the very basis of education and if you tell me that curiosity killed the cat, I say only the cat died nobly.

Arnold Edinborough

So, is it all rainbows and unicorns, this idea of operating from the inside out and getting student curiosity to flourish in every classroom?

In light of the grim reality of seemingly never-ending mandates, heavy-handed testing, and accountability schemes that have long driven U.S. education, some readers may think all of this talk of creating curious learners and "precision without prescription" is, well, hopelessly naïve. After all, the United States seems to have been the original "hot zone" of Pasi Sahlberg's colorfully coined G.E.R.M. (the Global Education Reform Movement), spreading high-stakes testing and top-down reforms like a contagion to the rest of the world. Given that, some might think that curiosity and inside-out change could *never* work in the United States like it did in Australia.

That thinking is half right.

It's also half wrong.

Getting What We Measure

The skepticism is *right* in that student curiosity and teacher professionalism are incompatible with a system of education narrowly focused on high-stakes tests, which, as research has found, tends to drive teachers to spend more effort "promoting basic skills while devoting less attention to helping students develop creativity and imagination" (Faxon-Mills, Hamilton, Rudnick, & Stecher, 2013, p. 16). And because what we measure is what we get, if we only measure basic, rudimentary knowledge and skills, then that's what we'll get (not to mentioned bored students and joyless teaching). So, if we are to create schools where curiosity can flourish, we must also re-engineer how we assess and measure learning.

Yet, it's wrong to abandon all hope of creating classrooms where curiosity can flourish or measuring learning in more thoughtful ways. For starters, if we resign ourselves to accepting the current *Twilight Zone* in which we find ourselves as our perpetual future, we may create a self-fulfilling prophecy. Moreover, as we'll describe in this chapter, a better approach to measuring student outcomes is not only possible, *it's already being done*. Across the United States, states and districts are beginning to tear down the old goal posts and replace them with better ones—measures that can drive better forms of teaching and learning.

In addition, as we'll discuss in the second half of this chapter, even if nothing changes and high-stakes tests remain, educators still have more power than they may realize to rethink how they respond to these policies: They can fixate in an unhealthy way on outcomes and measures, searching for ways to boost this score or that or bump this or that group of kids to the next performance band, *or* they can choose to focus on creating joyful learning environments for students and on professional collaboration for teachers and let the better results follow.

The Inconvenient Truth About Convenient Measures

For starters, though, let's acknowledge what many educators have long known: Standardized achievement tests are not the best way to measure student learning—just the most convenient. That's not to say the information bubble-sheet tests provide is entirely use-less. We might think of standardized testing as the equivalent of a doctor recording our weight and blood pressure when we go in for a check-up: It's important and can flag problems, but it doesn't really offer much insight about our overall health. For a deeper diagnosis, we need additional measures (e.g., blood work, testing, a review of personal and family medical history) and in-depth conversations with our doctor about our lifestyle and overall health.

For at least two decades now, though, our primary measure of student learning—and by extension, school performance—has been standardized achievement tests—which are comprised largely of multiple-choice questions. And according to an analysis conducted by the Fordham Foundation (Doorey & Polikoff, 2016), even the newly minted PARCC and Smarter Balanced tests, which were orig-inally heralded as overhauling testing in favor of more authentic, open-ended questions and long-form answers—still comprise just 8 and 10 percent, respectively, of these kinds of items; overwhelmingly, they consist of traditional single-answer multiple choice, multi-select (multiple-choice questions with more than one correct answer), technology-enhanced items (which require students to, e.g., drag and drop to match pairs or sequence—you guessed—it multiple-choice items), or some combination of these items.

Yet researchers (and educators) have long known that multiple-choice tests generally assess different kinds of knowledge than con-structed response or open-ended questions. Studies have shown, for example, that multiple-choice items are easier and require lower-level thinking than open-ended responses (Shohamy, 1984) and can mask learning gaps as students can skim a reading passage for key-words and phrases that match the answers in multiple-choice ques-tions, providing a "false positive" for comprehension, which becomes evident when they're asked to respond later to open-ended questions on the same passage (Lubliner & Smetana, 2003).

Multiple-choice assessments illustrate the maxim that not everything that matters can be measured and not everything that can be measured matters. Despite these obvious shortcomings, though, the need to simultaneously assess thousands of students at once coupled with the enormous expense and logistical complexity (not to mention psychometric concerns) of scoring more authentic assessments of student learning has left many schools in the United States forced to obsess over what often amounts to superficial assessments of students' recall and recognition of facts.

Confronting Campbell's Law

For the sake of argument, let's say that we *could* find the Holy Grail of assessment and devise a perfect test—one that truly measured students' breadth and depth of knowledge. Even if we could do that, we'd still bump into an inescapable reality of measurement first noted in the 1970s by Donald Campbell, then president of the American Psychological Association, who observed that "the more any quantitative social indicator is used for social decision making, the more subject it will be to corruption pressures and the more apt it will be to distort and corrupt the social processes it is intended to monitor" (1976, p. 49). In simple terms, what Campbell was saying (that's now referred to as "Campbell's law") was that the higher the stakes attached to a measure, the less valid that measure becomes.

Consider the dramatic gains reported over the years on some states' accountability assessments. If these gains reflected true increases in student learning, we'd expect to see students in those states demonstrating similar gains on other, lower-stakes measures of their learning of similar content, right? The reality, though, is that gains on high-stakes tests *do not* translate into gains on lower-stakes assessments. Harvard researcher Brian Jacob (2002), for example, found that while test scores for Chicago Public Schools students rose on a high-stakes assessment, the achievement of the same students dropped significantly on a low-stakes exam of the same knowledge, prompting Jacob to conclude that "despite its increasing popularity within education, there is little empirical evidence on test-based accountability" (p. 4).

In short, applying high stakes to a test may result in gains, but such spikes often do not reflect true gains in student learning, merely how well teachers have boosted students' test-taking abilities or narrowed instruction to the small band of knowledge covered by the test. In light of the performance plateaus we've seen on low-stakes measures such as the National Assessment of Education Progress (NAEP) during the same period of time that many states were reporting gains on their own high-stakes assessments, it would appear we have spent the past two decades confirming Campbell's law.

That's the bad news. The good news is that there is a solution.

According to Campbell, one of the best ways to prevent an indicator from becoming corrupted or distorted is to employ *multiple measures* of performance (1976). In addition, placing more emphasis on the collection and use of formative data helps to prevent an indicator from being corrupted. For example, it's been shown that using low-stakes classroom assessments created by teachers to guide instruction can have a strong, positive influence on student performance and motivation, especially when daily or weekly checks for understanding guide real-time changes to instruction (Wiliam & Thompson, 2007).

That said, formative assessments ought not be confused with so-called interim or benchmark assessments, which are often just large-scale assessments repackaged as monthly (or longer cycle) tests. Research shows that such tests do little or nothing to improve instruction (Popham, 2006). Moreover, they've led to another significant problem in education—an overwhelming proliferation of standardized tests for students.

Testing and More Testing

According to a recent survey by the Council of Chief State School Officers (CCSSO), between preschool and senior year of high school, U.S. students take an average of 113 standardized tests (Kamenetz, 2014). A study of 14 school districts conducted by the Center for American Progress found students in grades 3–8 taking an average of 10 and as many as 20 standardized tests per year (Lazarín, 2014). Perhaps not coincidentally, a growing chorus of parents, educators, and policymakers have begun expressing frustration and anger with the system of top-down accountability and high-stakes testing. Not too long ago in Colorado, thousands of high school seniors appeared to reach a breaking point when they walked out of state-mandated science and social studies exams (Gorski, 2014). "We have grown up taking standardized testing—since third grade," one student told the *Denver Post*. "This particular protest comes as a result of this frustration [of] taking these tests we don't feel are adequate." Nationwide, it's estimated that more than a half-million students opted out of state tests in 2016—including one in five students in New York state (Schweig, 2016). In response to the growing chorus of concerns, CCSSO and the Council of Great City Schools (2014) issued a pledge to cut back on unnecessary testing for students.

A Better Way: Rebalancing Assessments

So, is it time to jettison large-scale assessments altogether? Well, not necessarily. For starters, they can provide some useful comparative data and disaggregating those data has helped to keep the focus on helping all students succeed. However, multiple-choice tests, which, incidentally have ballooned into a $4.5 billion industry in the United States (Outsell, 2016) and are supported by a powerful lobby in Washington (Strauss, 2015), are far from the *only* way to measure learning, even on a large scale. There is a better way, one that starts with recognizing the power of two other kinds of long heralded, but often neglected, forms of assessment: *formative* and *performance* assessments.

Let's take a closer look at both.

Driving Change with Formative and Performance Assessment

Formative assessment is not simply frequent testing or interim benchmark assessments, such as those provided by test publishers. Rather, it consists of teachers themselves gathering evidence in the classroom during instruction using a variety of techniques, including observation, teacher and student questions, and quizzes, to provide real-time feedback to students and guide adjustments to teaching (Chappuis & Stiggins, 2002; Heritage, 2010; McManus, 2008; Wiliam, 2007; Wylie, 2008). Used well, formative assessment has been shown to help all students grow, with the greatest impact on lower-performing students (e.g., Black & Wiliam, 1998b; Brookhart, 2005; Hattie & Timperley, 2007; Shute, 2007)—an effect that far exceeds that of smaller class sizes and is on par with one-on-one tutoring (Black & Wiliam, 1998a).

Performance assessment, as Stuart Kahl, founder of the nonprofit assessment organization Measured Progress, describes it (Hofman, Goodwin, & Kahl, 2015), is analogous to the multi-stage process of getting a driver's license: We start with a multiple-choice test of basic facts, followed by a period of driving practice that culminates in a behind-the-wheel performance test. All three phases are important; to prepare for the multiple-choice test, we memorize the rules of the road. Testing our knowledge of these rules, however, does little to gauge our skill in applying that knowledge in an actual automobile on crowded streets; that takes time, practice, and lots of feedback. Only then are we ready for our performance assessment: the dreaded driving test.

Performance assessment works much the same way in classrooms: It requires students to demonstrate their ability to *apply* knowledge and skills through some form of product, presentation, or demonstration related to key aspects of academic learning (Pecheone & Kahl, 2014). Though these tasks may be relatively brief, they nonetheless require students to draw upon and demonstrate deep knowledge, synthesize, think creatively, and apply what they know in real-world settings. They also require students to demonstrate noncognitive skills, such as self-discipline, work habits, active learning, and goal orientation—dispositions that reflect a key (yet often missing) "x-factor" related to student success in college (Goodwin & Hein, 2016).

Research has shown that performance assessments offer a more complete picture of student learning than multiple-choice assessments alone while delivering several ancillary benefits (Darling-Hammond & Wood, 2008). For example, a study in Maryland (Lane, Parke, & Stone, 2002) found that after the state adopted an assessment program with more performance tasks, teachers reported placing greater emphasis on complex problem solving and reasoning in the classroom. RAND researchers have also found high-stakes testing can have positive or negative effects depending upon whether the assessments are, respectively, performance-based or multiple-choice (Soland, Hamilton, & Stecher, 2013).

The chief downside of performance assessments (and likely the reason they're not more prevalent) is that they can be prone to greater subjectivity in grading and, thus, scoring inconsistencies (Soland et al., 2013). Yet it is possible to create a statewide system of performance assessments that offers more authentic measures of student learning with the added benefit of not taking *any* time away from learning. How? By using curriculum-embedded performance assessments, or CEPAs for short.

Putting It All Together: Curriculum-Embedded Performance Assessment

A CEPA (see Figure 8.1 for an example) is a well-designed instructional unit that, like the process for getting a drivers' license, requires students to develop foundational knowledge, practice new skills, and demonstrate deep learning through a performance task. In so doing, it integrates the benefits of formative and performance assessment with all three drivers of Motivation 3.0, offering students *autonomy* in choosing performance tasks and how to approach them, delivering real-time feedback during the process to help them develop a sense of *mastery*, and offering real-world learning that provides a sense of *purpose* in what they're doing.

At the same time, CEPAs can also support state-level accountability systems by measuring what matters most, as described in a white paper from McREL and Measured Progress, a nonprofit testing company (Hofman, Goodwin, & Kahl, 2015). Over the course of the school year, teachers use the CEPAs for end-of-unit or end-of-course projects and assessments. Their results (e.g., scores on a five-point scale) are integrated into the state's large-scale assessment, providing a more robust picture of student- and school-level results. Each year, schools identify low-, mid-, and high-performing student work samples and submit those examples to the state (or other agency), where a state-appointed team of teacher specialists audit teachers' scoring practices and send audited scores back to schools, where they can be adjusted to reflect audited work samples/benchmarks.

Yes, it's complex work and comes at a time when resources are scarce. Yet it's the *right* work as it promotes deeper learning for students and capacity building for teachers. It also removes much of the "black box" mystery that surrounds testing for students by giving

Figure 8.1 | Sample CEPA

Here is a brief example of a CEPA. Fully developed, it would include content standards, learning targets, additional guidance for instruction and assessment, scoring rubrics, and sample student work.

Heat Transfer

Activity 1: Students, individually or in small groups, research methods of heat transfer. They discuss what they have learned about conduction, convection, and radiation (student-guided learning).

Activity 2: Teachers check student understanding of methods of heat transfer via ungraded quizzes, interviews, or class discussion (formative assessment evidence gathering, feedback, and adjustment).

Activity 3: In small groups, students design and conduct an experiment to determine which of two fabrics better protects against the winter cold. Materials required include tin coffee cans of different sizes (with lids), two different fabrics (e.g., plastic and wool), fasteners, thermometers (thermal probes), timers, and hot water (performance activity).

Activity 4: Students individually write up a formal lab report of their experiment (graded summative product).

Activity 5: Teachers, via questioning, lead class discussion of how methods of heat transfer played a role in the design and implementation of the research (formative assessment reflection and reinforcement).

Activity 6: Students individually research how a home heating system works and write a paper describing a home heating system and how different methods of heat transfer are involved (graded summative product).

everyone a clear picture of learning success and timely data on student progress. And perhaps most important, it can turn the collateral damage of high-stakes testing into collateral benefits by providing students with personalized learning experiences, real-world application, and more meaningful, real-time feedback.

Yes, It Can, and Is, Being Done

We know these ideas may not be met with immediate enthusiasm. Some may fear that doing all of this would be too time-consuming or impose yet another burden on already overburdened schools.

But curriculum-embedded performance assessments need not be an add-on; it can be the real work of schooling that gets included in regular coursework and grades.

Others may argue that the entire system would be too expensive. Yet when we consider the costs of the 100-plus standardized assessments students currently encounter between kindergarten and high school—and that states and districts in the United States spend an astounding $4.5 billion annually on large-scale tests—it's not difficult to see how we might shed some costs and redirect resources (and time) toward more effective measures of student learning by simply scaling testing back to key transition years (e.g., 4th and 8th grades) and late high school, as was common prior to the passage of No Child Left Behind.

Finally, it's important to note that curriculum-embedded performance assessments aren't simply wishful thinking; they've already been used in statewide pilot projects in Ohio and a districtwide effort in Buffalo, New York, as well as in places like New Technology High School in Sacramento and Leadership High School in San Francisco, where they were shown to demand more of students than anything they'd experienced with traditional selected-response exams. As a student at Leadership High School commented, "At other high schools, it's just 'you passed.' Kids can't tell what they got out of high school. Students here know what they've learned" (Darling-Hammond & Friedlaender, 2008).

Developing a Cure for G.E.R.M.

Admittedly, many educators may feel like small cogs in a hopelessly large and entrenched education machine. And policy conversations may seem important but distant. Understandably, many teachers and school leaders might simply want to know what *they* can do *right now* to inoculate their schools and classrooms from the counterproductive craziness of G.E.R.M. (the Global Education Reform Movement) while waiting for someone at higher levels of the system to bring balance and common sense back to assessing student learning.

The good news is there are things that teachers and leaders can do. And no, it's not simply to write your local representative or stage a walkout on test day. Let's start with leaders.

Leaders: Create and Follow a Recipe for Success

The first things leaders can do is stop fixating on large-scale assessment scores, student growth, percentages of kids proficient, and the like. Seriously.

Yes, we know this advice seems to fly in the face of everything you've probably been told about goal setting, creating data walls, engaging in data conversations, and focusing on achievement gaps. It really doesn't. The operative phrase here is *fixating on large-scale assessment scores*.

Given that these ideas of using data to improve performance have emanated from the business community, let's go ahead and take a closer look at some cautionary tales of some high-profile businesses that got it all wrong when it came to setting ambitious, data-driven goals—often at the expense understanding and sticking with what made them successful.

In his book *How the Mighty Fall*, Jim Collins (2009) profiles the decline of drug manufacturer Merck. For years, Merck had exemplified what Collins termed the "profit-seeking paradox"—that the most profitable companies focus less on profits and more on doing the right things. George Merck's philosophy was simple and inspiring: "We try never to forget that medicine is for the people," he was quoted as saying. "It is not for the profits. The profits follow, and if we have remembered that, they have never failed to appear." In contrast, the CEO of Pfizer, John McKeen, blustered, "So far as humanly possible, we aim to get profit out of everything we do."

Merck's fall from grace appeared to begin, perhaps not coincidentally, with its founder stepping down and a new generation of leaders stepping in and setting ambitious goals for profit growth, boasting in a letter to shareholders that its number one goal was to be "a top-tier growth company." With profits and growth as its chief goal, it began to heavily market Vioxx as a pain reliever (never mind the fact it wasn't really any more effective than aspirin) and failed to pull it from the shelves when it became apparent that it was causing dangerous side effects, including heart attacks and strokes. Mired in bad PR and lawsuits, Merck went into a decline.

What's far more important, and more likely to lead to long-term success, Collins observed, is for companies to figure out what makes them (or will make them) successful and stick to it. Indeed, one of the first signs of trouble among declining companies is that they lose "sight of the true underlying factors that created success in the first place" (p. 21).

The same could be said for schools. Lofty, ambitious goals are important, but if they're too tied to outcome data (e.g., achievement scores) and if people feel too much pressure to achieve the numbers, Campbell's Law suggests people tend to do the wrong things to hit those targets—as has happened in Georgia, where teachers were sent to jail for changing students' test responses to boost scores.

What's far more important is to get clear about the recipe for success—the handful of things that must be done well for students to succeed. As a starting point, we'd suggest the What Matters Most framework described in the book *Simply Better* (Goodwin, 2011c) or the 10 theories of action highlighted in this book. What's most important, though, is that school teams come together to agree on the key ingredients in their "recipe" for success and then devote their time and energies to following the recipe, trusting that if they've got the right recipe and follow it with precision, good things will follow.

As noted in the previous chapter, leaders can create a spirit of *kaizen* (where every defect is seen as a treasure) that allows people to feel comfortable surfacing and talking through challenges and seeking solutions with their colleagues. Effective leaders also help people see tests scores as just one data point—not the be-all-end-all of school performance. Moreover, they help people understand that achievement data is often just the tip of the iceberg. They model bringing questions to the data, helping people ask "five whys" to surface root causes of student performance.

Leaders: Focus on Your Bright Spots

Finally, without being Pollyannaish, leaders can help people spend as much time sifting through data to find things that are going *right* as they spend dwelling on everything that's going *wrong*. As Jerry Sternin discovered when helping Vietnamese villagers improve childhood nutrition, the answers usually lie in those bright spots. If a certain group of students is outperforming others in unexpected ways, everyone ought to be asking, why is that occurring? Is there something different in those students' learning environments? Is there something different in their attitudes about learning? If so, what? And how might we replicate that elsewhere?

Teachers: Focus on Better Teaching

As obvious as it sounds, if you're a teacher, you just need to focus on one thing: teaching your students well every day. The rest will follow. Although there's often a push to pore over data from externally imposed interim benchmark assessments to identify problems (or more kindly stated, opportunities for improvement), rarely, if ever, will these data tell you something you didn't already know. If anything, they should just confirm the patterns you're already seeing in the data you collect every day from your checks for understanding, classroom observations, classroom assessments, and reviews of student work.

You can spend the bulk of your data conversations with colleagues using the data to find the answers that are often already in the room. For example, if students in your classroom are struggling with a concept that students in another classroom are mastering, your colleague can share what she is doing to help students master that content. But those conversations should always circle back to a single, driving question: What can I do better?

Also, though it may be trendy, there's really no reason for teachers to use a data wall in their classrooms. No research to date shows that it helps kids (we've scoured all of the relevant databases and come up empty-handed) to display how they are doing for the world to see. Worse, it can violate the Family Educational Rights and Privacy Act (FERPA) if it calls out individual student performance. Also, as Caitlin Farrell, Julie Marsh, and Melanie Bertrand (2015) observed after studying teacher use of data in classrooms (including the practice of data walls), if not done thoughtfully, it can cement a fixed mindset—creating an impression that there are smart kids, average kids, and not-so-smart kids—and send a message that learning is all about external rewards instead of something students should do because they interested, engaged, or curious about what they're learning. Certainly, data are important; teachers should use them to guide student learning, but they can do that without putting work on display for everyone to see. There are better uses for your time and classroom wall space.

Teachers: Keep Calm and Carry On

Okay, that phrase has become a tired meme, but we mean it. Don't dwell too much on value-added measures (VAM). They're a crap shoot anyway. Research shows that teachers tend to pop in and out of performance categories due to the vicissitudes of student placement in their classrooms and a whole litany of factors beyond teachers' control (see, e.g., Goodwin & Miller, 2012, for a discussion of the many concerns around VAM). Perhaps the most damning statistic, though, is this one: Just one-third of teachers in the top quartile hold onto their status a year later, and only 10 percent of bottom-quartile teachers remain cellar-dwellers a year later (Goldhaber & Hansen, 2010). Some of that fluctuation may be due to actual changes in teacher performance, but some, according to researchers, "is simply due to *error in the measure* [emphasis added]" (p. 7).

Given these flaws, it's best for teachers not to get too much of their egos or self-esteem wrapped up in their annual VAM scores, despite how heavily they may be weighted in state-mandated evaluation systems. If a teacher is truly a low-performer year after year, that might be another matter, but in all likelihood, that fact will have become obvious long before it's revealed by a computer-generated score. In sum, the best advice for teachers when it comes to the VAM scores goes back to what we noted earlier: Just focus on good teaching.

Moving the Goal Posts in Greenhills

Victoria, Australia, was by no means G.E.R.M.-free. Student test scores were important—students in grades 3, 5, 7, and 9 were given the National Assessment Programme for Literacy and Numeracy (NAPLAN) test, and the Victorian Certificate of Education (VCE) exams served as a high-stakes test for graduating students, as their success on the test often determined their placement into university or Technical and Further Education (TAFE), not unlike the ACT or SAT in the United States. NAPLAN results were splashed across local newspapers and available on websites, on display for all to see; parents often used those scores to size up schools and "shop" for the best ones. Kayll and Gibson also were well aware of their school's data being on these sites. So were parents. And to a lesser extent, teachers.

It would have been easy to fixate on those data—to point to them, like a coach with a team down 10 points at halftime, exhorting everyone in the locker room to do better ("Dig! Dig! Dig!"). Kayll and Gibson never did that, though. "We really didn't market the NAPLAN as any measurable marker of success to parents and students," Gibson said. "The test was in May and we got results in September; it told us nothing that could assist teachers to improve current learning in classrooms."

As it turns out, the region's schools also tracked and used multiple measures for performance, including the following:

• Student surveys designed to measure a number of indicators of student well-being, including morale, distress, and opinions of their relationships with teachers and peers;

• Staff opinion surveys designed to measure the extent to which teachers felt they were working toward common goals with collegiality and professionalism and support for professional learning;

• Student pathways and transition data measuring effective transitions between grade levels, school retention rates, and exit destinations (e.g., whether graduating students went on to further education or training); and

• Parent opinion surveys of how well their children were being prepared for each transition in their schooling.

This broader data set made it possible to track "leading indicators" like student–teacher relationships and student engagement that can precede the "lagging indicators" of student performance. It also made it more difficult to game the system by focusing on just one outcome at the expense of others. Perhaps most importantly, though, it made the whole Curiosity and Powerful Learning effort possible by sending a strong signal from the outset that outcomes of schooling couldn't be measured with a single test score but must be tracked more holistically—looking at not only test results but also the kinds of learning environments schools were creating and their long-term impact on student success.

At the outset of their efforts, Kayll and Gibson paid close attention to all of these measures and began to see a somewhat bipolar picture emerge of a school where parents were mostly happy but didn't believe their children were being challenged; students enjoyed school but didn't feel confident in their own learning; and teachers appeared to be working together effectively but reported low job satisfaction. "If we had just looked at our student learning data, we might have just patted each other on the back and continued with the status quo," Gibson recalled. But by taking a more holistic view of the school, they saw they needed to focus on building positive relationships with teachers, students, and parents. "We knew that in the near future, we'd be using those relationships to improve our school from the inside out."

Rethinking Classroom Assessments

So instead of fixating on the NAPLAN scores or taking a deficit-minded approach of highlighting the kids who were falling behind, Kayll and Gibson opened up a different dialogue altogether by asking some simple, thought-provoking questions about the purpose of testing itself:

- What assessments are we using in our classrooms and why?
- What do the results of certain assessments tell us about student learning needs?

This simple "assessment audit" revealed that teachers were using a wide variety of assessments—some very purposeful, while others had little discernible purpose. Yet as teachers became more mindful of what assessments they were using and why, they began to quietly set aside certain kinds of tests and quizzes because they weren't really telling them, or their students, anything meaningful about their learning. "That was a bit of a turning point," Kayll noted. It began to move teachers toward a simple concept that Kayll called "diagnose and teach." For Kayll, it was an "idea that just makes sense. We can't just rely on gut feel when making judgments about what to teach our children next. We need to create more time in our teaching day by being more targeted in our teaching."

Diagnose and Teach

As the idea of "diagnose and teach" began to sink in, teachers began to flip the script on their own classroom assessments: No longer were there *summative* checkmarks or merit badges to give to students before moving onto something else. Rather, the bulk of classroom assessments were increasingly formative—providing a dashboard to guide student learning.

As teachers realized they needed better data to discern what students did and did not understand, they also began to develop their own practical, curriculum-embedded common assessments to track and discuss student growth at their professional learning community (PLC) meetings. They designed, for example, short (10–15 questions) math assessments to measure student understanding about particular concepts (such as subtraction) that spanned multiple grade levels of difficulty. Usually, the assessments began with a question that asked students to demonstrate the most basic understanding of a concept and ended with a challenge question that asked students to apply their knowledge to a complex task.

These tests were never designed with the intention that every student would get full marks—in fact, the goal was for kids to get around half of the answers right as part of a growth mindset that sought to stretch them to see which concepts (or parts of a concept) they had fully grasped, allowing teachers to give students feedback about what they needed to learn next.

"After about two terms [about six months] of using the new tests, that's when teachers' curiosity really kicked in," Gibson recalled. As teachers compared how students were progressing with their peers, they began to ask one another questions like "Your students are doing better than mine; what are you doing that I'm not?"

Initially, these new assessments left some parents scratching their heads. "What's the use of a test a kid can never get 100 percent on?" some would ask. But once parents understood that assessments were meant to be diagnostic (and not refrigerator artwork), parents' mindsets gradually became more growth oriented, leading them to celebrate when their children reached their personal learning goals.

Connecting Feedback to Personal Goals

Teachers soon began to see that assessment without feedback does little to improve learning; like a proverbial tree falling in the woods with no one around to hear it, a test score alone—no gold star or smiley face atop a paper—does little to guide or improve learning. As they reflected on their own practices, many teachers realized that they "praised" children, but seldom gave them real-time feedback on their own progress. "It took time for some teachers to understand that saying just 'great work' wasn't enough feedback for students to reflect on their performance and goals," Gibson recalled. "They needed to be saying something more like, 'This is great work; how about you take a look at your punctuation and we can set an editing goal together?'"

As teachers worked together to develop more *precision* with their feedback, they came to another realization: Feedback was inextricably linked to *personal* learning goals; after all, feedback is far more meaningful (and welcome) when it's on something we've committed to doing better. That realization led to more questions: Do our students know where they're going? Have they set personal goals for themselves?

Creating Personal Learning Goals and Performance Assessments

Here, teachers had to grapple with an inconvenient truth. Initially, many of them were a bit leery about letting students set their *own* learning goals; some harbored fears of anarchy breaking out in their classrooms. Yet they could see that without students owning their learning goals, teacher feedback often feels like unsolicited advice.

So, they embarked together on another line of inquiry: How can we help students set *personal* learning goals? Over time, they discovered that as they improved their formative assessments (i.e., developing a clearer understanding of student progress) and feedback (i.e., helping students understand what they needed to do to keep moving ahead), it became easier to help students set their own learning goals.

Using Performance Assessments to Demonstrate Mastery Learning

Attending to helping students set personal learning goals sparked another question: How should students demonstrate *mastery* of their learning. Should the goal of learning be to get an *A* on multiple-choice tests or something more meaningful—perhaps showing that they had grasped fertile ideas?

But how would they do that? Projects seemed like a logical answer, and before long, they decided that each school term (four per year) would culminate in projects and performance assessments related to the inquiry units students had been working on during the term. Younger students, for example, did a unit on toys—a science unit that would ask students to design, create, and market their own toy. And the school year would end with some kind of inquiry celebration of learning—for example, 5th and 6th graders would wrap up their history unit on the federation of Australia by writing and performing a play about it.

Looking back, Gibson struggled to retrace all of the steps that the leadership team and teachers at Greenhills took to arrive at a school where personalization, project-based learning, and student curiosity drove so much of what they were doing. "It was a messy process—there was really nothing linear about it," Gibson recalled. "We just went where we needed to go."

Of course, that's often the way it is with curiosity—one good question leads to another. And so it was with the Curiosity and Powerful Learning approach across the northern Melbourne region. Some schools, like Greenhills, engaged in shared inquiry with all teachers working through the same theory of action at the same time; other schools let teacher triads decide where to focus their efforts—which of the theories action they would dive deeply into during six-week learning cycles. But ultimately, they all embraced professional curiosity in all of its messiness—with its myriad of starting points, pathways, and forms.

PAUSE AND REFLECT

- What does your school "measure" that is truly valuable?
- How many summative tests are your students taking?
- What information do teachers use from student assessments to guide learning?
- How do teachers check for understanding in your school?
- How prevalent are performance assessments in your schools? What different kinds of learning do they encourage?
- How might you use data to create growth mindsets for students and teachers?

ENVISION A BETTER WAY

- Ask teachers to list the summative and formative assessments they administer during a school year.
- Ask teachers to identify the data they use to guide student learning and progress.
- Conduct a learning walk to identify different ways teachers check for student understanding.
- Identify assessment or testing measures that could be discarded at your school.

9

The Rest of the Story

The whole art of teaching is only the art of awakening the natural curiosity of young minds for the purpose of satisfying it afterwards.

Anatole France

One of the most iconic and perplexing Australian idioms is the expression "Fair dinkum?" Roughly, it translates into "Seriously?" or "Are you for real?" or "No kidding?" Sometimes it can be used as a declarative statement, as in "I'm telling you the truth." And at other times, it's used as a simple adjective, along the lines of "genuine," as in "He was born in EnZed (New Zealand) but is a fair dinkum Aussie now."

While an iconic phrase, Australians themselves remain divided as to its origins. Some historians say it emerged from Chinese immigrants in Australian gold fields as a rough translation of a Mandarin phrase for "good gold." Others say it comes from an old English word for "honest toil" or a hard day's work, while still others say it has roots in gold field ethics, which held that one of the shadiest things a person could do was stay sober while gambling, making "fair dinkum" a jocular admonition to engage in "fair drinking"—or keeping "transfusions of amber fluid" (beer drinking) apace with one's gambling buddies.

Whatever the etymology of the phrase, it's an apt response at this point in our book. If you were an Aussie, all of this talk of flipping the script—focusing on curiosity and inside-out approaches to change—might lead you to ask, Are you fair dinkum? Really? Does it work? As it turns out, the multiple indicators used in Victoria provided a robust data dashboard that schools across the region were able to use to see improvements in both leading and lagging indicators of student performance. Ultimately, what's most important about taking an inside-out approach to improvement that's borne out of curiosity is quite simply this: It works.

As curiosity began to take root in student learning, teachers developed greater precision without prescription, and school principals became more adept at empowering and guiding their schools through adaptive challenges, things began to change across the Northern Metropolitan Region.

Precision Without Prescription

One of the first noticeable differences surfaced on measures of implementation of the new teaching and whole-school theories of action. Using a scale developed by Hall and Hord (1987), external evaluators found that in at least three-quarters of the schools in the region, the new theories of action had become both "routine" (i.e., teachers were comfortable with the new approaches and using them in their classrooms) and "refined" (i.e., teachers were beginning to explore ways to use the approaches in continuous improvement) (Hopkins, 2011).

Let's pause for a moment to reflect on that data point alone.

As noted earlier in this book, the bane of most reform initiatives is poor implementation—as demonstrated by the weak implementation that afflicted the interventions put under glass for U.S. Department of Education-funded scientific studies (Goodwin, 2011b). Indeed, instead of demonstrating "what works," these scientific studies appeared to demonstrate that we still have much to learn about *how to do* what works.

Not Just Better Implementation, but Better Teaching

This dismal track record for implementation makes the fact that three-quarters of schools in the Northern Metropolitan Region could demonstrate fidelity to the Curiosity and Powerful Learning approach *without heavy-handed prescription or browbeating* all the more remarkable. Teachers were doing more than simply adopting someone else's approach; rather, they were refining and internalizing the approaches by working together to develop their professional capabilities.

At Greenhills, "fidelity of implementation was always a front-and-center concern," noted Gibson. "But it was never a prescriptive, 'thou-shalt-do-this' approach. Instead, we spent a lot time, before we asked teachers to do anything, making sure we were all on the same page. We really used those rubrics to develop shared understandings about good teaching." At the same time, "throughout each implementation cycle, we gave teachers several opportunities to reflect on and share their trials and successes," Kayll added. "We knew that if implementation was to be successful, our whole staff would need to be engaged in cycles of continuous improvement, grounded in our shared belief that every student can learn and will show growth."

Across the region, as Greenhills and other schools began to implement the theories of action with greater precision, students were among the first to notice the difference. Annual surveys showed steady increases in how students viewed their teachers' effectiveness, as shown in Figure 9.1. From the inception of the effort in 2006, students in every grade level that was measured—from 5th grade to 12th grade—perceived their teachers' effectiveness to be increasing. Prior to the effort, students in the NMR rated their teachers below the mean rating for the state of Victoria. Within four short years, they rated their teachers on par with and often better than the average rating for teachers across the state.

At Greenhills, the morale of 5th graders climbed from the 50th to the 90th percentile, ratings of teacher effectiveness climbed from roughly the 35th to the 70th percentile, and ratings for the extent to which students were experiencing "stimulating learning" also climbed from below the 25th percentile to above the 75th percentile compared to the entire state. At the same time, although Greenhills teachers' ratings of their work demands increased from approximately the 25th to the 75th percentile, so, too, did their sense of empowerment. Moreover, their ratings for "supportive leadership" climbed from just above the 10th percentile to nearly the 80th percentile. In short, staff were working harder, but feeling more supported and empowered.

Figure 9.1 | **Students' Ratings of Teacher Effectiveness in the Northern Metropolitan Region**

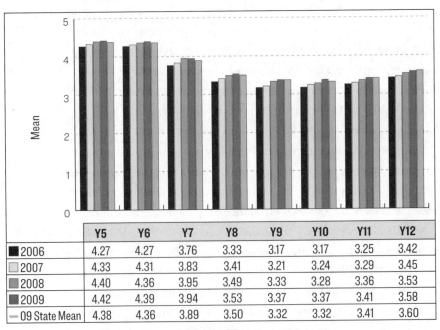

	Y5	Y6	Y7	Y8	Y9	Y10	Y11	Y12
■2006	4.27	4.27	3.76	3.33	3.17	3.17	3.25	3.42
□2007	4.33	4.31	3.83	3.41	3.21	3.24	3.29	3.45
■2008	4.40	4.36	3.95	3.49	3.33	3.28	3.36	3.53
■2009	4.42	4.39	3.94	3.53	3.37	3.37	3.41	3.58
— 09 State Mean	4.38	4.36	3.89	3.50	3.32	3.32	3.41	3.60

■2006 □ 2007 ■2008 ■2009 — 09 State Mean

A Rising Tide Begins to Lift All Boats

As teachers became more effective, achievement also began to rise across the spectrum. The percentages of students scoring in the bottom two (of six) achievement bands on the Australian national test (called the NAPLAN) shrank as the percentages in the top two began to rise (Hopkins, 2011). Between 2008 and 2009, for example, the percentage of students in the district who were scoring in the bottom bands of the NAPLAN assessment decreased from 18.5 percent to 15.9 percent, while the percentage of students scoring in the top two bands increased from 30.3 percent to 39.0 percent—significant changes for a large system (of more than 75,000 students) with a prior history of chronic low performance.

Let's consider what that means in raw student numbers. Nearly 3,000 students who had previously been off-track or languishing in the bottom performance bands were brought up to proficient levels, making their futures much brighter. At the same time, nearly 7,000 students who had been in the middle of the pack rose to the top performance bands, increasing their opportunities for post-secondary success and making their futures brighter as well. In short, flipping the script in Melbourne was able to raise both the floor and ceiling for student performance—something that has eluded districts and states in the United States during a decade-plus of high-stakes testing and heavy accountability pressure wrought by No Child Left Behind.

From Blight Spot to Bright Spot

In 2012, two years after the merger at William Ruthven, the school's grade 7 and grade 9 students were demonstrating marked gains in state test scores, and fully 93 percent of the school's grade 12 students were going on to university, technical schools, or community college, and the rest found jobs (Maslen, 2013). By 2013, the average score on the state's exit exam for grade 12 students, the Victorian Certificate of Education (VCE), had climbed from 25 to 28.2, bucking national trends that showed a widening gap between wealthy schools and low-income ones like William Ruthven (Milligan, 2014).

As teachers began to focus more on building student curiosity and motivation, they also noticed a difference in student attitudes. Two years after the merger, Karen Money observed that it was as if all the trauma of the integration had never occurred, "Teachers say the kids are talking more about their learning than the politics of the merger" (Maslen, 2013).

Through it all, even as she was focusing on improving teacher performance and keeping everyone focused on the whole-school theories of action and teacher theories of action, Money's approach to improvement remained decidedly inside out. She used a government grant to hire two extra teachers to serve as coaches and allow the school's more accomplished teachers to carve time out of their days to coach peers on the Curiosity and Powerful Learning framework. As teachers' classroom practices became more precise, the entire school began to undergo a transformation in teaching—nothing short of a "small revolution," as described by a news report from the Australian Broadcast Corporation (ABC) (Milligan, 2014, np).

Kevin Kapeke was one of the students who benefited from this small revolution. Five years after his family emigrated from Zimbabwe, he had become one of the school's star public speakers with plans to enroll in university to study economics and politics. In an interview with the ABC, he spoke of the passion for social justice he had found at William Ruthven. "I would like to be sort of like a barometer for social justice, for people out there who can't help themselves . . . whether that's through politics or through lawmaking or through the court or the parliament, that's just what I want to try and attain right now" (Milligan, 2014). Amir Mallelari similarly found his passion in mathematics and related to the ABC how he had learned to push himself to learn more every day: "On tests I'll get like 97 percent and I'll ask myself, 'Where'd I get that 3 percent wrong?'" (Milligan, 2014). In short, he had become a consummate questioner, constantly reflecting on his own learning, becoming self-motivated to fill in the gaps of knowledge—which is, of course, the very definition of curiosity.

Flourishing with New Goal Posts

A small revolution occurred at Greenhills, too. What the teachers and leaders there—and all across the region—managed to do was move the goal posts for learning—not only setting a higher bar for students but also making their learning goals more meaningful for them. One student in particular—we'll call him Glenn—stands out in Gibson's mind. He was bright, but so bored (and often angry) in class that his mother was being called up almost every day for something he was doing or had done. But when the focus of his classrooms began to shift to inquiry-based learning, he found things to be interested in and his behavior improved markedly. For Glenn and many other students like him, unleashing curiosity brought welcome change in their behavior.

Before long, the word got out that Greenhills was doing things differently. Parents from outside the region were calling in, wanting to send their kids there. Enrollment grew from 425 to 537—well beyond what was supposed to have been a cap of 500. And applications to work at the school also tripled. For one job—a 12-month contract position for an entry-level teacher—180 people applied.

All along, Kayll and Gibson had, somewhat counterintuitively, de-emphasized the importance of NAPLAN inside the school. It was just an indicator, not the be-all, end-all. Doing this served to reduce students' anxieties on test day. And then a strange thing happened.

Test scores went up.

Across the board—reading, writing, and mathematics achievement of grade 3 and grade 5 students (the two grades tested) improved. For example, over the course of four years the average starting point for grade 3 students on the numeracy assessment rose a full band level, with many students showing achievement well above their peers statewide; so, too, for grade 5 numeracy scores, with some students illustrating success at grade 7 standards. By not focusing on NAPLAN, but on developing excellent teacher and whole-school practices, the school's NAPLAN scores grew consistently for an extended period. Greenhills demonstrated what companies have learned—the key isn't to focus on the bottom line but rather to focus on the recipe for success that produces the bottom line. Fixating on bad test scores in an effort to improve them may be as counterproductive fixating on falling asleep to combat insomnia.

For Kayll, the emphasis has always been on good teaching. "Our teachers are working on the right things . . . their practice," he reflected. "The children at Greenhills are getting a better deal as a result of this journey we've taken. We have really unlocked their potential by exposing them to curriculum well beyond their grade level—and giving them an opportunity to surprise us." And those little surprises, Kayll noted, "are what keep us coming back as teachers every day."

10

The Road Less Traveled Awaits

We keep moving forward, opening new doors, and doing new things, because we're curious and curiosity keeps leading us down new paths.

Walt Disney

As human beings, we enter the world asking questions. Such questions lie at the heart of our innate curiosity. The most productive among us never stop asking them. Perhaps now, more than any other time in recent memory, it's time for educators at all levels of the system to ask this question: After a quarter century of going down the same road of top-down, carrot-and-stick approaches to reform, are we ready to flip the script and take a road less traveled—one that starts with student curiosity in the middle and builds, inside out, from there?

Why *not* start with student curiosity and engagement? Are we so convinced that what we've been doing is the right approach that we ought to continue along this path? At what point do we acknowledge that we're trying the same thing, yet expecting different results?

Why *not* start something new, something that might make everything else we're trying to do a lot easier ... and a whole lot more joyful?

Finding a New Path

Parents, students, and educators worldwide recognize the problems with the current approach and appear to want something different. Ken Robinson's talk on the need to change our paradigms in education has been viewed more than 13 million times on YouTube as of this writing, and as noted earlier, students across the United States are opting out of state assessments en masse. Certainly, it's easy for educators today to feel constrained by federal mandates, state laws, and local board decisions. Could it be, though, that these constraints are more perceived than real? Has a quarter century of test-driven accountability left school systems in a state of learned helplessness, so focused on trying to avoid the looming threat of sanctions by moving groups of "bubble kids" from one performance band to the next that we've lost sight of what we're really trying to do—or have we lost the courage or empowerment to try something new?

If all of this sounds hopelessly naïve or like wishful thinking, consider the backlash that's brewing against the amount of time students now find themselves taking tests instead of learning. Congress appears to have listened to these concerns, signing into law the Every Student Succeeds Act to replace the No Child Left Behind Act. The new law has considerably fewer mandates for testing and places greater control over education in the hands of states and districts. It also gives states the freedom to adopt new indicators such as measures of student social-emotional learning. And it calls for professional development to be job-embedded and supported by peer coaching—a core tenet, of course, of inside-out change.

A New Day Full of Promise and Peril

This shift back to state and district control, while full of promise, brings with it some peril. On the one hand, states and districts could use their greater autonomy to experiment with new measures of student learning and approaches to school reform that encourage student curiosity and inside-out approaches to improvement. On the other hand, without a clear vision or abiding sense of moral purpose, greater autonomy could devolve into unfocused systems of education where students aren't challenged, their curiosity isn't piqued, and too many are left to fall through the cracks.

With so many things in flux at the moment—sweeping changes in Washington, a growing backlash against testing, highly stressed educators reaching breaking points and leaving the profession, and a nagging sense of unease about whether our improvement efforts are really improving anything—perhaps what's needed at this time, more than any other time in recent memory, is a clear, compelling vision of where we *ought* to be going in education. Certainly, numerous writers, including Ken Robinson, Tony Wagner, and Yong Zhao, have begun articulating what a better future for education might look like. Hopefully, this book, in some small way, might add to that conversation—not as the final word or blueprint for the future of education, but as a starting point with some new next steps that could challenge us to contemplate how our system of education might look different and result in different outcomes for students if we placed curiosity at the center.

Getting there, of course, will require that not only students but also *we adults* remain curious, asking tough questions about our current approaches, stepping back, and wondering why are we doing this? Is it important? Will it help students become more literate, numerate, or curious?

Being *truly* curious, though, means being more than just pessimistic naysayers, wondering why everything seems to have gone so hopelessly wrong. As Daniel Pink (2013) points out, one of the most effective questions we can ask ourselves is the same one as the children's television character Bob the Builder asks when he encounters a problem: Can we fix it? According to Pink, what's so powerful about this particular question is that it doesn't gloss over the challenge but rather prompts us to think through what actions we must take to make things better.

Doing so can also encourage a sense of wonderment about our profession as educators, calling upon us to experiment with new approaches to support deeper learning and highly engaged learners. Hopefully by providing real-life examples of educators who have placed student curiosity and a radically different approach to improvement at the heart of their efforts, this book may help make a brighter future seem less like a far-off imaginary place and more like a reality that we can begin shaping now.

But Will It Work Here?

That said, we understand that the pressure of G.E.R.M. remains all around us and is tough to ignore. For educators presently consumed with stress of these demands (e.g., test scores, teacher evaluations, college entrance exams) not to mention the tyranny of daily fires to put out (e.g., social media policy, building maintenance, and school board members' pet issues) or the very real issues of students in trauma or communities in strife—nurturing student curiosity and improving schools from the inside out may seem like lofty ambitions that have little to do with the daily muck and mire of running a district, school, or classroom.

Yet if that's all we focus on, it's likely that's all we'll ever focus on, never building toward something better. In the sage words of the old cartoon character Pogo Possum, "You can spend your whole life looking down at the yuck and the muck and mire and all around your feet … or you can look up and see the sky." When we do, others will, too— like those famous psychology experiments when one person looks up at the sky, others do as well to see what has captured her gaze.

Is the Public Ready for a Change?

Others may fear, *My community would never go for this; they're too comfortable with the old ways of doing things—pinning those 10/10 quiz scores on their collective refrigerators.* Yet the reality is that the public may have *always* been more supportive of taking a different path. Years ago, at the outset of the No Child Left Behind era, we conducted a series of community forums and focus groups as part of a national dialogue on education to determine what the public wanted schools to be accountable for doing (Goodwin, 2003). Way back then, we heard parents, taxpayers, and community members all voicing the opinion that "standards are meaningless without tests, but accountability should be based on more than just test scores" (p. 2). Moreover, they told us that "the biggest problems with public schools have little to do with standards or academics"—parents were concerned with "safety, discipline, character, and values," and business leaders said their "chief concerns revolved around character issues such as personal responsibility, attitudes, and work ethic" (p. 2).

Recently, state leaders from Kansas discovered much the same thing when they surveyed hundreds of community members and went on a listening tour across the state to ask stakeholders in 287 focus groups the question: What characteristics, qualities, abilities, and skills do we want 24-year-old Kansans to have? Fully 70 percent of community groups cited "nonacademic skills such as professionalism, teamwork, and communications as essential to success" (23 percent cited more traditional academic skills) and fully 81 percent of business groups cited "soft skills" as key (Nguyen, 2016, p. 2).

Consider that for a moment. Kansas is one of the most conservative states in the United States; it hasn't voted for a Democratic presidential candidate since Lyndon Johnson in 1964. Yet there, in the heart of so-called "red state" America, the public wants to see schools have more than a myopic focus on test-taking abilities.

What Will the Neighbors Say?

Nonetheless, many educators may wonder, would the public and taxpayers in my community support inside-out approaches to change? Or would they view it as a pie-in-the-sky approach that will let teachers off the hook instead of putting their feet to the fire?

Consider this, though: The same strange bedfellows of liberals and conservatives that came together 15 years ago to support No Child Left Behind with its heavy federal involvement in (some would say intrusion into) education now seem to have reunited to dismantle it with the passage of the Every Student Succeeds Act (ESSA), which has shifted much of the control for education back to states and districts.

At the same time, many businesses, which were enamored with "rank-and-yank" approaches to hiring and firing 15 years ago, have seen the error of their ways and are now replacing annual performance reviews with individual goal setting and real-time feedback for improvement. Microsoft, for one, realized that its get-tough approach to employee appraisal, including grading employees on a curve, led to a decade of stagnation by causing its employees to become more risk-averse and less collaborative. According to analysis by the Organisation for Economic Cooperation and Development (OECD, 2014) the same thing appears to have happened to U.S. schools, perhaps not coincidentally in the years that mirror the era of No Child Left Behind; from 2000 to 2011, the United States was among the worst performers in terms of school (organizational) and classroom (pedagogical) innovations.

Tapping into a Rich Vein of Culture and Pride

Perhaps the best way to think about inside-out approaches is that at their heart, they are designed to encourage schools to become more innovative and entrepreneurial, finding better ways to help students learn and pursue their own intellectual passions and talents—all the while maintaining a healthy skepticism and reliance on data to make sure new approaches and ideas are working.

And who could argue with that?

In fact, much of what we've talked about in this book reflects deeply held American ideals and sources of pride. Since the days of Ben Franklin and Thomas Jefferson, we've taken pride in our American ingenuity and exceptionalism—of being a light to the rest of the world with our "crazy" notions of flying kites in electrical storms and declaring our allegiance not to monarchs but to world-changing ideas like people being created equal and endowed with certain inalienable rights.

Finland's remarkable rise in education was rooted in a deeply held shared cultural value called *sisu*—a sort of rugged determination to never give up and to act rationally in the face of adversity (Sahlberg, 2011); the Finns tapped into *sisu* to declare that they would develop an education system on par with the best in the world to ensure their own self-determination and an education system that would serve as a great equalizer, helping all students be successful in life.

In Melbourne, Wayne Craig and David Hopkins found that helping children become critical thinkers (literate and numerate) and curious were ideas that everyone could rally around as a "catch cry." Communities in America and elsewhere might quickly gravitate to similar ideas or put their own twist on them—and that's as it should be. Ultimately, inside-out change begins and ends with what's deep inside us as individuals—not what's foisted upon us by far off bureaucrats (or even suggested to us by writers tapping away on their laptops), well-meaning though all parties may be.

When we find what's deep inside each of us, we almost always find that others share those same values, too—like wanting to see our children happy, productive, and fulfilled and our communities thriving, peaceful, and full of hope for the future. Therein lies the power of taking time to engage people in deep conversation about their hopes and dreams for education—and their driving moral purpose for everyone's children.

A Place Called Here, a Time Called Now

Over the years, there's been a lot of talk about creating more engaging learning environments for students. Admittedly, one of the more disheartening aspects of researching this book was finding brilliant quotes and then realizing they had been written decades earlier. Good ideas, however, are timeless. Just because we've talked about them or tried them unsuccessfully does not mean they are no longer worth pursuing: consider freedom, justice, and equity—grand, simple ideas that people grasp immediately but spend a lifetime (or longer) trying to achieve.

Most rallying cries are like that, though—simple and readily understandable, yet difficult to achieve. So, too, it may be with curiosity and more joyful, intrinsically motivated approaches to learning and improving schools. Both are deceptively simple and familiar ideas that, like pebbles cast into a still pond, can have ripple effects across the entire system of education if we place them at the *heart* of what we're trying to accomplish.

Flipping the script and introducing new vocabulary could fill tired educators with a renewed sense of purpose. In new and meaningful ways, students might value and take ownership of their learning. Communities and parents might feel a renewed connection to their schools, especially when they see students filled with excitement about coming to school and accomplishing more than they ever before thought was possible.

Make no mistake, though, if we were to place the simple concept of student curiosity at the heart of what we're trying to accomplish as educators, nothing may ever again be the same—for ourselves or for our students; it has the power to transform learning as we know it. Sure, there will still be pessimists and naysayers who might insist on staying the course or doubling down on our bets with high-stakes testing, accountability pressure, and rank-and-yank evaluations for teachers. Let's hope for our students' sake, though, that the rest of us feel enough curiosity and courage to take the next step forward and continually ask the question: *Can we fix it?*

We started this book with an homage to *The Twilight Zone* in Rod Serling's distinctly clipped narrative style. Of course, as every *Twilight Zone* fan knows, the show's appeal lay in its twist endings, flipping the script on itself—like the bookworm with Coke-bottle glasses who awakens alone in a post-apocalyptic world rejoicing that he finally has enough time to read to his heart's content before (spoiler alert!) accidentally breaking his glasses, or the episode in which a strange object crashes to earth and causes neighbors to turn against one another in a witch hunt for extraterrestrials before the camera pulls away to reveal that aliens have, in fact, invaded and are conquering the earth by simply manipulating humans into attacking one another.

Not all episodes of *The Twilight Zone* have such dark endings, though. Nor need this one. Let's envision a happier ending for our own narrative:

> Our journey through the land of unintended consequences ends with a question from a child, a stranger to this land, who hasn't yet been taught to stop asking questions: Why are we doing things this way?
>
> It's a simple question, but it leads to another and then another. String them together like a strand of lights and they illuminate a path out of the twilight zone.
>
> Couldn't happen, you say? But it has happened. And it can happen in your school, too. You see, often the keys to the chains that bind us are simply thoughts, hopes, and ideas—once discarded, but awaiting rediscovery. If you're interested as to where find them, you might look them up under "C" for curiosity.

Appendix

These tables provide the rubrics of the six teacher theories of action used in Melbourne.

Rubric: Harnessing Learning Intentions, Narrative, and Pace

Teacher usually sets clear learning intentions and desired outcomes.	Teacher mostly sets clear learning intentions, shares an engaging narrative, and paces lessons well.	Teacher usually sets clear learning intentions, develops a clear narrative, and creates a lively pace.	Teacher sets clear learning intentions and plans lessons that engage students with the lesson narrative. Students set an effective pace.
❑ Most lesson plans clearly identify desired objectives.	❑ Lesson objectives are mostly crafted so that the lesson prepares students to demonstrate their understanding of the question and the big picture.	❑ Every lesson is part of the big picture, and every lesson question prepares students for mastery.	❑ Every aspect of the lesson is connected to the objectives.
❑ Objectives are shared with students when the lesson starts.		❑ Usually the narrative is maintained because the sequence of lessons prepares learners for what comes next.	❑ Every lesson builds on what students have already done and prepares them for what they need to do next.
❑ Objectives may be referred to infrequently during the lesson.	❑ A narrative is mostly created by objectives that link lessons together.	❑ Clear learning intentions are explained and discussed with students.	❑ Clear learning intentions and success criteria mean all students know where they are going, monitor their progress, and know what to do next to make further progress.
❑ To engage and enthuse students, the teacher uses a range of strategies that are mostly constructed to help students achieve the objectives.	❑ The learning intention, outcomes, and success criteria support the lesson's narrative.	❑ The lesson narrative connects prior learning and lesson objectives.	
	❑ Objectives mostly define a learning outcome.	❑ Students largely self-regulate, and there is little deviation from the lesson intentions.	❑ Feedback is used to make real-time changes in teaching, check misconceptions, and fill gaps in understanding.
❑ Lesson pace is usually good, though learners occasionally lose the thread of the lesson and engage in disruptive behavior.	❑ Pace is good, and there is little deviation from the lesson narrative.	❑ The learning intention for a lesson or series of lessons clearly describes what the student will know, understand, and be able to do as a result of the lesson's learning and teaching activities.	❑ The lesson narrative assists all students to know what they are learning to do and why.
❑ The teacher tracks student learning against the intended outcomes and sometimes shares observations about progress and misconceptions.	❑ Teacher uses a range of strategies that engage and enthuse students and sets a good pace for the lesson.		❑ Students know the aim of the fertile question. They identify gaps in their thinking. They decide how to plug the gaps and how to deepen understanding.
	❑ Activities align with outcomes and are deployed at the correct time.	❑ Pace keeps the lesson lively, and increasing tempo ensures there is little or no low-level disruption.	
❑ Usually students can monitor their progress and thinking against the objectives, though sometimes there is a lack of clarity about the lesson narrative, learning intentions, or connections to the big picture.	❑ Most learners engage with the narrative and share in the lesson success.	❑ Learning is aided by chunking the lesson into manageable and connected phases.	❑ Learner thinking is monitored via student feedback.
	❑ At times some learners disengage because the lesson is teacher-intensive for long stretches.	❑ Teacher and students check understanding at the end of each chunk before moving on.	❑ Students take responsibility for the pace of the lesson, with no distractions.
			❑ Every lesson ends with the question to be addressed at the start of the next lesson.

Rubric: Set Challenging Learning Tasks

Teacher is aware of strategies that create challenge in the classroom.	Teacher uses teaching strategies that are usually matched to most students' needs.	Teacher matches teaching strategies to most students' needs.	Teacher uses well-judged and often inspirational teaching strategies. Students learn optimistically and independently.
❑ Tasks allow many students to avoid challenge while still meeting success criteria. ❑ Teacher uses subject-specific language to explain concepts. ❑ Some students use subject-specific language to explain concepts. ❑ Some students are often passive and display off-task behavior. ❑ A minority of students engage in higher-level cognitive tasks. ❑ Teacher sets low-level cognitive tasks that ask students to repeat, reproduce, match, or sequence.	❑ Most tasks set by the teacher challenge students and require them to use subject-specific language to explain concepts. ❑ Some students are challenged to demonstrate subject expertise. ❑ Occasionally the teacher mismatches challenges and students' levels of understanding. This is apparent from flagging pace, engagement, and motivation. ❑ Students demonstrate some autonomy. They often require teacher input before deciding what they need to do to improve their performance.	❑ Most tasks are differentiated and set within the zone of proximal development for all students. ❑ All students demonstrate progress. ❑ Students are encouraged and supported to use subject-specific language to explain their thinking. ❑ Students are asked to perform high-level cognitive tasks, such as arguing, justifying, analyzing, and evaluating. ❑ Students demonstrate autonomy through task choice. ❑ Students can talk about the gap between their current performance and the desired performance.	❑ All tasks are precisely targeted. Each student makes greater than expected progress. ❑ All students understand the desired learning outcome and regulate their performance against it. ❑ Students are engaged by, and able to complete, tasks that require them to find contradictions or tensions in knowledge and to expose assumptions in knowledge. ❑ Students know subject-specific language and use it to talk about their thinking. ❑ Students confidently formulate counter-knowledge and generate new knowledge. ❑ Students have the autonomy and expertise to monitor their learning. They ask questions and work independently on increasingly complex tasks.

Rubric: Frame Higher-Order Questions

Teacher often asks questions that require students to repeat information.	Teacher often asks questions that allow students to demonstrate their thinking.	Teacher usually asks questions that assist teacher and students to revise tasks and review explanations in ways that improve learning.	Teacher uses questions skillfully to check understanding and uses student responses to intervene in ways that have a noticeable effect on learning.
❑ Most teacher questions are low order, relating to task compliance, knowledge acquisition, and comprehension.	❑ The ratio of low-order and high-order questions is about 50/50.	❑ Teacher uses strategies to ensure students demonstrate thinking skills in their answers.	❑ Teacher uses strategies to ensure students demonstrate thinking skills in their answers.
❑ Some questions are directed at developing thinking skills and knowledge application.	❑ Most teacher questions are referenced to the question, the learning intention, and task objectives. Some questions are not referenced, and students and teacher may lose sight of the lesson's narrative.	❑ Teacher uses student responses and student questions to control the direction of the lesson.	❑ Teacher uses student responses and student questions to control the direction of the lesson.
❑ Response to student answers is often "yes," "no," or praise for correct answers rather than praise for effort and thinking strategy.	❑ Responses are not always well acknowledged or validated.	❑ Teacher uses high-order questions to identify and address misconceptions and gaps in understanding.	❑ Teacher uses high-order questions to identify and address misconceptions and gaps in understanding.
❑ Student responses occasionally inform pace and direction of a lesson and occasionally develop a lesson's narrative.	❑ Teacher uses questioning to tease out evidence of student thinking.	❑ Teacher uses questions to determine how ready students are to move more deeply into an idea and to judge the pace of escalation and the level of complexity.	❑ Teacher uses questions to determine how ready students are to move more deeply into an idea and to judge the pace of escalation and the level of complexity.
❑ Teacher asks around one question a minute, and frequency produces low engagement.	❑ Teacher sometimes asks volunteers to answer a question, enabling some students to take a backseat or to disengage.	❑ Students are encouraged to respond to questions with analysis and explanation.	❑ Students are encouraged to respond to questions with analysis and explanation.
❑ Teacher may ask questions to manage off-task behavior.	❑ Teacher uses questioning that encourages discussion, such as wait time.	❑ Teacher uses questioning strategies that focus students on their responsibility to think carefully about their responses.	❑ Teacher uses questioning strategies that focus students on their responsibility to think carefully about their responses.

Rubric: Connect Feedback to Data

Teacher uses assessment data to provide general feedback to students about whether their constructed responses meet expectations.	Teacher uses assessment data to provide general feedback to students about how well their constructed response met expectations.	Teacher uses assessment data to provide general feedback to students about how well their constructed response met expectations.	Teacher always uses assessment data to provide specific feedback to students about how to improve their constructed responses.
❏ Students rarely have the opportunity to reflect on feedback and improve their work before assessments are submitted.	❏ Criterion-referenced feedback is used for some assessment tasks.	❏ Criterion-referenced feedback is used effectively for most assessment tasks.	❏ Students reflect on gaps in their approach and modify later drafts.
❏ Feedback is mostly one way, from teacher to student.	❏ Time is usually built into the lesson following the assessment or drafting for students to reflect on feedback.	❏ Time is always built into the lesson following the assessment for students to reflect on feedback.	❏ Time is always built into the lesson following the assessment for students to reflect on feedback.
❏ Students rely on the teacher for feedback and for prescribing the next steps required.	❏ Teacher talks with students about the link between effort and achievement and helps students to recognize that progress is incremental.	❏ Students act on a belief that learning is a process and that knowledge can be developed and contested. They connect effort and achievement.	❏ As peers, students seek and provide task- and knowledge-specific feedback.
❏ Feedback sometimes orientates students within the learning narrative.	❏ Teacher-student relationship mostly reflects a master–novice model and occasionally reflects an expert–apprentice model.	❏ Teacher elicits feedback from students about their current thinking to inform lesson planning.	❏ Students evaluate their work as they produce it, reviewing it against success criteria and a model constructed response.
❏ Students are mostly passive learners—they have occasional opportunities to take control of the learning process.	❏ Teacher often engages students in discussion about the link between effort and success.	❏ Feedback is two way—teacher and students are learning at the same time about student thinking, misconceptions, and knowledge gaps.	❏ Students connect effort and achievement and see effort as an investment rather than a risk.
❏ Teacher occasionally engages students in discussion about the link between effort and success.	❏ Teacher sometimes discusses with students that improvement is incremental.	❏ Teacher plans opportunities for students to seek and provide task- and knowledge-specific feedback from each other.	❏ Teacher elicits feedback from students about their current thinking to inform lesson planning and readiness for assessment.
			❏ Teacher focuses on mastery, modeling, and discussing skill development as incremental and subject specific.

Rubric: Commitment to Assessment *for* Learning (AfL)

Teacher gathers evidence through feedback and mostly uses it after a lesson to assess the progress students are making in their thinking.	Teacher checks understanding several times a lesson and, if necessary, recaps ideas before moving on.	The teacher carefully plans for and uses various AfL strategies many times in a lesson and across a series of lessons.	Teacher constantly uses a range of assessment strategies to connect current learning to the big picture.
❑ Teacher occasionally uses AfL strategies to elicit evidence of student thinking.	❑ Teacher clearly describes what success looks like for each learning task and activity.	❑ Teacher actively cultivates a classroom ethos in which students are a resource for one another.	❑ Students actively maintain a classroom ethos in which students are a resource for one another.
❑ Teacher occasionally uses evidence gathered through feedback to assist lesson planning and delivery.	❑ Teacher often uses AfL strategies to elicit clear evidence of student thinking.	❑ Students are familiar with their role as peer reviewers.	❑ Students can explain where they are going, describe their current performance, and
❑ Teacher often sticks closely to a lesson plan even if students are not keeping up or are venturing down a different pathway.	❑ Teacher often uses evidence gathered through feedback to assist lesson planning and delivery.	❑ Before moving on, teacher elicits feedback to ensure that understanding is consolidated.	identify what they need to do next to keep making progress.
❑ Teacher sometimes defines success vaguely so that students are unable to grasp where they are on their learning journey and where they are trying to get to.	❑ Teacher uses feedback from students to ensure most students achieve success and to keep the class on track.	❑ All students know where they are going and what they need to do next to keep making progress.	❑ Students know how to review one another's work and how to construct appropriate, helpful feedback.
❑ Teacher sometimes is unclear about the link between tasks, learning intentions, and the question—consequently, students experience difficulty in peer review and group learning activities.	❑ Students know where they are in their learning journey and what the learning intention is for the lesson.	❑ Teacher uses AfL systematically to develop increased learner autonomy and metacognition.	❑ Students share an understanding of the model of mastery they are working toward and constantly review their progress against it.
	❑ Teacher is sometimes unclear about strategies students can use to make progress in their thinking or on a learning task.	❑ Teacher uses feedback from students to inform lesson planning.	❑ Peer feedback is connected to the model of expertise students are working toward.
	❑ Teacher provides supported opportunities for peer review.	❑ Teacher uses feedback from students to alter lesson plans in real time.	❑ Teacher ensures all students have multiple opportunities for drafting and redrafting their constructed responses.
		❑ Students set short-term task completion goals to achieve the overall learning goal for the question.	

Rubric: Implement Cooperative Groups

Teacher plans and implements cooperative group structures.	Teacher plans and effectively implements cooperative group structures.	Teacher uses cooperative group structures at the right time and matches them to students' needs.	Teacher and students decide when to use cooperative group structures to best enable successful learning.

❏ Teacher is working toward a good match between group structures, challenging tasks, and learning intention.
 	
❏ Tasks allocated to group work are usually problem-solving tasks that require group work rather than individual work.
 	
❏ Teacher usually plans group work activities that ensure students work together.
 	
❏ Teacher usually sets ground rules to enhance cooperation in groups and monitors compliance with the rules.
 	
❏ Teacher occasionally has difficulty in determining which grouping of students is best suited to the task.
	❏ Teacher usually has a coherent plan that matches cooperative group work with the learning intention.
	
	❏ The cooperative structure and task usually model effectively to students how experts in that subject or field think and act to achieve a desired outcome.
	
	❏ The structure of group work tasks usually requires students to explain their thinking and communicate their resolutions to the problem.
	
	❏ Teacher usually plans activities that ensure students work together so that all learn.
	
	❏ Teacher usually uses small groups of three and only uses groups of five or more for specific purposes.
	
	❏ Teacher decides whether mixed ability or settled groups are required, depending on the task.
	
	❏ Teacher usually sets clear ground rules to enhance cooperation in groups.
		❏ Teacher plans effectively so that cooperative group structures enable students to make rapid progress in their understanding.
		
		❏ Teacher creates a context for learning that supports diverse learning abilities within the activity.
		
		❏ Group work is used at the right time in the learning cycle to build on prior learning and prepare students for future learning.
		
		❏ Teacher uses cooperative group work to enable students to talk through their current thinking using everyday language.
		
		❏ Teacher always plans activities that ensure students work together so that all learn.
		
		❏ Teacher always sets clear ground rules to enhance cooperation in groups and encourages students to monitor the group's compliance with the rules.
			❏ Teacher and students collaborate to determine and direct learning tasks that are best managed in a cooperative group structure.
			
			❏ Students are orientated in the learning narrative and know what the problem is that they are trying to solve.
			
			❏ Teacher uses cooperative structures as a tool that enables students to develop more sophisticated levels of thinking once they have collected and interpreted the data needed to solve the problem.
			
			❏ Students in each group can answer the following questions:
			  ❏ Where am I going?
			  ❏ How am I doing?
			  ❏ What do I need to do next?
			
			❏ Students know why and how working in small groups helps develop more sophisticated responses to a question and when working in a group adds little value.
			
			❏ Teacher offers professional learning for colleagues on using cooperative structures and how to develop learner autonomy through group work.

References

Adams, G., & Carnine, D. (2003). Direct instruction. In H. L. Swanson, K. R. Harris, & S. Graham (Eds.), *Handbook of learning disabilities* (pp. 403–416). New York: Guilford Press.

Ahn, T., & Vigdor, J. (2014, September). *The impact of No Child Left Behind's accountability sanctions on school performance: Regression discontinuity evidence from North Carolina.* Working Paper No. 20511. Cambridge, MA: National Bureau of Economic Research.

Ainsworth, M. D. S., Blehar, M. C., Waters, E., & Wall, S. (1978). *Patterns of attachment: A psychological study of the strange situation.* Hillsdale, NJ: Erlbaum.

Anderson, J. (2012, February 19). States try to fix quirks in teacher evaluations. *New York Times*, A1.

Aron, A. R., Shohamy, D., Clark, J., Myers, C., Gluck, M. A., & Poldrack, R. A. (2004). Human midbrain sensitivity to cognitive feedback and uncertainty during classification learning. *Journal of Neurophysiology, 92*(2), 1144–1152.

Baggio, R. (2002, May 18). Do you remember when . . . My penalty miss cost Italy the World Cup? *The Guardian.* Retrieved from http://www.theguardian.com/sport/2002/may/19/worldcup-football2002.football/print

Bailey, F., & Pransky, K. (2014). *Memory at work in the classroom: Strategies to help underachieving students.* Alexandria, VA: ASCD.

Baker, S., Gersten, R., & Lee, D. S. (2002). A synthesis of empirical research on teaching mathematics to low-achieving students. *Elementary School Journal, 10*, 51–73.

Barber, M., & Mourshed, M. (2007). *How the world's best-performing school systems come out on top.* London: McKinsey and Company.

Barber, M., Moffit, A., & Kihn, P. (2011). *Deliverology 101: A field guide for educational leaders.* Thousand Oaks, CA: Corwin.

Baxter, K. (2010, July 9). In World Cup, penalty shootouts kick up controversy. *Los Angeles Times*. Retrieved from http://articles.latimes.com/2010/jul/09/sports/la-sp-world-cup-penalty-kicks-20100710

Bean, C. E. W. (1946). *Anzac to Amiens*. Canberra: Australian War Memorial.

Beesley, A. D., & Apthorp, H. S. (2010). *Classroom instruction that works, second edition: Research report*. Denver, CO: McREL.

Benjamin, A. S., & Bjork, R. A. (2000). On the relationship between recognition speed and accuracy for words rehearsed via rote versus elaborative rehearsal. *Journal of Experimental Psychology: Learning, Memory, and Cognition, 26*(3), 638–648.

Béteille, T., Kalogrides, D., & Loeb, S. (2011). *Stepping stones: Principal career paths and school outcomes*. Working paper 17243. Cambridge, MA: National Bureau of Economic Research. Retrieved from http://www.nber.org/papers/w17243

Bill & Melinda Gates Foundation. (2013). *Ensuring fair and reliable measures of effective teaching: Culminating findings from the MET Project's three-year study* [Policy and practice brief]. Seattle, WA: Author.

Bishop, B. (2010). *Beyond basketballs: The new revolutionary way to build a successful business in today's post-product world*. Bloomington, IN: iUniverse.

Black, P., & Wiliam, D. (1998a). Assessment and classroom learning. *Assessment in Education: Principles, Policy & Practice, 5*(1), 7–74.

Black, P., & Wiliam, D. (1998b). Inside the black box: Raising standards through classroom assessment. *Phi Delta Kappan, 80*(2), 139–144, 146–148.

Bloom, H. S., Hill, C. J., Black, A. B., & Lipsey, M. W. (2008). Performance trajectories and performance gaps as achievement effect-size benchmarks for educational interventions. *Journal of Research on Educational Effectiveness, 1*(4), 289–328.

Bridgeland, J. M., DiIulio, J., & Morison, K. B. (2006). *The silent epidemic: Perspectives of high school dropouts*. Washington, DC: Civic Enterprises.

Bridges, W. (2009). *Managing transitions: Making the most of change* (3rd ed.). Philadelphia: Da Capo Lifelong Books.

Brinson, D., & Rhim, L. M. (2009). *Breaking the habit of low per-formance: Successful school restructuring stories.* Lincoln, IL: Academic Development Institute.

Bronson, P., & Merryman, A. (2013). *Top dog: The science of winning and losing.* New York: Twelve.

Brookhart, S. M. (2005, April). *Research on formative classroom assessment.* Paper presented at the annual meeting of the American Educational Research Association, Montreal.

Brooks, D. (2016, May 10). Putting grit in its place. *New York Times,* A23.

Bryk, A. S., Gomez, L. M., Grunow, A., & LeMahieu, P. (2015). *Learning to improve: How America's schools can get better at getting better.* Cambridge, MA: Harvard Education Press.

Butrymowicz, S., & Garland, S. (2012). New York City teacher ratings: How its value-added model compares to other districts. *Hechinger Report.*

Calligeros, M. (2015, March 4). Melbourne: The world's sixth most expensive city. *The Melbourne Age.*

Campbell, D. T. (1976). *Assessing the impact of planned social change.* Hanover, NH: Public Affairs Center, Dartmouth College.

Chappuis, S., & Stiggins, R. J. (2002). Classroom assessment for learning. *Educational Leadership, 60*(1), 40–44.

Chenoweth, K. (2007). *It's being done: Academic success in unex-pected schools.* Cambridge, MA: Harvard Education Press.

Chenoweth, K. (2009). *How it's being done: Urgent lessons from unexpected schools.* Cambridge, MA: Harvard Education Press.

City, E. A., Elmore, R. F., Fiarman, S. E., & Teitel, L. (2009). *Instruc-tional rounds in education: A network approach to improving teaching and learning.* Cambridge, MA: Harvard Education Press.

Collins, J. (2009). *How the mighty fall: And why some companies never give in.* New York: HarperCollins.

Council of Chief State School Officers, Council of Great City Schools. (2014). Commitments from CCSSO and CGCS on high-quality assessments. Retrieved from https://www.cgcs.org/cms/lib/DC00001581/Centricity/Domain/4/CSSO_CGCS_AssessmentCommitments%20October%2015%202014.pdf

Csikszentmihalyi, M., Rathunde, K., & Whalen, S. (1993). *Talented teenagers: The roots of success & failure.* New York: Cambridge University Press.

Cushman, K. (2010). *Fires in the mind: What kids can tell us about motivation and mastery.* San Francisco: Jossey-Bass.

Daly, A. J., Moolenaar, N., Bolivar, J., & Burke, P. (2010). Relationships in reform: The role of teachers' social networks. *Journal of Educational Administration, 48*(3), 20–49.

Darling-Hammond, L., & Friedlaender, D. (2008). Creating excellent and equitable schools. *Educational Leadership, 65*(8), 14–21.

Darling-Hammond, L., & Wood, G. (2008). *Assessment for the 21st century: Using performance assessments to measure student learning more effectively.* Washington, DC: Forum for Education and Democracy.

Datnow, A., Park, V., & Kennedy-Lewis, B. (2013). Affordances and constraints in the context of teacher collaboration for the purpose of data use. *Journal of Educational Administration, 51*(3), 341–362.

Dean, C. B., Hubbell, E. R., Pitler, H., & Stone, B. (2012). *Classroom instruction that works: Research-based strategies for increasing student achievement* (2nd ed.). Alexandria, VA: ASCD.

Deci, E. L., Ryan, R. M., & Koestner, R. (1999). A meta-analytic review of experiments examining the effects of extrinsic rewards on intrinsic motivation. *Psychological Bulletin, 125*(6), 627–668.

Deming, D. J., Cohodes, S., Jennings, J., & Jencks, C. (2016). When does accountability work? *Education Next, 16,* (1) 71–76.

Deutschman, A. (2006). *Change or die: Three keys to change at work and in life.* New York: HarperBusiness.

Doorey, N., & Polikoff, M. (2016). *Evaluating the content and quality of next generation assessments.* Washington, DC: The Fordham Foundation.

Drummond, K., Chinen, M., Duncan, T. G., Miller, H. R., Fryer, L., Zmach, C., & Culp, K. (2011). *Impact of the Thinking Reader software program on grade 6 reading vocabulary, comprehension, strategies, and motivation* (NCEE 2010-4035). Washington, DC: National Center for Education Evaluation and Regional Assistance.

Duggan, K. (2015, December 15). Six companies that are redefin-
ing performance management. *Fast Company*. Retrieved from
http://www.fastcompany.com/3054547/the-future-of-work/
six-companies-that-are-redefining-performance-management

Duhigg, C. (2012). *The power of habit: Why we do what we do in life
and business*. New York: Random House.

Duhigg, C. (2016). *Smarter faster better: The secrets of being productive in life and business*. New York: Random House.

Dweck, C. (2006). *Mindset: The new psychology of success*. New York:
Ballantine Books.

Engel, S. (2011). Children's need to know: Curiosity in schools. *Harvard Educational Review, 81*(4), 625–645.

Engel, S. (2015). *The hungry mind: The origins of curiosity in childhood*. Cambridge, MA: Harvard University Press.

Engelhard, G., & Monsaas, J. A. (1988). Grade level, gender and
school-related curiosity in urban elementary schools. *Journal of
Educational Research, 82*(1), 22–26.

Engelhard, G. (1985). *The discovery of educational goals and outcomes: A view of the latent curriculum of schooling* (Unpublished
doctoral dissertation). University of Chicago, Chicago, IL.

Fantz, A. (2015, April 15). Prison time for some Atlanta
school educators in cheating scandal. *CNN*. Retrieved
from http://www.cnn.com/2015/04/14/us/
georgia-atlanta-public-schools-cheating-scandal-verdicts/

Farrell, C. C., Marsh, J. A., & Bertrand, M. (2015). Are we motivating
students with data? *Educational Leadership, 73*(3), 16–21.

Faxon-Mills, S., Hamilton, L. S., Rudnick, M., & Stecher, B. M.
(2013). *New assessments, better instruction? Designing assessment systems to promote instructional improvement*. Santa
Monica, CA: RAND.

Fernández-Aráoz, C. (2014). 21st century talent spotting. *Harvard
Business Review, 92*(6), 46–56. Retrieved from https://hbr.
org/2014/06/21st-century-talent-spotting

Finnigan, K., Daly, A. J., & Che, J. (2012). Mind the gap: Learning,
trust, and relationships in an underperforming urban system.
American Journal of Education, 119(1), 41–71.

Fryer, R. (2010). *Financial incentives and student achievement: Evidence from randomized trials.* Cambridge, MA: Harvard University.

Fullan, M. (2001). *Leading in a culture of change.* San Francisco: Jossey-Bass.

Fullan, M. (2011). *Choosing the wrong drivers for whole system reform.* Summary of Seminar Series Paper No. 204. Melbourne, Australia: Centre for Strategic Education.

Garet, M. S., Cronen, S., Eaton, M., Kurki, A., Ludwig, M., Jones, W. et al. (2011). *The impact of two professional development interventions on early reading instruction and achievement.* Washington, DC: U.S. Department of Education, Institute of Education Sciences.

Gawande, A. (2009). *The checklist manifesto: How to get things right.* New York: Metropolitan Books.

Goldhaber, D., & Hansen, M. (2010). *Is it just a bad class? Assessing the stability of measured teacher performance.* CEDR Working Paper 2010-3. Seattle, WA: University of Washington.

Goldstein, D. (2017, March 21). School choice fight in Iowa may preview the one facing Trump. *New York Times,* A1.

Goodson, B., Wolf, A., Bell, S., Turner, H., & Finney, P. B. (2010). *The effectiveness of a program to accelerate vocabulary development in kindergarten* (VOCAB) (NCEE 2010-4014). Washington, DC: National Center for Education Evaluation and Regional Assistance.

Goodwin, B. (2003). *Digging deeper: Where does the public stand on standards-based education?* Aurora, CO: McREL.

Goodwin, B. (2011a). Don't wait until 4th grade to address the slump. *Educational Leadership, 68*(7), 88–89.

Goodwin, B. (2011b). Research says: Implementation counts. *Educational Leadership, 69*(2), 82–83.

Goodwin, B. (2011c). *Simply better: Doing what matters to change the odds for student success.* Alexandria, VA: ASCD.

Goodwin, B. (2015a). Getting unstuck. *Educational Leadership, 72*(9), 8–12.

Goodwin, B. (2015b). To go fast, direct. To go far, empower. *Educational Leadership, 72*(5), 73–74.

Goodwin, B., Cameron, C., & Hein, H. (2015). *Balanced leadership for powerful learning: Tools for achieving success in your school.* Alexandria, VA: ASCD.

Goodwin, B., & Hein, H. (2016). The X-factor in college success. *Educational Leadership, 73*(6), 77–78.

Goodwin, B., & Hubbell, E. R. (2013). *The 12 touchstones of good teaching: A checklist for staying focused every day.* Alexandria, VA: ASCD.

Goodwin, B., & Miller, K. (2012). Use caution with value-added measures. *Educational Leadership, 70*(3), 80–81.

Gorski, E. (2014, November 13). Thousands of Colorado high school students refuse to take state tests. *Denver Post.* Retrieved from http://www.denverpost.com/news/ci_26930017/hundreds-colorado-high-school-students-refuse-take-sate

Gottfried, A. E., Fleming, J., & Gottfried, A. W. (2001). Continuity of academic intrinsic motivation from childhood through late adolescence: A longitudinal study. *Journal of Educational Psychology, 93*(1), 3–13.

Greene, P. (2015, August 6). TNTP: Why does professional development suck? *Curmudugation* [blog post]. Retrieved from http://curmudgucation.blogspot.com/2015/08/tntp-why-does-professional-development.html

Gruber, M. J., Gelman, B. D., & Ranganath, C. (2014). States of curiosity modulate hippocampus-dependent learning via the dopaminergic circuit. *Neuron, 84*(2), 486–496.

Guskey, T. R., & Yoon, K. S. (2009). What works in professional development? *Phi Delta Kappan, 90*(7), 495–500.

Hackman, J. R. (2011). Six common misperceptions about teamwork [blog post]. Retrieved from *Harvard Business Review* at http://blogs.hbr.org/2011/06/six-common-misperceptions-abou

Hall, G. E., & Hord, S. M. (1987). *Change in schools: Facilitating the process.* Albany, NY: State University of New York Press.

Hansen, M. (2009). *Collaboration: How leaders avoid the traps, create unity, and reap big results.* Cambridge, MA: Harvard Business Review Press.

Harpaz, Y., & Lefstein, A. (2000). Communities of thinking. *Educational Leadership, 58*(3), 54–57.

Hattie, J. (2009). *Visible learning: A synthesis of over 800 meta-analyses relating to achievement.* New York: Routledge.

Hattie, J., & Timperley, H. (2007). The power of feedback. *Review of Educational Research, 77*(1), 81–112.

Heath, C., & Heath, D. (2007). *Made to stick: Why some ideas survive and others die.* New York: Random House.

Heath, C., & Heath, D. (2010). *Switch: How to change things when change is hard.* New York: Crown Business.

Heifetz, R. A., & Laurie, D. L. (1997). The work of leadership. *Harvard Business Review, 75*(1), 124–134.

Henderson, B. B., & Moore, S. G. (1980). Children's responses to objects differing in novelty in relation to level of curiosity and adult behavior. *Child Development, 51*(2), 457–465.

Heritage, M. (2010). *Formative assessment and next-generation assessment systems: Are we losing an opportunity?* Paper prepared for the Council of Chief State School Officers, Washington, DC.

Heshmat, S. (2015, January 22). The addictive quality of curiosity: Curiosity as an antidote to boredom and addiction [blog post]. *Psychology Today.* Retrieved from https://www.psychologytoday.com/blog/science-choice/201501/the-addictive-quality-curiosity

Hill, H. (2015). *Review of* The Mirage: Confronting the hard truth about our quest for teacher development. Boulder, CO: National Education Policy Center.

Hindle, T. (2008). *Guide to management ideas and gurus.* London: Profile Books.

Hitchcock, J., Dimino, J., Kurki, A., Wilkins, C., & Gersten, R. (2010). *The impact of Collaborative Strategic Reading on the reading comprehension of grade 5 students in linguistically diverse schools* (NCEE 2011-4001). Washington, DC: National Center for Education Evaluation and Regional Assistance.

Hochbein, C. (2012). Relegation and reversion: Longitudinal analysis of school turnaround and decline. *Journal of Education for Students Placed at Risk, 17*(1-2), 92–107.

Hofman, P., Goodwin, B., & Kahl, S. (2015). *Re-balancing assessment: Placing formative and performance assessment at the heart of learning and accountability.* Denver, CO: McREL.

Hollingsworth, J., & Ybarra, S. (2009). *Explicit direct instruction (EDI): The power of the well-crafted, well-taught lesson.* Thousand Oaks, CA: Corwin.

Hopkins, D. (2007). *Every school a great school: Realizing the potential of system leadership.* Berkshire, UK: McGrawHill Education.

Hopkins, D. (2011). *Powerful learning: Taking educational reform to scale.* Melbourne, Australia: Education Policy and Research Division Office for Policy, Research, and Innovation, Victoria Department of Education and Early Childhood Development.

Hopkins, D. (2013). *Exploding the myths of school reform.* East Melbourne, Victoria, Australia: Centre for Strategic Reform.

Hopkins, D., & Craig, W. (2011). Going deeper: From the inside out. In D. Hopkins, J. Munro, & W. Craig (Eds.), *Powerful learning: A strategy for systemic educational improvement* (pp. 153–172). Camberwell, Austrialia: Australian Council for Educational Research Press.

Horn, I. S., Kane, B. D., & Wilson, J. (2015). Making sense of student performance data: Data use logics and mathematics teachers' learning opportunities. *American Educational Research Journal, 52*(2), 208–242.

Howell, R. J. (2011). Exploring the impact of grading rubrics on academic performance: Findings from a quasi-experimental, pre-post evaluation. *Journal on Excellence in College Teaching, 22*(2), 31–49.

Iyengar, S., & Lepper, M. (2000). When choice is demotivating: Can one desire too much of a good thing? *Journal of Personality and Social Psychology, 79*(6), 995–1006.

Jacob, B. A. (2002). *Accountability, incentives, and behavior: The impact of high-stakes testing in the Chicago Public Schools.* Cambridge, MA: National Bureau of Economic Research. Retrieved from www.nber.org/papers/w8968.pdf?new_window=1

Jacob, B. A., & Lefgren, L. (2008). Can principals identify effective teachers? Evidence on subjective performance evaluation in education. *Journal of Labor Economics 26*(1) 101–36.

Jao, L. (2013). Peer coaching as a model for professional development in the elementary mathematics context: Challenges, needs and rewards. *Policy Futures in Education, 11*(3), 290–297.

Jonsson, A., & Svingby, G. (2007). The use of scoring rubrics: Reliability, validity and educational consequences. *Educational Research Review, 2*, 130–144.

Jordet, G., & Hartman, E. (2008). Avoidance motivation and choking under pressure in soccer penalty shootouts. *Journal of Sport & Exercise Psychology, 30*(4), 450–457.

Joyce, B., & Showers, B. (2002). *Student achievement through staff development* (3rd ed.). Alexandria, VA: ASCD.

Joyce, B., Hopkins, D., & Calhoun, E. (2014). Winning with coaching: Strengthening the links between professional learning, CCSS, and STEM. *Changing Schools, 72*(3), 8–10.

Kamenetz, A. (2014). Testing: How much is too much? *National Public Radio.* Retrieved from http://www.npr.org/blogs/ed/2014/11/17/362339421/testing-how-much-is-too-much

Kane, A. A., Argote, L., & Levin, J. M. (2005). Knowledge transfer between groups via personnel rotation: Effects of social identity and knowledge quality. *Organizational Behavior and Human Decision Processes, 96*(1), 56–71.

Kane, T. J., Taylor, E., Tyler, J. & Wooten, A. (2011). Identifying effective classroom practices using student achievement data. *Journal of Human Resources, 46*(3), 587–613.

Kashdan, T. B., & Roberts, J. E. (2004). Trait and state curiosity in the genesis of intimacy: Differentiation from related constructs. *Journal of Social and Clinical Psychology, 23*(6), 792–816.

Kashdan, T., & Steger, M. (2007). Curiosity and pathways to well-being and meaning in life: Traits, states, and everyday behaviors. *Motivation and Emotion 31*(3), 159–173.

King, A. (1991). Improving lecture comprehension: Effects of a meta-cognitive strategy. *Applied Cognitive Psychology, 5*(4), 331–346.

Kleinfeld, J. (1972). *Effective teachers of Indian and Eskimo high school students.* Fairbanks: University of Alaska, Institute of Social, Economic, and Government Research.

Kohn, A. (1993). *Punished by rewards: The trouble with gold stars, incentive plans, As, praise, and other bribes.* New York: Houghton Mifflin Company.

Lane, S., Parke, C. S., & Stone, C. A. (2002). The impact of a state performance-based assessment and accountability program on mathematics instruction and student learning: Evidence from survey data and school performance. *Educational Assessment, 8*(4), 279–315.

Larson, L. R., & Lovelace, M. D. (2013). Evaluating the efficacy of questioning strategies in lecture-based classroom environments: Are we asking the right questions? *Journal on Excellence in College Teaching, 24*(1), 105–122.

Lash, A., Makkonen, R., Tran, L., & Huang, M. (2016). Analysis of the stability of teacher-level growth scores from the student growth percentile model (REL 2016–104). Washington, DC: U.S. Department of Education, Institute of Education Sciences, National Center for Education Evaluation and Regional Assistance, Regional Educational Laboratory West. Retrieved from https://ies.ed.gov/ncee/edlabs/regions/west/pdf/REL_2016104.pdf

Lazarev, V., Newman, D., & Sharp, A. (2014). Properties of the multiple measures in Arizona's teacher evaluation model (REL 2015–050). Washington, DC: U.S. Department of Education, Institute of Education Sciences, National Center for Education Evaluation and Regional Assistance, Regional Educational Laboratory West. Retrieved fromhttps://ies.ed.gov/ncee/edlabs/regions/west/pdf/REL_2014050.pdf

Lazarín, M. (2014). *Testing overload in America's schools*. Washington, DC: Center for American Progress.

Levitt, S. D., List, J. A., Neckermann, S., & Sadoff, S. (2012). The behavioralist goes to school: Leveraging behavioral economics to improve educational performance (NBER Working Paper Series No. 18165). Cambridge, MA: National Bureau of Economic Research.

Loewenstein, G. (1994). The psychology of curiosity: A review and reinterpretation. *Psychology Bulletin, 116*(1) 75–98.

Lorinkova, N., Pearsall, M., & Sims, H. (2013). Examining the differential longitudinal performance of directive versus empowering leadership in teams. *Academy of Management, 56*(2), 573–596.

Lowry, N., & Johnson, D. W. (1981). Effects of controversy on epistemic curiosity, achievement, and attitudes. *Journal of Social Psychology, 115,* 31–43.

Lubliner, S., & Smetana, L. (2003). Recognition or recall: What reading comprehension tests really measure. Paper presented at the Annual Meeting of the American Educational Research Association (Chicago, IL).

Martin, P. (2016, March 25). Population surge: Melbourne booms as locals leave Sydney. *Sydney Morning Herald.* Retrieved from http://www.smh.com.au/federal-politics/political-news/population-surge-melbourne-booms-as-locals-leave-sydney-20160324-gnqfd2.html

Marzano, R. J. (1998). *A theory-based meta-analysis of research on instruction.* Aurora, CO: McREL.

Marzano, R. J., & Kendall, J. S. (1998). *Awash in a sea of standards.* Aurora, CO: McREL.

Marzano, R. J., Waters, J. T., & McNulty, B. A. (2005). *School leadership that works: From research to results.* Alexandria, VA: ASCD.

Maslen, G. (2013, June 16). Leading from the front but lacking support. *Sydney Morning Herald.* Retrieved from http://www.smh.com.au/national/education/leading-from-the-front-but-lacking-support-20130614-2o8pk.html

McGregor, D. (1960). *The human side of enterprise.* New York: McGrawHill.

McMillen, A. (2013, August 6). School's out early for overworked and under-supported young teachers. *The Guardian.* Retrieved from https://www.theguardian.com/education/2013/aug/06/teachers-leave-profession-early

McManus, S. (2008). Attributes of effective formative assessment. Paper prepared for the Formative Assessment for Teachers and Students (FAST) State Collaborative in Assessment and Student Standards (SCASS) of the Council of Chief State School Officers (CCSSO), Washington, DC.

McTighe, J., & Wiggins, G. (2013). *Essential questions: Opening doors to student understanding.* Alexandria, VA: ASCD.

Medina, J. (2008). *Brain rules: 12 principles for surviving and thriving at work, home, and school.* Seattle, WA: Pear Press.

MetLife. (2013). *The MetLife survey of the American teacher: Challenges of school leadership.* Retrieved from https://www.metlife.com/assets/cao/foundation/MetLife-Teacher-Survey-2012.pdf

Milligan, L. (2014, October 23). Gap between rich and poor schools is widening but some schools are bucking the trend. Australian Broadcast Corporation. Retrieved from http://www.abc.net.au/7.30/content/2014/s4113474.htm

Moore, S. G., & Bulbulian, K. N. (1976). The effects of contrasting styles of adult-child interaction on children's curiosity. *Developmental Psychology, 12,* 171–172.

Mourshed, M., Chijioke, C., & Barber, M. (2010). *How the world's most improved school systems keep getting better.* New York: McKinsey & Company.

Munro, J. (2015). *Curiouser and curiouser.* Denver, CO: McREL.

Murray, S., Ma, X., & Mazur, J. (2009). Effects of peer coaching on teachers' collaborative interactions and students' mathematics achievement. *Journal of Educational Research, 102*(3), 203–212.

National Center for Education Statistics. (1997). *Time spent teaching core academic subjects in elementary schools: Comparisons across community, school, teacher, and student characteristics.* Washington, DC: Author.

National Commission on Excellence in Education. (1983). *A nation at risk: The imperative for educational reform.* Washington, DC: U.S. Government Printing Office.

Nguyen, A. (2016). Kansas loops stakeholders in on conversation about K–12 Policy. *State Innovations, 21*(3), 1–3.

Nichols, S. L., Glass, G. V., & Berliner, D. C. (2012). High-stakes testing and student achievement: Updated analyses with NAEP data. *Education Policy Analysis Archives, 20*(20). Retrieved from http://nepc.colorado.edu/files/EPSL-0509-105-EPRU.pdf

OECD (Organisation for Economic Cooperation and Development). (2011). *Strong performers and successful reformers in education: Lessons from PISA for the United States.* Paris: Author. Retrieved from www.oecd.org/dataoecd/32/50/46623978.pdf

OECD (Organisation for Economic Co-operation and Development). (2014). *Measuring innovation in education: A new perspective.* Paris: OECD Publishing.

Olson, L. (2004, May 5). England refines accountability reforms. *Education Week, 23*(34), 1, 20–22.

Outsell, Inc. (2016). *Outsell forecasts steady growth for the US K–12 testing and assessment market.* [Press release]. Burlingame, CA: Author.

Paige, R. (2002). *What to know: No Child Left Behind.* Washington, DC: U.S. Department of Education.

Patall, E., Cooper, H., & Robinson, J. C. (2008). The effects of choice on intrinsic motivation and related outcomes: A meta-analysis of research findings. *Psychological Bulletin, 134*(2), 270–300.

Payne, C. M. (2008). *So much reform, so little change: The persistence of failure in urban schools.* Cambridge, MA: Harvard Education Press.

Pecheone, R., & Kahl, S. (2014). Where are we now: Lessons learned and emerging directions. In L. Darling-Hammond & F. Adamson (Eds.), *Beyond the bubble test: How performance assessments support 21st century learning* (pp. 53–91). San Francisco: Jossey-Bass.

Pianta, R. C., Belsky, J., Houts, R., & Morrison, F. (2007). Opportunities to learn in America's elementary classrooms. *Science, 315*(5820), 1795–1796.

Pink, D. (2013). *To sell is human: The surprising truth about motivating others.* New York: Riverhead Books.

Pink, D. H. (2009). *Drive: The surprising truth about what motivates us.* New York: Riverhead Books.

Popham, J. (2006). All about accountability. Phony formative assessments: Buyer beware! *Educational Leadership, 64*(3), 86–87.

Raine, A., Reynolds, C., Venables, P. H., & Mednick, S. A. (2002). Stimulation seeking and intelligence: A prospective longitudinal study. *Journal of Personality and Social Psychology 82*(4), 663–674.

Randel, B., Beesley, A. D., Apthorp, H., Clark, T. F., Wang, X., Cicchinelli, L. F., & Williams, J. M. (2011). *Classroom assessment for student learning: The impact on elementary school mathematics in the Central Region* (NCEE 2011-4005). Washington, DC: National Center for Education Evaluation and Regional Assistance.

Ravitch, D. (2010). *The death and life of the great American school system: How testing and choice are undermining education.* New York: Basic Books.

Rawson, K. A., & Kintsch, W. (2005). Rereading effects depend on time of test. *Journal of Educational Psychology, 97*(1), 70–80.

Reio, T. G., & Wiswell, A. (2000). Field investigation of the relationship among adult curiosity, workplace learning, and job performance. *Human Resource Development Quarterly, 11*(1), 5–30.

Ricci, C. (2015, October 18). Teachers' pay varies widely and affects the quality of students entering the profession. *Sydney Morning Herald.* Retrieved from http://www.smh.com.au/national/education/teachers-pay-varies-widely-and-affects-the-quality-of-students-entering-the-profession-20151012-gk76f5.html

Ringelmann, M. (1913). Recherches sur les moteurs animés: Travail de l'homme [Research on animate sources of power: The work of man]. *Annales de l'Institut National Agronomique, 12,* 1–40.

Ripley, A. (2010, April 19). Should kids be bribed to do well in school? *Time.* Retrieved from http://www.time.com/time/magazine/article/0,9171,1978758,00.html

Rosenthal, R., & Jacobson, L. (1992). *Pygmalion in the classroom.* New York: Irvington.

Rowe, M. B. (1986). Wait time: Slowing down may be a way of speeding up! *Journal of Teacher Education, 37*(1), 43–50.

Sahlberg, P. (2011). *Finnish lessons: What can the world learn from educational change in Finland?* New York: Teachers' College Press.

Schmoker, M. (2014, September 23). The Common Core is not ready. *Education Week.* Retrieved from http://www.edweek.org/ew/articles/2014/09/24/05schmoker.h34.html

Schneider, M. (2011, December 15). The accountability plateau. *Education Next.* Retrieved from http://educationnext.org/the-accountability-plateau

Schweig, J. (2016, May 9). The opt-out reckoning: An ever-growing call to opt out of standardized tests is prompting serious questions in education. *USA Today.* Retrieved from http://www.usnews.com/opinion/articles/2016-05-09/who-does-the-movement-to-opt-out-of-standardized-testing-help

Shohamy, E. (1984). Does the testing method make a difference? The case of reading comprehension. *Language Testing, 1*(2), 147–170.

Shute, V. J. (2007). *Focus on formative assessment.* (ETS Report No. RR-07-11). Princeton, NJ: Educational Testing Service.

Sinek, S. (2011). *Start with why: How great leaders inspire everyone to take action.* New York: Portfolio.

Skinner, B. F. (1969). *Contingencies of reinforcement: A theoretical analysis.* New York: Merrick.

Smarick, A. (2015, September 30). What "The Mirage" gets wrong on teacher development. [blog post]. Retrieved from http://edexcellence.net/articles/what-the-mirage-gets-wrong-on-teacher-development

Smithers, A. (2005). Education. In A. Seldon & D. Kavanagh (Eds.), *The Blair Effect: 2001–2005.* Cambridge, UK: Cambridge University Press.

Soland, J., Hamilton, L., & Stecher, B. (2013). *Measuring 21st century competencies: Guidance for educators.* Retrieved from http://asiasociety.org/files/gcen-measuring21cskills.pdf

Somech, A. (2006). The effects of leadership style and team process on performance and innovation in functionally heterogeneous teams. *Journal of Management, 32*(1), 132–157.

Souza, D. A. (2011). *How the brain learns* (4th ed.). Thousand Oaks, CA: Corwin.

Spillane, J. P. (2000). *District leaders' perceptions of teacher learning* (CPRE Occasional Paper Series OP-05). Philadelphia: Consortium for Policy Research in Education.

Strauss, V. (2015, June 12). Why so many teachers leave—and how to get them to stay. *The Washington Post.* Retrieved from https://www.washingtonpost.com/news/answer-sheet/wp/2015/06/12/why-so-many-teachers-leave-and-how-to-get-them-to-stay/

Stringfield, S., Reynolds, D., & Schaffer, G. (2010). *Toward highly reliable, high quality public schooling.* Paper presented at the McREL Best in the World Consortium Meeting, Denver, Colorado.

Sullivan, B., & Thompson, H. (2013). *The plateau effect: Getting from stuck to success.* New York: Penguin.

Swan, G. E., & Carmelli, D. (1996). Curiosity and mortality in aging adults: A 5-year follow-up of the western collaborative group study. *Psychology and Aging, 11*(3), 449–453.

Symons, C. S., & Johnson, B.T. (1997). The self-reference effect in memory: A meta-analysis. *Psychological Bulletin, 121*(3), 371–394.

Taylor, E. S., & Tyler, J. H. (2012, Fall). Can teacher evaluation improve teaching? *Education Next, 12*(4).

TNTP. (2015). *The mirage: Confronting the hard truth about our quest for professional development.* Brooklyn, NY: Author.

Torrance, P. E. (1963). The creativity personality and the ideal pupil. *Teachers College Record, 3,* 220–226.

Torrance, P. E. (1965). *Rewarding creative behavior: Experiments in classroom creative behavior.* Englewood Cliffs, NJ: Prentice Hall.

Vescio, V., Ross, D., & Adams, A. (2008). A review of research on the impact of professional learning communities on teaching practice and student learning. *Teaching and Teacher Education, 24,* 80–91.

von Stumm, S., Hell, B., & Chamorro-Premuzic, T. (2011). The hungry mind: Intellectual curiosity is the third pillar of academic performance. *Perspectives on Psychological Science 6*(6), 574–588.

Wallace, J. C., Little, L. M., Hill, A. D., & Ridge, J. W. (2010). CEO regulatory foci, environmental dynamism, and small firm performance. *Journal of Small Business Management, 48*(4), 580–604.

Warren, T. (2013, November 12). Microsoft axes its controversial employee ranking system. *The Verge.*

Waters, J. T., & Marzano, R. J. (2006). *School district leadership that works: The effect of superintendent leadership on student achievement.* Denver, CO: McREL.

West, M. (2012). Global lessons for improving U.S. education. *Issues in Science and Technology, 28*(3), 37–44.

Wijekumar, K., Hitchcock, J., Turner, H., Lei, P. W., & Peck, K. (2009). A multisite cluster randomized trial of the effects of Compass Learning Odyssey Math on the math achievement of selected grade 4 students in the Mid-Atlantic Region (NCEE 2009-4068). Washington, DC: National Center for Education Evaluation and Regional Assistance.

Wiliam, D. (2007). Keeping learning on track: Classroom assessment and the regulation of learning. In F. K. Lester (Ed.), *Second handbook of mathematics teaching and learning.* Greenwich, CT: Information Age Publishing.

Wiliam, D. (2011). *Embedded formative assessment.* Bloomington, IN: Solution Tree Press.

Wiliam, D., & Thompson, M. (2007). Integrating assessment with instruction: What will it take to make it work? In C. A. Dwyer (Ed.), *The future of assessment: Shaping teaching and learning* (pp. 53–82). Mahwah, NJ: Erlbaum.

Williams, P. (2015, November 12). Former "'teacher of the year'" alleges pressure to change grades. NewsChannel 5 Network. Retrieved from http://www.newschannel5.com/news/newschannel-5-investigates/former-teacher-of-the-year-alleges-pressure-to-change-grades

Wylie, E. C. (2008). *Formative assessment: Examples of practice.* Paper prepared for the Formative Assessment for Teachers and Students (FAST) State Collaborative in Assessment and Student Standards (SCASS) of the Council of Chief State School Officers (CCSSO), Washington, DC.

Yazzie-Mintz, E. (2010). *Charting the path from engagement to achievement: A report on the 2009 High School Survey of Student Engagement.* Bloomington, IN: Center for Evaluation & Education.

Zbar, V. (2013). *Generating whole-school improvement: The stages of sustained success.* East Melbourne, Victoria: Centre for Strategic Education.

Index

The letter *f* following a page number denotes a figure.

About the Authors

Bryan Goodwin is president and CEO of McREL International. For 20 years at McREL, he has translated research into practice, scanning the world for new insights and best practices on teaching and leading, and helping educators everywhere adapt them to address their own challenges. A frequent conference presenter, he is the author of *Simply Better: Doing What Matters Most to Change the Odds for Student Success* and coauthor of *The 12 Touchstones of Good Teaching* and *Balanced Leadership for Powerful Learning: Tools for Achieving Success in Your School.* He writes a monthly column for ASCD's *Educational Leadership* magazine. Before joining McREL in 1998, Goodwin was a college instructor, a high school teacher, and an award-winning business journalist.

Tonia Gibson, a McREL International project consultant, works with schools, districts, and other stakeholders to develop sustainable plans for improving the professional practices of teachers and school leaders. Gibson began her career in Australia, teaching all grades from K–6. As a lead teacher, she focused on curriculum, assessment, and implementation, as well as developing effective practices and protocols for effective professional learning communities. As an assistant principal, Gibson's focus was on developing the capacities of teachers and school leaders to improve student engagement, student achievement, and teacher confidence. Gibson earned a master's degree in school leadership from the University of Melbourne and a bachelor of education in primary/adult learning from RMIT University.

Dale Lewis is senior director of research, evaluation, and technical assistance at McREL International. Lewis also serves as deputy director of the Regional Educational Laboratory for the Pacific Region. Before joining McREL, he served as principal technical assistance consultant for the American Institutes for Research, with primary responsibilities as director of the Texas Comprehensive Center. Lewis has extensive experience guiding and leading others in the application of the Concerns-Based Adoption Model to support the implementation of new educational programs and initiatives. He is a certified educational diagnostician and special education teacher. Lewis holds an MA in special education and a PhD in education–school improvement from Texas State University.

Kris Rouleau is senior director of learning services and innovation at McREL International. Prior to working at McREL, Rouleau was a classroom teacher, curriculum specialist, elementary school principal, and district-level curriculum administrator. Among her accomplishments, she designed and led her district's first centralized literacy coach cadre for K–12 teachers. Rouleau earned her administrative credentials at the University of Washington, her master's in curriculum and teaching from Michigan State University, and a bachelor's degree in elementary education from Western Michigan University. As of this writing, she is a doctoral candidate in leadership for educational equity from the University of Colorado–Denver.

About McREL

McREL International is an internationally recognized nonprofit education research and development organization, headquartered in Denver, Colorado, with offices in Honolulu, Hawai'i; Nashville, Tennessee; Charleston, West Virginia; and Melbourne, Australia. Since 1966, McREL has helped translate research and professional wisdom about what works in education into practical guidance for educators. Our 120-plus staff members and affiliates include respected researchers, experienced consultants, and published writers who provide educators with research-based guidance, consultation, and professional development for improving student outcomes. Contact us if you have questions or comments or would like to arrange a presentation, workshop, or other assistance from McREL in applying the ideas from this book in your district, school, or classroom.

Related Resources

At the time of publication, the following resources were available (ASCD stock numbers in parentheses).

Print Products

The 12 Touchstones of Good Teaching: A Checklist for Staying Focused Every Day by Bryan Goodwin & Elizabeth Ross Hubbell (#113009)

Balanced Leadership for Powerful Learning: Tools for Achieving Success in Your School by Bryan Goodwin & Greg Cameron with Heather Hein (#112025)

Simply Better: Doing What Matters Most to Change the Odds for Student Success by Bryan Goodwin (#111038)

Cultivating Curiosity in K–12 Classrooms: How to Promote and Sustain Deep Learning by Wendy L. Ostroff (#116001)

Fighting for Change in Your School: How to Avoid Fads and Focus on Substance by Harvey Alvy (#117007)

Learning to Choose, Choosing to Learn: The Key to Student Motivation and Achievement by Mike Anderson (#116015)

For up-to-date information about ASCD resources, go to www.ascd. org. You can search the complete archives of *Educational Leadership* at www.ascd.org/el.

ASCD myTeachSource®
Download resources from a professional learning platform with hundreds of research-based best practices and tools for your classroom at http://myteachsource.ascd.org/

For more information, send an e-mail to member@ascd.org; call 1-800-933-2723 or 703-578-9600; send a fax to 703-575-5400; or write to Information Services, ASCD, 1703 N. Beauregard St., Alexandria, VA 22311-1714 USA.